D1985088

The Life Of Sethos V1

Jean Terrasson

In the interest of creating a more extensive selection of rare historical book reprints, we have chosen to reproduce this title even though it may possibly have occasional imperfections such as missing and blurred pages, missing text, poor pictures, markings, dark backgrounds and other reproduction issues beyond our control. Because this work is culturally important, we have made it available as a part of our commitment to protecting, preserving and promoting the world's literature. Thank you for your understanding.

Jean Terrasson.

THE

LIFE

OF

SETHOS.

TAKEN FROM

PRIVATE MEMOIRS

OF THE

Ancient *EGYPTIANS.*

Translated from a *Greek* MANUCSRIPT into FRENCH.

And now faithfully done into *English* from the *Paris* EDITION;

By Mr. *LEDIARD.*

IN TWO VOLUMES.

VOL. I.

LONDON:
Printed for J. WALTHOE, over-againſt the *Royal-Exchange* in *Cornhill.*
M.DCC.XXXII.

THE

PREFACE.

THE Greek Manuscript, of which I here offer the Publick a Translation, was found in the library of a foreign nation, extremely jealous of this sort of treasure. Those who procured me the reading of it would admit of my publishing this Translation upon no other terms, but that of concealing the library in which the Original is deposited. The author is no where named: But we find by several Passages in this work, that he was a Greek born, and lived at Alexandria, under the reign of Marcus Aurelius.

THERE is no room to doubt but this work is a fiction. The event of sundry enterprizes proving in a manner such as a reader would wish or hope, the unexpected return and rencounter of several personages, but above all, the great number of discourses directly from the Persons themselves, sufficiently evince, that our author has not tied himself down to such real facts, which the common circumstances of life make liable to a greater confusion; and that he takes upon him the entire disposal, not only of the actions, but even of the thoughts of those persons he brings upon the stage.

THE particular advantage, which he proposed to himself, obliged him to employ his pen in this kind of writing. History, *properly so call'd, has beyond dispute its excellencies. It is an Improvement of the Mind, which we expect from every one who undertakes to cultivate education. History is essential to the professions of some, and a recreation almost universally coveted by others, whose main business seems the most distant from it. It is one of the chief springs of true philosophy, by the knowledge it gives us of human passions and prejudices. It is accounted the most sure guide in politicks, by furnishing one single person with the experience of all preceding ages.*

ages. In short, it is looked upon by some as a great foundation of moral instructions, by the reiterated examples it lays before us of good and evil.

BUT with regard to this last property; I believe, when we come to examine the matter narrowly, we shall find history fall far short of fiction; when the latter is employed in such a manner as becomes every prudent writer; that is, with an Eye to form the manners of men. History, in itself, is but a collection of facts, guided by providence, for ends generally unknown to us: and tho' every thing be wonderfully well ordered, pursuant to the mysterious views of the divine wisdom and justice; the consequences of mens actions are frequently to our eyes but a series of disappointed projects and crimes unpunished. A view of what has happened in the world is, strictly speaking, no other than a view of what passes in a place of publick resort, neither the one nor the other is in any-wise moral but by the reflections of the spectator or relator. In a Word, mere history is rather an object than a doctrine.

BUT in a fictitious work the case is very different. The moral Author, if his undertaking be narrative, generally makes it his business to represent his hero adorned with all the virtues proper to his state and con-

dition. He places him in all such circumstances as may give him room to exercise these virtues. He sets him in opposition not only to wicked men, but to such whose virtues are weak and wavering; that their different characters may make that of his hero shine forth with the greater lustre. His images are accompanied with judgments already formed, and explicit advices. In a word, his instructions are rendered perfect, as well by doctrine as example. We might combine and melt down numbers of the great Men in history, and unite the events of many ages; before we should find those materials for wonder and imitation, which a judicious author of a fiction will often produce in but a small part of the life of one single hero.

THE two works we have hitherto seen of this kind, Telemachus and the Travels of Cyrus perfectly answer this idea. It is not a comparison with history, which is of a quite different nature, but a comparison of good fictitious works, which will more and more discover the pernicious folly of romances, when by that term we mean an advantageous, or if but a favourable representation of the frailties or disorders of love. But a yet more important effect of good fiction will be to explode false heroism. That cruel ambition and implacable revenge celebrated by so many orators and poets under the epithet of valour, will be divested of the lustre they have cloathed it with, and we shall soon look upon

whatever

whatever has contributed to raise these false virtues to such an eminence, as the deceitful beauties of eloquence, or poetry.

THIS happy effect seems to be already infused in the minds of men. The spoil of nations does now no longer appear an object of emulation; at least among civilized people. Panegyricks upon conquests and devastations are no more patterns in the education of princes; and good poets have done with extolling them for making arms alone their pastime. I find no reason to repent of what I formerly said speaking of Telemachus: That if the happiness of mankind could be said to arise from a poem, it would be from that. And tho' princes may not often apply themselves much to reading, yet those who have the care of their education, knowing as well the origine as progress of learning, don't suffer them to be ignorant, either in those principles of morality or maxims of lenity, which even their own times may have produced and established. Princes now ascend the throne endued with a knowledge of true glory, and imbibing the very same sentiments on this head with the publick, they concur in supporting it in that tranquility and happiness which is expected from them.

A peace, the long continuance of which has no precedent in our history, is unquestionably owing to the wisdom of a great minister. And the French nation acknowledges all the obli-

gations due to him for that unwearied administration which is the support of their tranquility. But the princes he has to treat with would perhaps more strenuously oppose his measures, if an education advanced by a work, which is of service to all the kings in the universe, had not reconciled them to the same dispositions of mind as the young and august monarch, in whose kingdoms Telemachus took its birth. If we are allowed to assert, that the encrease of literature has introduced a politeness and good taste in all the courts and cities of Europe, we may justly attribute, at least in part, that fondness for peace, which at this time seems to be the favourite passion of all nations, to those works which contain an excellent moral, set off with all the embellishments that can render it agreeable. We may certainly number them among the causes of that just and pacifick temper of mind, which every one is seemingly big with, and which by degrees extirpates those animosities among nations, which the bare remoteness of their former inducements, began to render unjust and reproachful; and in the place of which a mutual value for the virtues, talents, and every commendable quality of their neighbours is daily substituted.

A natural consequence of the success of Telemachus *next to reforming our judgments, and softening our manners, ought to be laying a foun-*

a foundation for a new kind of work. The first poems of antiquity produced imitations of the same form and denomination, as Epopeas, *Tragedies, Idylls and the like; but the author of Telemachus has only been imitated in the essential part; that is by the same intention or zeal to produce the same effects. Thus Telemachus is an epick poem; but the Travels of* Cyrus, *in conformity to their title, contain only the hero's rambles in search of instructions from all the wise men of his times, in order to introduce into his own dominions whatever he found good and profitable in the different customs of the most celebrated kingdoms and commonwealths.*

THE Work before us is, with regard to the moral design of it, of the same species with both; but more different in the form of it, than they are one from the other. They are both properly a system of education: and tho' Cyrus *was more advanced in years than Telemachus; both heroes only treasured up instructions for practice, or made trial of what they were to put in use; the former in the management of a little kingdom, and the latter in the government of a vast empire. My author, on the contrary, displays a compleat life, or the actual application of those principles and sentiments, which his hero had imbibed in the course of a most excellent education. So that in this history, which is divided into ten books, the hero, from the fourth, is in a condition to instruct others; and in the whole sequel acts alone upon his own motives. Mov'd by a true heroism, he employs the time of a tedious exile in the quest of unknown people, whom he frees from the bondage of the most barbarous superstitions, and becomes their law-giver. In his return, he, by his valour, relieves a mighty republick from an enemy, that was at its very gates; but demands no other reward for his labour, than the preservation of the people he had vanquished, whose king or tyrant had been the aggressor. Being at last returned into his native country, he becomes a benefactor to those he had reason to look upon as his enemies and rivals; rejoicing in those junctures, which engaged his honour to sacrifice his own interest to theirs, and made the happiness he obtained for them his duty.*

SETHOS is not alone virtuous by a natural disposition or from a habit. The motives of his conduct are drawn from durable and enlightened principles, which he displays in different rencounters. And he forms to himself such decisions, as, tho' always tending towards the highest perfection, and even to heroism, are more recommendable by their accuracy than their severity. Hence we have reason to suppose, that our author, who liv'd in the second century, had some knowledge of morals far superior to those of paganism. From these morals, it is very plain

be

he borrows those adequate definitions of the virtues and vices, which he sometimes puts into the mouth of his hero, and some others of his personages. And upon this it is I build the confidence I have in affirming, that this work contains a more refined and profound moral *than has hitherto been seen in any book, the product of mere literature, or of the number of those which may be stil'd prophane.*

AS our author, however, leaves his hero a pagan; he confines himself, in this history or life, wholly to moral virtues; and the recommendation of such to the practice of mankind is not without its advantage. It is by means of them, if I may be allowed the expression, we can have intercourse with the manners of those nations, who differ the most from us in point of religion. It is by them, that even in religion itself, we are able to keep up that humanity and probity, so necessary for the publick good, in men who have the unhappiness of not enough perceiving those motives of another kind, which are of greater importance to them. To conclude, by them we can shew those too zealous persons, who seem to despise such virtues as are merely moral, that christian virtues are in regard to moral virtues what faith is with respect to reason; superior, but never contradictory.

ANOTHER of our author's views has been to lay hold of the opportunity of an Egyptian tion hero to throw into his work a great number of learned curiosities, concerning that once so famous people: And farther, as he makes his hero travel over a great part of the globe, he had carefully got together the primary notions of the ancient geography. This was, without doubt, one of his reasons for giving his work the turn of a history or life, preferable to that of a poem or romance. In reality, the examples of Herodotus, Polybius, Diodorus, and especially of Plutarch, sufficiently justified his inserting in this narrative, not only political or military antiquities, but even historical passages relating to the rise and progress of human knowledge. These great writers looked upon such digressions as very curious for the common part of readers, who want time or patience to have recourse to other springs.

I must own, however, that upon a view of my whole translation, I began to fear the inconveniency of interruptions, either too frequent or too prolix, in a life built upon fable, the contexture of whose parts ought to render it more engaging than common lives. Of all the particulars on this head in the original, I have therefore only preserved such as were necessary to give an adequate idea of the education of a hero, who stood in need of great lights, to undertake a very long voyage, not before attempted; and then to give proper laws to the different nations, which were civilized by him. The academies of Memphis, which he frequents in his most tender youth, and the observatory of Thebes, which he visits before he imbarks for his voyage, were preparations essential to the carrying on of this design. And so the reader will find a plan of the former in the first book, and a sketch of the other in the fifth. But even in these hints I have considerably abridged our author's historical comparison between the sciences of the Egyptians and those of Greece.

NEVERTHELESS, the general impression which will arise from the body of the work, is sufficient to give even a pretty extensive idea of the Egyptians, Phœnicians, and some other nations: And even the fiction will be no hinderance to a search into the grounds of their understanding and manners. Many people have no other notion of the Greeks and Romans but what they have taken from Tragedy; and a certain principle, not very easy to define, teaches them to distinguish that which may reasonably be supposed to be true from what is probably the product of invention only. This advantage has been improved even in romances, and the ninth part of Cleopatra gives us as faithful a picture of the recesses of Agustus's court, as we could expect from the Abbot of St. Real. But here the reader will find plainer

indications

indications than are to be found either in tragedies or romances.

WE may at first view rely upon the particular circumstances, as well of Egypt as of other nations, which the author confirms by quoting any known writers. He seems himself to have separated the real from the fictitious, by alledging his anecdotical authors for those facts which are wholly the children of his own invention, or for such customs as are founded upon truth, but are refined and amplified in the relation. Fiction has a right of sacrificing the accuracy of facts, not only to moral virtues, but even to the embellishment of the narration; supposing besides that the end of such embellishment is to render the instruction more agreeable. An example of this conduct in our author, is the important article of initiation, which alone fills two whole books. But even this article is very conformable to the essential part of this renowned institution; as far as it could break thro' that rigid silence which cover'd it, and as we find any traces of it in those authors, either Pagan or Christian, who have mentioned it. The whole work is full of manners and customs, part of which I myself have confirmed by notes added to the text. As to some other less considerable passages, for the proof of which I have designedly avoided over-

charging

charging this work with quotations. I dare venture to affirm, that the more my readers may have examined, the more they will find our author agree with those testimonies which are either collected or dispersed in the different writings we have left of antiquity. For tho' my intent was to clear this work from all tedious erudition, I never designed to deprive it of the advantage and support of curious enquiries: but had always my author's chief aim in view, who adding his love for learning to that of virtue, looks upon literature in a nation, taken in general, as the source and support of every humane and civil virtue.

TO conclude, our author seems to have drawn all the probability, that can be expected from a fictitious writer, concerning the knowledge he could be supposed to have of the actions and sentiments of his hero, from the place where he lived. He is treating of an Egyptian prince, born in the century preceding the Trojan war, a time in which ancient Egypt was in its greatest splendor. Now this period so remote can have furnished no publick memoirs to any other writer either of Italy or Greece. But it is very natural to suppose that a citizen of Alexandria may have been master of memoirs taken in the confusion of war from the sacred archives of Egypt, and unknown even to the Egyptian

priests

priests of his times; and besides those priests who accompanied Sethos in his travels, may have been the authors of them. It was to give a like sanction to her history that Madam de Scudery in the preface to her Cyrus, a hero posterior to ours by seven or eight hundred years, studies to have it thought the translation of an ancient manuscript found in the Vatican library.

IN the second place, as our author mentions the sciences of the Egyptians only comparatively with those of the Greeks, from whom alone the Romans had any knowledge of ancient Egypt; the second century, or the latter end of the first, and the beginning of the second, in which he lived, was the most proper time for this comparison. A time which may justly be termed the most favourable to the sciences both for the Romans and Greeks, then under the same empire. M. de St. Evremont has already remarked that the days of Augustus were only noted for poetry; and that we must look something farther back for the days of eloquence. Our best writers in point of painting and sculpture, M. Felibien and M. de Piles, seem on the other hand to refer the period of sciences among the Romans, to that interval of time included in the reign of Vespasian and the Antonines. The names of Pliny, Ptolemy and Galienus alone give us reason to fix

fix their greatest eminency thereabouts; and the reader will find in this life sundry evidences to prove, that Alexandria was then their principal seat, even for the Romans themselves. These considerations were sufficient to justify our author with regard to what I have thought proper to omit on this head, and may perhaps give him more credit with regard to that little I have retained.

LICENCE.

By Order of the Lord Keeper of the Seals, I have read a Manuſcript, entitled: *The* Life *of* Sethos; *taken from private Memoirs of the ancient* Egyptians, *tranſlated from a* Greek *Manuſcript*. This Work, which contains excellent Leſſons of the moſt refin'd Morality, and is full of ſolid, and the moſt extenſive Learning, can't fail of being equally inſtructive and curious.

Paris, Jan. 29. 1731.

Lancelot.

ERRATA.

VOL. I. *P.* 64, *l.* 24. *read* advantage. 103,6. *r.* adopted. 114,2. *in the notes for* his *r.* the. 160,2. *for* lanes *r.* lines. 185,23. *r.* complaiſance. 240,16. *r.* I had, *&c.* 279,9. *r.* the diſcretion. 354,5. *after* ramparts *add a* (,). 358,13. *dele* (,). 383,22. *dele* (,). 386,19. *r.* ruling. 390,3. *r.* companion.

VOL. II. *P.* 62, *l.* 5. *after* ſettlement *add* in the city. 68,27. *r.* predeceſſor. 275,20. *r.* governor. 315,18. *after* they *add* likewiſe. 324,2. *dele* (,) *after* were, *and place it after* yet. 341,15. *after* judge, *add* only. 342,1. *r.* beſieger. 432,24. *for* ſtill *r.* ſwell.

THE LIFE OF SETHOS.

BOOK I.

THE Egyptians, who go farther back in the relations of their origine than our histories reach, say the Gods were their first kings. They name seven: Vulcan, the Sun, Agathodemon, Saturn, Osiris, Isis and Typhon. By Vulcan, to whom they assign no beginning, their philosophers meant that elementary fire, which is diffused every where. This same fire, re-united into one globe, is the Sun, the son of Vulcan. Agathodemor, defin'd by his very name, was their good genius or principle. Saturn, or Time, was the father of Osiris and Isis, brother and sister, husband and wife, the two sexes of nature. Typhon, their third brother, was always regarded by them as their evil principle.

HORUS was the son of Osiris and Isis, reason, or human wisdom, and he began the reign of the demi-gods. These were nine in number, Horus, Mars, Anubis, Hercules, Apollo, Ammon, Tithoes, Sosus, and Jupiter, or Menes. I shall not speak of every one of these in particular, most of them being pretty well known to the Greeks and Romans, even in their allegorical signification. I shall only observe, in order to set the times of my hero in a clearer light, that the latter of these demi-gods began the reign of men. He was indeed look'd upon but as a man in his life-time: but after having rul'd all Egypt alone by the name of Menes, he was, after his death, in consideration of his happy reign, number'd with the gods by the name of Jupiter. He had four sons, Thot or Mercury, Æsculapius, Athotes and Curudes, of which the two first were, as well as himself, advanced to the skies. Menes, to render the succession to his states equal, divided Egypt into four kingdoms. Mercury reign'd in Thebes, Æsculapius at Memphis, Athotes at This, and Curudes at Tanis. This was the rise of the four great Dynasties of Egypt, which were collateral or cotem-

cotemporary for ſixteen hundred years, to the time of the famous Seſoſtris, king of Thebes, and conqueror of Aſia. * The other Egyptian dynaſties, which ſome hiſtorians mention, to the number of twenty, from the times of Menes to Seſoſtris, were but ſeparate branches of theſe four chief diviſions; and the different names they give them, as Heracleopolites, Xoites, Elephantins, and the like, were taken from the reſidence of ſome of the kings of each dynaſty in different cities of the ſame kingdom.

As for the Shepherd Kings, who were foreigners, and having dwelt in Egypt during the ſpace of three or four ages, ſeem to have interrupted this ſucceſſion; they never had any ſettled poſſeſſion on this ſide Tanis, on the borders of Delta, tho' they obliged the natural kings of thoſe regions to retire to Heliopolis. But as theſe foreigners, originally Arabians, made frequent incurſions into the other parts of Egypt, the Egyptians, being reunited, attack'd, and having vanquiſh'd them, oblig'd them, and their deſcendants, to furniſh all Egypt with ſlaves. This victory was obtain'd near two hundred years before the birth of Seſoſtris, who found Egypt in a ſtate of tranquillity, and made it very flouriſh-

* The preceding genealogies are conformable to thoſe of Marſham; but what follows ſeems to agree with the chronology of father Pezron.

ing. This hero had the ambition to ſet the god Oſiris for his pattern, and like him, according to the Egyptian traditions, viſited a great part of the earth, teaching the inhabitants to cultivate it, and to form agreeable and uſeful ſocieties; thus Seſoſtris was the firſt king, of the race of men, who bore arms in Aſia, and there introduced and eſtabliſh'd the laws and ſciences of Egypt. He even rul'd all the four kingdoms of Egypt, not indeed by a ſovereign power, but by the ſuperiority of his genius, his virtues and reputation.

HIS firſt ſucceſſors ſupported for a time, eſpecially with regard to foreign provinces, the ſplendor of ſo great an empire; and we find, about one hundred years after Seſoſtris, Mendes or Memnon, king of Thebes, ruler of Suſa and Phrygia, chaſtizing the revolted Bactrians, and re-eſtabliſhing order among the people conquer'd by his anceſtor. But Rameſſes, who ſucceeded Memnon, wanting both the courage and conduct of his forefathers, loſt, by his weakneſs, all the conquer'd dominions, and, by his pride, a title which he had till then retain'd above the other kings of Egypt. His immediate predeceſſors having need of all their cunning as well as force, to keep the diſtant provinces under the yoke of obedience, had treated theſe kings with diſcretion, and had
not

not abus'd that right, which they perceived had in truth only devolv'd upon Sesostris, on account of his personal merit. But young Ramesses * soon discover'd his character by two obelisks, which he caus'd to be inscrib'd with titles so ostentatious and false, with regard to him, that in latter ages they have been thought to relate to Sesostris. This young prince, whose whole study was to deck himself with a vain and momentaneous glory, the ignominious consequences of which he never foresaw, took upon him to send these kings, who were now become his equals, his commands in form. But they soon gave him to understand, that they insisted upon Egypt's retaining its pristine form of four dynasties, which had been always independant since the four sons of Menes. They alledg'd, that Sesostris himself had not interrupted them: and that the kings their predecessors, in his life-time, reserving the royal title and dignities, had accepted of diverse regulations, by him proposed, only because they appear'd to be equally advantageous to the whole nation. Such was the division he had made of all Egypt into thirty-six nomes † or provinces, the particular governors of which could with greater ease keep a watchful eye over the productions of

* Kirk. Oed. Ægyp. tom. 4 p. 162. & Marsham, p. 431. ed. in fol.

† Diodorus, l. 1.

nature and art, which they furniſh for foreign commerce; and over the taxes they were in a condition to contribute in caſe of a general war. It was to him, they ſaid, were owing thoſe temples which were erected in each city, to the honour of its tutelar god; the wall which extended from Peluſa to Heliopolis, and put a ſtop to the inroads of the Syrians, and bordering Arabians of the deſarts, a people under no manner of diſcipline; the great canal, by which a communication was open'd between the Mediterranean and the Red-ſea, and the whole eaſtern and weſtern commerce made to paſs thro' Egypt; and laſtly thoſe dykes and ſluices, which taking in the whole ſpace from the Cataracts of the Nile, to its mouth or entrance into the ſea, between the mountains of Libya, and the coaſts of the red-ſea, ſtopp'd or received, as occaſion requir'd, the inundations of that river. But they added, that, all theſe undertakings being finiſhed, they knew how to maintain them, each in his own dominions, without the advice of Rameſſes, from whom they abſolutely refuſed to receive any commands. This oppoſition put an end to a diſpute, which a king, more wiſe than he, might have kept undecided; and he was obliged to take up with the title of king of Thebes the great, which devolv'd to Seſoſtris by right of his anceſtors.

ABOUT

ABOUT two hundred years after the death of Rameſſes, and fifty or ſixty years before the Trojan wars; Oſoroth, a prince advanced in years, ſucceeded to the crown of Memphis, a dynaſty but little inferior in power to that of Thebes, but by far preferable to it with regard to the lenity of its climate, and the beauty of its ſituation. The city of Memphis, the metropolis of the dynaſty, was ſituate on the weſtern bank of the Nile, near the place where that only river of Egypt divides itſelf into ſeven arms, of which thoſe two, which are at the greateſt diſtance one from the other, encloſe the Delta, and all together form ſeven mouths at their entrance into the great ocean (the Mediterranean.) All Egypt has, from the antienteſt account of time, been ſtil'd a gift of the Nile; being ſuppos'd to be only a heap of earth, which the waters of this river has ſucceſſively carry'd away with its ſtream from the ſouth to the north. But the formation of the Delta is held to be more recent: becauſe according to thoſe * monuments, which may well be look'd upon as hiſtorical truths, the Pharus of Alexandria, which is now join'd to the continent, was formerly twenty-four leagues diſtant from it in the ſea. This region is ſo delightful, that, according to fable, the gods form'd it upon

* Plin. lib. 2. c. 35. Sen. quæſt. nat. lib. 6. c. 26.

the constellation of the triangle, which passes vertically over the Delta every Day in the year.

OSOROTH, not long before his accession to the throne, had marry'd Nephte, daughter of the king of This, a third dynasty, situate between Memphis and Thebes, to the west of the river Nile. Of this princess he soon had the prince, whose life I am about to write. He was the eldest of the three sons of Osoroth, mentioned in the annals of † Manethon only by the name of the Anonymi. But tho' this famous historian was a priest, and even keeper of the sacred archives of Heliopolis; as he did not write till the reign of Ptolomeus Philadelphus, two hundred years after the devastation of Egypt by Cambyses, the remains of those memoirs he was possess'd of were but very imperfect. I have, by means not to be related, discover'd those which are more ample, and have been preserv'd more entire; and which give to the first of these Anonymi of Manethon the name of Sethos, and the surname of Sosis, or Preserver, for a reason that will be shewn in the sequel of his life.

† See the Egyptian origines of Perizonius, p. 47. under the column, ex African. also the 38, and 49 pages, in which Manethon is alledg'd to be the first author of the sequels of Africanus and Eusebius.

THE

THE birth of this prince fill'd the whole kingdom with joy; ſo great was the love the people bore to their king, or rather to the queen, who, tho' but young in years, govern'd them with an admirable wiſdom and goodneſs: For Oſoroth, whoſe character it would be difficult to trace in one ſingle picture, and which will not be well underſtood till towards the concluſion of this hiſtory, immediately entruſted the reins of government in the hands of the queen. This prince did not aſcend the throne till the 50th year of his age: And king Seſonchis his father, more jealous of his preſent authority than attentive to the future felicity of his ſon and ſubjects, had kept him ignorant of the affairs of his realm, even to the moment he left him his ſucceſſor. So Oſoroth, having fortify'd his natural indolence by a life given up to ſloth and inactivity, had no other taſte of the ſweets of royalty, but that of independency, and ſought how to disburthen himſelf of the weight of government. This part fell, as it were of itſelf, into the hands of the queen, more capable than any other of receiving it; and what appear'd in the eye of the people to be a judicious choice, was in reality the mere effect of ſupineneſs in Oſoroth. He was one of thoſe kings, who being of themſelves neither good nor bad, become the very beſt or worſt of princes,

just

juſt as they happen by mere accident to fall into the hands of good or wicked miniſters: Unhappy the ſituation of a people ſubject to a prince whoſe very errors are without controul!

NEPHTE, from the firſt dawn of her power, had fill'd her ſubjects with the hopes of a gentle government. They were the more ſenſible of it, as their deceas'd king, otherwiſe a great prince, was rigid and ſtern in his manners. The minds of the people were ſenſible of a relief, even before the queen had eas'd them in the publick burden; becauſe, without diminiſhing the king's revenue, ſhe had found means of rendring it leſs perceptible. Even the riches of private perſons encreas'd by the confidence they plac'd in her, and in one another. She, at the ſame time, brought up her only ſon with all the affection of a mother, and the foreſight of a wiſe queen. She earneſtly deſir'd to ſee him attain to that age in which ſhe might, in her turn, deliver up to him that adminiſtration, which ſhe look'd upon but as a truſt committed to her charge. In the mean time ſhe took as an aſſiſtant in the conduct of her affairs, an excellent perſon, call'd Amedes; who, tho' he had not in the late reign paſs'd thro' all the offices of dignity wherewith he might have been inveſted, yet had acquitted himſelf with great honour in

ſeveral

ſeveral eminent ſtations, as well civil as military, and in negotiations with foreign princes; and who now adviſ'd the queen (as he had before the late king) to conceal from the publick the honour ſhe did him, to avoid exciting the jealouſy of the great, and that murmuring of the people, which is often raiſ'd againſt thoſe miniſters who are moſt zealous for the publick felicity. Hence the queen, reſerving Amedes for her cabinet counſellor, without any title of note, preferr'd the beſt of her ſubjects, among thoſe whom the different degrees of birth ſeem'd to preſent for every place that became vacant. Thus her ſovereign authority was employ'd in diſtinguiſhing merit, without ſubverting order; and the number of the diſaffected was very ſmall, and even they were apprehenſive of uttering thoſe complaints, which they knew the voice of the publick would condemn.

WHILE the queen intirely devoted herſelf to affairs of ſtate, the king gave himſelf up to all the amuſements of a glittering court. But as theſe were never reliev'd by any thing ſerious, they could ſcarce keep him from uneaſineſs, and manifeſted in the king of a great people, a man whoſe very leiſure ſate heavy upon him. Among the ladies who were about him was one, whoſe name was Daluca, the widow of a great lord of the court. She had no children, and had already

paſs'd

paſs'd thoſe years in which the ladies only cultivate their beauty in order to carry on their gallantry, and was enter'd into thoſe, in which they are ſtudious of making the remains of it ſubſervient to their ambition. This lady had form'd a deſign of gaining an aſcendant over the king The eſteem and regard the queen was in had deterr'd every one elſe from the like attempt. Daluca herſelf, who was perfectly acquainted with Oſoroth's temper, was very cautious of ſaying any thing to him againſt Nephte, that might excite any diſagreeable emotions in his mind. She made it her buſineſs to be continually near him; and had the art of pleaſing by that obſequiouſneſs and thoſe complacencies, which have by much a greater power over kings ſomewhat advanc'd in years, than youth and beauty, void of ſtratagem and private views. And ſhe did not find it difficult to gain the favour of a prince ſo unguarded and indolent. She might perhaps have already rais'd her ambition to a greater height, upon obſerving that the queen was not in the beſt ſtate of health. But without renouncing the view of a more remote happineſs, her vanity was for the preſent ſatiſfy'd by being a diſtinguiſh'd object among the courtiers, and by ſtanding in ſome manner in competition with the queen.

NEPHTE,

NEPHTE, by the dignity of her perſon, as well as the ſituation of affairs, was far above the uneaſineſſes which generally affect thoſe who perceive themſelves inveſted only with a borrow'd power. Wherefore, tho' ſhe ſoon obſerv'd the ſtratagems and intrigues of her rival, ſhe fear'd nothing with regard to herſelf; but then her foreſight laid her under the greater apprehenſions for her ſon. He had then attain'd but his eighth year, and ſhe ſaw with grief, that if ſhe ſhould be ſnatch'd away before his father had ſettled the ſucceſſion upon him, the fate of this young prince would be deliver'd into the hands of the raſh Daluca. The right of primogeniture was indeed eſtabliſh'd in Egypt: But the choice of a father was of great weight; and hiſtory furniſh'd more than one example of a ſecond or third ſon being preferr'd to the eldeſt. And oftentimes this incertitude had been the occaſion of quarrels among brothers, which the fortune of the ſword could alone decide. Thus, tho' the queen had then no ſymptoms that foreboded any approaching diſtemper, yet the thoughts of a doubtful futurity caſt her into great uneaſineſſes. Wherefore recommending her ſon, by means of the prieſts, to the protection of all the deities of Egypt, ſhe apply'd herſelf with the greater earneſtneſs to the performance of her duty, that ſhe might

might engage heaven to ſecond intentions ſo worthy of her maternal care: but the gods, who are the ſole arbiters of the rewards of the juſt, do not always diſpenſe them in the courſe of this mortal life.

THE queen's too aſſiduous application to buſineſs, even beyond her ſtrength, and perhaps her too great apprehenſion of ſickneſs, caus'd her in a ſhort time to fall into an indiſpoſition, which, being at firſt but ſlight, ſhe ſtrove to conceal, in hopes of overcoming it. But the fever increaſing, the diſtemper was ſoon look'd upon as a thing not to be trifled with; and the reflections ſhe made upon the circumſtances of her ſon, threw her into the utmoſt deſpair. Unhappy princeſs! cry'd ſhe, whatever my fears have hitherto ſuggeſted is now coming to paſs! Why muſt my life be of ſuch moment to my ſon? Tho' in bloom of youth, I have taſted enough of the bitterneſs of life to leave it without regret, if no one elſe was concern'd; yet, alas! 'tis I who die; and 'tis I who mourn for my ſon! Theſe words were follow'd by a torrent of tears, which heighten'd her diſeaſe, without alleviating her affliction. In vain her diſconſolate damſels, who took care to keep the prince from her ſight, ſtudy'd to appeaſe her by perſuaſion and entreaty. Alas! ſaid ſhe, I plainly perceive by the confuſion in your diſcourſes, and the cruelty with which you

you conceal my ſon from my eyes, that my fate is fix'd, and all hopes of a recovery loſt. My ſon! my deareſt ſon! cry'd ſhe, in the greateſt agitation of mind, thou alone makeſt death my terror! Death, who is the end of all others pain, is the origin of mine! I ſhall be deny'd even the peace of the grave! Madam, anſwer'd the moſt venerable of her attendants, who by her birth, virtue and affection was deareſt to her, whither do the hurry of your thoughts carry you? Do you conſider, that, by giving way, as you do, to an exceſs of grief, whereby you render your diſtemper mortal, which otherwiſe is but dangerous, you at the ſame time offend the providence of the gods, the ſovereign arbiters of yours and your ſon's deſtiny? That virtue, madam, which you have hitherto ſtrictly profeſs'd, is not perfectly diſtinguiſhable till exercis'd in ſuch trials as this. Well, anſwer'd the queen, I ſubmit to your advice, and devote myſelf with an abſolute reſignation to the will of the gods. Acquaint me only when the time of my diſſolution approaches, that I may take my laſt meaſures with regard to my ſon, upon whoſe fate I foreſee depends the happineſs of my people.

THIS lady, whoſe friendſhip was ſincere and reſolute, having promis'd the queen what ſhe demanded, Nephte from that moment endeavour'd to preſerve her mind in a ſtate of of tranquillity; but the leſs viſible her anxieties appear'd in her outward behaviour, the greater effect they had upon her mind.

IN the mean time the moſt celebrated phyſicians of the kingdom, who were then the prieſts, were aſſembled in the palace, even by order of the king; tho', that it might not break in upon his pleaſures, he always ſuppos'd the queen's diſtemper to be of no dangerous conſequence. Egypt, the mother of arts and ſciences, claim'd the honour, before all other, of having given birth to the medical art. Æſculapius, one of the ſons of Menes, had even reign'd in Memphis, as we have already obſerv'd, while his brother Mercury was king of Thebes; and the ſix volumes * which the former had compil'd upon phyſick, added to the ſix-and-thirty wherein Mercury had given the principles of all the other ſciences, form'd that famous treaſure of learning, by which the prieſts boaſted of having been inſtructed by the gods themſelves. Be that as it will, theſe phyſicians, truly accompliſh'd in their art, put in practice, with regard to the queen, whatever their reading, reflexions, and experience could ſuggeſt. They at firſt treated her according to their ancient rules, which were enjoyn'd them under penalty of death: for

* Clem. Alex. Strom. 6.

every physician, who deviated from them, was answerable for his patient, and in case of ill success, the death of the one surely brought on the death of the other. This indeed often serv'd for a pretext to treat those patients, who were indifferent to them, with negligence, and not to exceed the letter of the law. But that concern with which they were sensibly affected for the preservation of a queen, such as Nephte, and the lamentations of a people, who recommended their sovereign, whom they styl'd their mother, soon engag'd them to have recourse to new remedies. They indeed disguis'd them under ancient names, whereby they found means to justify themselves by some of the innumerable instances with which their books were fill'd. They even by turns waited at the gate of the palace to hear all who might have any advice to offer for the queen's recovery: and afterwards gave their opinion of them in their consultations. For it was of importance to them in so critical a juncture, in some measure, to comply with an ancient custom, of placing their sick before the doors of their houses, that they might enquire of all who pass'd by, if they knew of any remedy for the distemper in question.

ON the other hand, the temples of the gods were open day and night to a vast concourse of people, who continually resorted thither to supplicate the recovery of their queen. They began at the † temple of Vulcan, built by Menes, the common anceſtor of all the kings of Egypt, which had been preſerv'd during the ſpace of 1600 years in all the ſplendor it was left in by the founder. From thence they went to thoſe of Serapis and Venus: But it was in the temple of Oſiris, his wife Iſis, and their ſon Horus, that they were the moſt aſſiduous, on account of the remarkable relation there happen'd to be between theſe three deities, and the perſons of whom the royal family then conſiſted. The ſucceſſive concourſe of innumerable people continually fill'd not only the court, the porch, and body of the temple, but all the parts contiguous to the ſanctuary, notwithſtanding their large extent.

IN the middle of the ſanctuary, upon a very high pedeſtal, and all of one ſingle piece of caſt metal, were plac'd theſe three deities, in ſuch ſort, that Oſiris, whoſe image was the higheſt, held Iſis * ſtanding before him, and ſhe Horus in the ſame manner: For what Strabo ſays of the temples of Egypt being without ſtatues, or at moſt having only the figure of ſome animal in the middle of them, is not to be underſtood of the times antecedent to the invaſion of Cambyſes. The

† Strab. l. 17. Herod. l. 2.
* Vid. Kirch. tom. 1. p. 113.

head

head of Osiris was incircled with a radiant sun. Isis was crown'd with a bushel, and had her face cover'd with a veil. Under her left arm she held an urn bow'd downwards, and at her feet lay the bird Ibis. And Horus was describ'd holding his finger upon his lips. There it was that numerous troops of musicians sung to slow musick, and in a mournful tone, hymns, taken from their ancient rites, and adapted to the present occasion. *

OSiris, pow'r, from earliest times, that springs,
Victor and patron of this mighty ball,
Branch of our gods, and stem of all our kings,
Husband of Isis, sovereign lord of all:
Save from too hard, but, ah! impending fate,
A pious monarch's wife and watchful mate,
Religion's prop, and safeguard of the state.

Isis, sole goddess; thro' the world ador'd;
In mysteries conceal'd; in bounties seen;
One deity by various names implor'd,
In various places; of those regions queen,
Where springs, and is reserv'd, the sacred flood,
Which being gives, and proves earth's vital blood,
When from thy urn thou pourst th' irriguous good.

* This hymn has a conformity to the inscriptions upon the columns of Osiris and Isis, mention'd by Diod. l. 1. Apul. Metam. l. 11. and others.

Type of our queen, and anceſtor, ordain,
  If to thy virtues, as thy worſhip, true,
Memphis ſhe gave again to feel thy reign,
  That theſe our tears fate's rigour may ſubdue.
In ſaving Nephte, thy own glory ſave,
The ſpouſe, the ſubjects, and the ſon you gave,
All doom'd alike to periſh in her grave.

Horus, thou god of ſilence, wiſdom taught,
  Who ſhield'ſt from harms the weakneſs of the
To full maturity by years unbrought: [good,
  Protect our prince, thy image, and thy blood.
O guard his royal youth with tender care,
Aſſume the task thy mother Iſis bare
For thee, of equal years, her infant heir.

WHILE this and the like hymns were repeating, the prieſts (in robes of linnen, with chaplets of lotus on their heads, and ſandals of the plant papyrus on their feet) were continually offering ſacrifices upon three triangular altars plac'd before the triple ſtatue. Theſe holy men, worn away with auſtere faſting, which had continu'd from the inſtant the queen's diſtemper begun, and fainting under the cruel ſcourgings with which they accompany'd their invocations, were hardly able, notwithſtanding their great number, to put up the prayers the people demanded of them, or which they offer'd of their own accord.

BUT

BUT what avail temples, and all the vows offer'd in them, againſt the irrevocable decrees of fate! The queen, however ready to conform to all the preſcriptions of her phyſicians, declin'd daily. The moſt powerful medicines, tho' apply'd even before ſhe was reduc'd to extremity, ſeem'd to have no more effect upon her than common remedies; and the phyſicians, who had been leſs apprehenſive of any extraordinary event, than of that inſenſible decay they perceiv'd in her, never let fall the leaſt word of hopes. Convinc'd of her own fate, ſhe reſolv'd at laſt to conſult the moſt ancient oracle in the world, which was in the neighbourhood of Memphis, with regard to her ſon. It was the oracle of Latona, the nurſe of Horus, at Butos, a city lying between the Sebennitick and Polbitinick gulph, oppoſite to which was the then floating iſland Chemnis. * And this it was which gave the Greeks a notion of their iſland of Delos floating till the birth of Apollo, the ſon of Latona. The prieſts of the oracle, inform'd of the queen's ſickneſs, had anticipated her deputation, and made great preparations for obtaining the goddeſs's anſwer. They offer'd up their ſupplications to her in a vaſt temple, dug under that which appear'd. In that above the ſacrifices were offer'd, and

* Pomp. Mela.

the ceremonies perform'd, in the ſight of all the people; but to the myſteries celebrated in the ſubterranean temple, none were admitted but thoſe who were initiated. There it was that ſo many human victims were ſacrific'd, particularly upon ſuch occaſions as this, and the gods entreated to accept of other young perſons, in exchange for a prince or princeſs greatly belov'd. There are few nations known, but what may be reproach'd with the ſame ſhameful barbarity: But the Egyptians, more ſuperſtitious than other nations, have, in former days, carry'd it ſo far as to ſacrifice every foreigner at the tomb of Oſiris, in the city of Heliopolis. This tomb was call'd Buſiris; and fable has related it as of a king of Egypt, a tranſgreſſor of the laws of hoſpitality. However, Amoſis, * one of the anceſtors of Seſoſtris at Thebes, had the courage and authority to aboliſh this bloody cuſtom in every city. In the room of theſe human victims were then ſubſtituted images of wax, ſince ſo much made uſe of in magick ſuperſtitions.

THE prieſts deputed to conſult the oracle being arriv'd, after one day's journeying, at Butos, with the noble offerings the queen had ſent, went the ſame evening into the temple. All the people having conducted

* Euſeb. Præpar. Evan. l. 4. c. 16. ex. Porph.

them

them thither, were oblig'd to attend without; and they enter'd into that part of the temple adjoining to the chapel in the superior temple, of which Herodotus makes mention, and which was hewn out of one single square ſtone, the inſide whereof was ſixty foot every way. After having paſs'd a good part of the night in this place, they received the anſwer of the oracle, and were let out privately by another door, and made the beſt of their way for Memphis.

THE queen, who counted every moment of their journey, and her life, waited their return with an impatience that added to the ardor of her fever. That ſorrow which had ſo tortur'd her mind in the firſt periods of her indiſpoſition, and which ſhe ſtill continu'd to ſuppreſs, was now as viſible in her attendants. They look'd upon her death as an irrevocable decree of fate; and the conſequences of it, which they foreſaw, as well with regard to themſelves as the ſtate, threw them into an inexpreſſible anguiſh of mind. It was not only that tender affliction ariſing from the approaching and eternal ſeparation from a miſtreſs, and a friend, to whom they were entirely devoted: Their concern was like to that of perſons who imagin'd they beheld all their fair poſſeſſions on the point of being laid in aſhes, by the impetuous ravages of ſome ſudden fire, which would reduce them from a ſtate of plenty, to that of extreme indigence: or to the conſternation of a city brought to extremity by a barbarous enemy, ready to deſtroy its religion and laws. The anguiſh of deſpair was ſo viſible in their faces, that the moſt beautiful were become ghaſtly; and thoſe amongſt them, who were endu'd with the greateſt preſence of mind, could not conceal their diſtraction, even in their attendances upon the queen, who ſtill kept a profound ſilence.

THE deputies being at laſt return'd, and taking the young prince, with the faithful Amedes, whom they found attending him, with them, they enter'd the queen's apartment; where, in the preſence of both, and of her confident, without any other witneſſes, the chief of the deputation thus unfolded the anſwer of the oracle, which the ſequel of the life of Sethos ſo exactly verifies, that the author of my memoirs may perhaps be ſuſpected of having copy'd from thence. Vertuous ſpouſe, generous mother, and wiſe queen (ſaid he) the gods, adverſe, and at the ſame time propitious, ſend you this anſwer: Be comforted in that death for which you are already prepar'd. It is only an unhappineſs to thoſe in whom it puts an end to a wicked life, and when it loads the memory of the deceas'd with the hatred and maledictions of the living. The gods are attending

ing to beſtow upon you that reward which is due to the good works you have perform'd, and even to thoſe you deſign'd. You will ſtill live in the hearts of your people, and your ſon will one day reſtore to them that felicity, which the loſs of you is now about to deprive them of. He himſelf however will not be happy, according to the idea common ſouls form to themſelves of the proſperity of princes: But the gods promiſe him all that heroick virtue has moſt ſatisfactory in itſelf, and all that the glory which attends it can indulge him with. Born for the good of mankind, he will become a benefactor to nations; preſerver of Egypt; and a conqueror of himſelf. But let thoſe who now hear me keep as an inviolable ſecret, whatever concerns the prince, and ſuffer the cloud which will overſhadow his firſt years to diſperſe of itſelf.

THE prieſt had hardly made an end of ſpeaking, when the queen, embracing young Sethos, ſaid: My ſon, my death is no longer a trouble to me, the gods deprive you of my relief only to give you a more eminent merit and luſtre in thoſe great actions they propoſe to effect by your means. Be faithful to the deſtiny they have prepar'd for you, and fulfil all their deſigns. And then, addreſſing herſelf to the prieſts, Return, ſaid ſhe, to your temples, and continue your vows

vows for my ſon, whom I have long ſince recommended to you: The preſents I deſign for the gods ſhall immediately follow you; may they vouchſafe to accept of theſe ſlender marks of my gratitude.

THESE preſents were all the ornaments of a domeſtick chapel, which ſhe had caus'd to be built contiguous to the apartment ſhe ſlept in. She had brought them from This, the place of her nativity, where the news of her lamented death was ſoon going to ſhorten the days of the king her father. Amongſt theſe ornaments were ſtatues of gold, ſome of the height of a cubit, which repreſented the common deities of all Egypt, and in particular of Apollo, who was held in peculiar veneration at This, and at Abydus, which was dependant upon it. Having thus previouſly ſent to the gods what was moſt dear to her, ſhe addreſs'd herſelf to Amedes in the following diſcourſe. Wiſe and faithful counſellor, ſaid ſhe, the kingdom will not be ſo happy to have you for its ſupport, under the adminiſtration which will ſucceed my death; devote yourſelf to my ſon, and be his governor and council. The gods aſſure me that thoſe virtues they have promis'd him will be the effects of your inſtructions and example. Amedes immediately embracing young Sethos with the reſpect due to him; My prince, ſaid he, to you I entire-

entirely devote the remains of my ſtrength and life. All the ſervices I am capable of rendering my country, are included in the education I ſhall have the honour of giving to him, to whom the ſovereignty of it will one day of right belong.

IN that inſtant the king, who, not to be wanting in his devoirs, had made it a rule to viſit the queen twice a day, enter'd her apartment. My lord, ſaid ſhe, upon ſeeing him approach, the oracle has pronounced my doom. It may not be ſeemly to recommend a ſon to his father; but, ſince he is going to be deprived of me, vouchſafe to accept my entreaty, that you will be to him a father and a mother. Madam, anſwer'd the king, my ſon is dear to me for my own ſake, and will be ſtill dearer to me for yours; but I don't yet deſpair of moving the gods to pity for your preſervation. Upon which, covering his eyes with his hand, he departed.

THE next thing the queen did, was to diſtribute jewels to all her attendants, according to their birth and quality. That ſerenity which appeared in her countenance had chang'd their deſpair into gentle tears. At laſt, turning to the young prince; For you, my ſon, ſaid ſhe, I have reſerved this casket: in it you will find jewels to an ineſtimable value, and ſufficient for your ſupport,

ſupport, to whatever ſtate fortune may reduce you. Amedes will keep them for you, or employ them for your ſervice. But for this emerald, ſet in the form of a heart, which I have hitherto cauſed you to wear about your neck, and which you ſhall convert into a ring, when you put off the habit of a child, never part with it on any account. About four years ſince, your father caus'd us all three to be repreſented in relievo upon the ſame ſtone; himſelf in the form of Oſiris, me in the reſemblance of Iſis, and you like Horus, ſtanding between us. The ingenious workman afterwards, by his command, cut this ſtone into three pieces, according to the bigneſs of the figures. One of them is that you wear, another is ſet in the ring I now take from my finger, and put into your casket. Theſe two, when diveſted of their ornaments, will exactly correſpond with the third, which your father has himſelf upon his finger. Adieu, my ſon! may the gods protect you, and receive me! Sethos, touch'd with all the ſentiments his tender years were ſuſceptible of, reply'd; I receive, madam, what you are pleas'd to beſtow upon me; I have given attention to what you have ſaid; and when I am of riper years, I will endeavour to do as you have done. The queen preſs'd his hand, and made a ſign for him to be remov'd. She ſpoke no more, and an hour afterwards yielded to the fatal ſtroke.

I WILL not pretend to give a defcription of the grief which overfpread Memphis, and all the provinces of the kingdom, as this melancholy news reach'd them. The tears which were fhed upon a bare apprehenfion of this cataftrophe may give fome idea of it. * The Egyptians in former days were fo much devoted to their fovereigns, that a mourning in the royal manfion was generally a domeftick mourning in every family. They gave teftimony of it in publick for forty days, by appearing with their garments rent, and in private by their auftere faftings. But this laft lofs, the confequence of which every one was apprehenfive of in his private concerns, fill'd each heart with inexpreffible grief; infomuch that the priefts, who, upon the like occafions, were wont to countenance the publick affliction, to do honour to the memory of their deceas'd kings, found themfelves oblig'd, in the prefent incident, to calm the minds and hearts of the people, in order to preferve that decorum which was, as they faid, becoming a civiliz'd nation, and to render to the manes of the deceas'd queen an homage more agreeable to her virtues. They declared, that fhe died in peace, and that the oracles had removed her apprehenfions for the deftiny of her fon and people.

* Diodor. l. 1.

They alledged the ſtate of reſt and felicity, into which they had ſo much reaſon to hope the gods would admit her at her approaching obſequies. They endeavour'd in ſhort, by all manner of conſolatory advices, to aſſwage the pain of that wound, which time alone could heal, and which they, however, fear'd time might render more ſenſible.

PREPARATIONS were in the mean time making for the funeral pomp. No people ever came up to the Egyptians in this particular. Their authors, and even ours ſay, * that they were the firſt who had any notion of the immortality of the ſoul. And, indeed, it appears by the ſimplicity of their palaces, in compariſon with the magnificency of their tombs, that they were more ſollicitous for the eternal manſions of a future life, than for the tranſitory abodes of this. We muſt however allow, that their doctrine on this head was not very conſiſtent. For, not to mention the Metempſychoſis, which Pythagoras was for eſtabliſhing among them, and which made the ſouls of men, when freed from the body, paſs from one animal to another, till after the ſpace of three thouſand years, they again enter'd into human bodies; the wiſeſt men allow'd of a place of torment in hell, for the ſouls of the

* Herodotus, l. 2.

wicked, and delightful fields for those of the good. So that either opinion, or a mixture, such as it was, of both, left nothing in those costly tombs, but a dead corpse, which was very far from being eternal; but which, however, by the art they had of embalming, was more durable than the tombs themselves.

THOSE who were appointed to perform this last function, had already taken charge of the queen's corpse. † They were officers of the second rank, very much respected in Egypt, for the knowledge they had of the secrets of the priesthood, though they were no other than domesticks of the priests. The operation was thirty days in performing. Having, by means of a lateral incision in the body, taken out all the intestines, excepting the heart and reins, they anointed it both outwardly and inwardly with a certain gum compos'd of cedar, myrrh, cinnamon, and other perfumes; which not only preserved it for several ages, but caus'd it to diffuse an agreeable odour. They had, besides, the secret of giving a corpse its pristine form; insomuch that the deceas'd seem'd to have retain'd the air of his countenance, and the port of his person. The hairs, not only of his head, but of his eye-brows and eye-lids, were di-

† Diodorus, l. 1. sect. 2.

ſtinctly preſerv'd; and what is yet more ſurprizing, they reſtor'd to him an appearance of plumpneſs, and a colour and freſhneſs as natural, as in the healthieſt part of his life. Some private perſons choſe rather to preſerve the bodies of their relations, thus embalmed, in cloſets made for that purpoſe, than to depoſite them in ſepulchres already made, or to erect new ones for them; and it was a ſingular ſatisfaction to them to behold their anceſtors with the ſame phyſiognomies, and in the ſame attitudes as when living.

BUT it was not ſo with reſpect to kings: for, if they did not make any particular diſpoſition to the contrary, they were all, in which-ever dynaſty they reign'd, convey'd to the labyrinth ſituate in the middle of the lake Moeris, on the borders of Libya. This edifice, which in magnificence ſurpaſs'd all the labours of Greece put together, even according to the teſtimony of the Greeks themſelves, was not built, as Herodotus imagin'd, by the twelve kings who reign'd at one and the ſame time, after the retreat of Sabacon the Ethiopian: For he did not make himſelf maſter of Egypt till two or three hundred years before the invaſion of Cambyſes: whereas this labyrinth was by far more antient than Seſoſtris himſelf, and was erected when Egypt was only divided into twelve provinces. The kings of the four dynaſties, being all at peace,

peace, had all contributed to this memorable work, of which the upper part was dedicated to the ſun, and the ſubterranean to the infernal deities. And this it was occaſion'd * Homer's calling the entrance into hell the gates of the ſun. The twelve immenſe palaces, which it contain'd, repreſented, according to their deſign, all Egypt; and for that reaſon they mark'd out their ſeveral ſepulchres, for them and their ſucceſſors, in the ſubterranean vaults. But the imaginations of the people, added to the ceremonies performed by the prieſts before they admitted a corps into theſe gloomy manſions, where few of the living had ever enter'd, gave occaſion to a great deal of fiction. It was an article of religion to believe, that the innumerable windings, with which they were told, and with truth, that theſe ſubterraneous paſſages abounded, conducted their good kings to delightful regions, but that tyrants were forbidden even an entrance into the labyrinth. The manner of theſe ceremonies was this. When the corpſe was brought to the bank of a lake call'd Charon, over which the paſſage lay to the gate of the infernal deities, it was there ſtopp'd by an incorruptible tribunal, compos'd of ſixteen prieſts of the labyrinth, with their chief, and two judges choſen out of each

* Odyſſ. 24.

of the twelve ancient nomes. The high-priest, who conducted the deceas'd king, having there made an harangue, the president of the tribunal gave leave to all the assistants to lay such charges against the deceas'd, as they could prove. They then proceeded to judgment, by which the corpse was either sentenc'd to be deliver'd to their ferryman, whom they call'd Charon, or to be depriv'd of sepulture. This sentence pass'd by scrutiny, that is, by certain tickets, which the judges threw into that terrible urn, the very idea of which was powerful enough to keep the ancient kings within the bounds of justice.

To conclude, To whatever sepulchre the corpse of kings, or even of private persons, were carry'd, they were liable * to an examination before judges, who were always men of the greatest reputation and probity. They were only eligible out of those who were initiated; and, if for a private person, they were upon every occasion chosen by men taken out of each class of the freemen of a city, or of the subjects of the kingdom, when for a sovereign. And the tickets in which the names of the judges were written, were open'd and number'd in publick view. But for those kings who were to be interr'd

* Diodor. l. 1. §. 2.

in the labyrinth, all Egypt, according to the division of the twelve ancient nomes, had their suffrage in the election of the judges. And besides, at this labyrinth alone was perform'd that great number of other ceremonies, from whence Orpheus the poet, whom we shall soon see in Egypt, and who being present at the obsequies of another king, borrow'd thence the greater part of that description of hell which he has given us in his verses; and which was afterwards copy'd by Homer in Greek, and by Virgil in Latin.

THE fortieth day after the queen's decease being now come, all was ready for setting forward with the funeral procession, which was to march the forty leagues between Memphis and the labyrinth in ten days and ten nights, according as the several stages were regulated. The porch of the palace was clos'd up from all approaches of the sun, and illuminated with lamps: Under it was plac'd a large chariot with four wheels, all cover'd over with gold. At the hinder part of the chariot was erected a throne, with an ascent of three steps, cover'd with a large crown of gold, richly adorn'd with precious stones, and supported by a sphinx of the same metal, with large wings display'd, upon the head of which the edge of the crown rested. From the top of the crown fell down in large folds, between the sphinx's wings, a cloth of purple in the form of a pavilion, cover'd with hieroglyphicks richly emboſſed in gold, and repreſenting all the virtues. The two extremities of this pavilion join'd and croſs'd one another at the front of the chariot. This chariot had two poles, and was drawn by ſixteen horſes, four in front. Their harneſs was exceeding magnificent, as on a day of triumph. But nothing was comparable to the richneſs and elegancy with which the queen was array'd. She was plac'd upon the throne in a ſitting poſture, and ſo artfully faſten'd into it, that no jolt, however violent, could give her any motion, which might make her have the appearance of a corpſe. The whole machine was moreover in ſuch manner ſuſpended between its ſhafts, that nothing could bring it out of a level. And beſides, the roads, which of themſelves were very good in Egypt, had been levell'd for the conveniency of this proceſſion. In a word, this chariot ſeems to have ſerv'd as a model for that in which afterwards the corpſe of Alexander was tranſported from Babylon to * Alexandria. The queen, who had her face and boſom bare, but her eyes clos'd, ſeem'd to enjoy the ſweets of an agreeable ſlumber amidſt the noiſe of trumpets and kettle-drums, with which the air reſounded while the proceſſion was rang'd

* Diodor. l. 18.

in order. What melancholy reflexions were there not renew'd in the hearts of thoſe who lov'd her, and had been depriv'd of her ſight ſince her death, or ſince her ſickneſs! They ſaw her, they ſpoke to her; but ſhe was no more. Thoſe who had been the neareſt devoted to her, the better to ſuppreſs their affliction, avoided looking on her for a time; but overpower'd at laſt by their curioſity and affection, they caſt their eyes upon her, and finding yet the ſame features, and the ſame graces, they immediately turn'd them away, and melted into tears.

IN the mean time the queen's houſhold, conſiſting of ſix thouſand horſe, march'd in the front, leaving the care of the royal corpſe to the prieſts. Theſe officers were rang'd four and four, with their arms pointed downwards: The din of their warlike inſtruments ſounding in mournful tone, and mix'd with periodical intervals of ſilence, pierced to the ſoul. Next to theſe follow'd the ſocieties of the city of Memphis, diſtinguiſh'd by proper habits, but cover'd with black crape, on horſe-back, as the former. And among this number of people, which already amounted to twelve thouſand, not a ſingle word was utter'd during the whole proceſſion. The great officers of the court, and after them the princes, excepting the king and the preſumptive heir to the crown, who never appear'd publickly at funerals, came next, four and four, as the former, clad in purple robes, sitting in a kind of niches, cover'd with black, and plac'd upon shafts, having the ensigns of their dignities at their feet, and carry'd each upon the shoulders of eight slaves. These three numerous troops began their march by day; and at the close of the evening the ladies, who made the most doleful part of the procession, began to appear. They were seated four and four in sixty chariots, cover'd above, but open on the sides, and drawn each by eight horses, two and two. Both horses and chariots were in a manner bury'd under their coverings of black silk, strew'd all over with tears of silver. These ladies, muffled up in their veils from head to foot, resembled so many spectres. In the last chariot sate the chief lady of the deceas'd queen's court, holding before her a child, who, being veil'd like herself, was known by none, but respected by all. However, the most prudent did imagine that Amedes, not only willing to let the young prince see the solemnity of a trial of the dead in the bloom of his youth, was at the same time cautious of leaving him in the palace in the absence of all his deceas'd mother's servants.

AFTER these ladies, whose sobs and groans heighten'd the grief of the spectators, and who were continually ſeen drying away their tears under their veil, as a contraſt which could not but be very affecting, immediately follow'd all thoſe inſtruments of muſick which in Egypt were made uſe of at their higheſt feſtivals, as the citterns, ſhalms, and hautboys; which were anſwer'd periodically by trumpets and kettle-drums, to proclaim the approach of the queen's chariot. Thoſe who ſounded theſe inſtruments, and even the leaders of the chariot, and the twelve body-ſlaves who march'd on the right and on the left of it, were clad in their feſtival habits, which contradiction to their mournful aſpects and profound ſilence, was to the ſpectators a lively emblem of the deceitfulneſs and brevity of human joy. The queen herſelf was adorn'd with a ſort of ſcarf of flowers, which croſſing over her left ſhoulder, met and join'd under her right arm; and in her hands ſhe held feſtoons, which hanging over her knees, reach'd down to her feet. This cuſtom of the Egyptians was to ſignify, that tho' the death of virtuous perſons was a matter of ſorrow to the ſurviving, it was to them the entrance into peace, a happineſs, and a triumph. The queen's chariot was follow'd by the prieſts. The high-prieſt of Memphis, who was to preſent the queen to the judges, was carry'd next to the chariot, ſtretch'd out at length in an open coffin, like a corpſe, clad in white, and his head and face cover'd with a white veil. All the other priests, clad and veil'd in the same manner, leaning with one hand on an augur's wand, curb'd at the top, and holding in the other a ring or circle of gold, to which hung a sort of Tau, march'd on foot in two single lines of five hundred each, and as far distant from one another as the breadth of the roads would allow. In the middle between these two lines, at certain distances, were carry'd standards, on which were represented the several deities, or the symbols of the deities of Egypt, as the Apis of Memphis, the Colossus of Abyddus, the Eagle of Thebes, the Spar-hawk of Tanis, the Anubis of Cynopolis, the Vase of Canope, the Goat of Mendez, the Wolf of Hermontis, the Lamb of Sais; and so of the rest. For there were priests out of all the cities of Egypt at the funerals of their kings, even tho' they were actually in war with one another. And the class of priests, with those of the labourers and traders, were never involv'd in the differences of the states. On the other hand, the death of kings was a means of reconciling the priests of different cities, who seem'd to have very hot disputes concerning the various, and oftentimes contrary deities they ador'd. Our historians speaking of Egypt * have remark'd, that those kings, who had many cities of

* Vid. Plut. Treatise of Osiris and Isis, and others.

different worſhip in their dominions, were glad to keep up this ſpirit of diſſention among the prieſts; leſt, if they ſhould unite, their influence, which was very great over the vulgar, might ſet them up above their kings. To conclude, the whole proceſſion was clos'd by a great number of baggage-waggons, which kept off the people that follow'd.

THEY frequently paſs'd thro' cities, ſome greater, ſome leſs. The number of them, as well on this road, as every where elſe, had given occaſion to the opinion of old, that there were more cities in Egypt alone, than in all the world beſides. In theſe cities it was that the ſtages were mark'd out at almoſt equal diſtances; and near every one of them was the houſe deſtin'd for their entertainment; from which they march'd out again to take their ſtations at ſet-times. The queen's chariot was plac'd under tents, which were erected for that end at every ſtage, where it was guarded by other prieſts, not belonging to the proceſſion. This chariot, by which the whole proceſſion was rul'd, never mov'd but in the night-ſeaſon, and but three hours together, during which time it advanc'd about two leagues; and then, reſting four hours, reſum'd the march again till day-light, and ſo lay by, waiting the return of the evening.

THE whole procession being arriv'd, was rang'd in order upon the plain to leave a free passage for the queen's chariot, and the people that had follow'd the procession behind the waggons. They then advanc'd to the brink of the lake Charon, * and there were plac'd on each side of the chariot on a spacious plain, on the right and on the left: And the priests remain'd rang'd behind the chariot in a strait line. At the approach of this awful tribunal, compos'd of judges, who were rever'd as the gods themselves, the high-priest, who was to be the queen's advocate, and all those who were concern'd for her memory, were seiz'd with unexpected terrors: For if those things which are really good, are sometimes accounted bad by the injustice of men, it is more to be apprehended, that those causes which to us appear good, may be really bad in the judgment of the gods.

THE judges were plac'd upon a large and deep scaffold in the form of an alcove, rais'd two steps; about which their seats, to the number of forty one, form'd a semi-circle. Their under-habits were a sort of tunicks, or white vests, like the priests or initiates, over which they wore scarlet robes like judges. Round their necks they had chains of gold,

* By comparing the relations of the ancients to those of the moderns, the labyrinth seems to have been situate between the two lakes Charon and Mœris.

at

at each of which hung an emerald, with the image of truth * engraven upon it; and they were rang'd in the following order: The high-prieſt, who preſided over the tribunal, was plac'd in the center on a ſeat rais'd ſomewhat higher than the reſt, and on both ſides of him ſat the two judges elected by the nome of Memphis, who were only initiates, of whom Amedes was the chief. Below them on either ſide were the ſixteen prieſts of the labyrinth, and then the twenty-two initiates appointed by the other nomes. The urn was plac'd in the front of the tribunal, on the brink of the uppermoſt ſtep; and the officers of the ſecond order were ſeated upon the lowermoſt, in habits proper for the functions they were to perform after judgment given. Every thing being thus diſpos'd, the horſes taken out of the queen's chariot, and the poles and pavilion remov'd; the high-prieſt of Memphis, who directed the proceſſion, being mounted upon the foot of the chariot, ſtanding, and with his head uncover'd, made the following oration:

" INEXORABLE deities of hell! behold here " our queen, whom you have appointed a " victim, in the bloom of her years, and in " the greateſt neceſſity of her people. We " come to intreat you will vouchſafe her

* Diodor. l. 1. §. 2. & Ælian. variar. hiſt. l. 14.

" that

" that repoſe, of which her loſs may ſhortly
" deprive us. She has been faithful in every
" duty to the gods. She has not diſpens'd
" with the outward exerciſe of religion un-
" der pretext of affairs of ſtate; nor has that
" exerciſe alone ſupply'd in her the place of
" virtue. Amidſt the cares which employ'd
" her in her counſels, and that gaiety which
" ſhe ſometimes put on at court, the divine
" law, which was ever preſent to her mind,
" and rul'd in her heart, was always viſi-
" ble, Of all the feſtivals, at which the
" ſuperiority of her rank, the ſucceſs of her
" undertakings, or the love of her people,
" have engag'd her to be an aſſiſtant, none
" have been ſo agreeable and pleaſant to
" her, as thoſe which have call'd her to
" our temples. She has not ſuffer'd herſelf
" to be led into the paths of injuſtice, as
" many kings have done, in hopes of ma-
" king ample ſatisfaction by her offerings;
" and her magnificence towards the gods,
" has been the fruits of her piety, not the
" tributes of remorſe. Inſtead of counte-
" nancing animoſity, vexation and perſecu-
" tion, by the counſels of an ill-tim'd piety,
" ſhe has drawn no other maxims from reli-
" gion but thoſe of lenity; and has never
" put ſeverity in practice, but when the
" common courſe of juſtice, and the ſecu-
" rity of the ſtate, has demanded it. She has
" exercis'd all the virtues of the beſt of kings
" with

" with that modest diffidence, which has
" hardly allow'd her to enjoy that happiness
" which she procur'd for her people. A
" glorious defence of the frontiers, peace
" settled both at home and abroad, and
" every other ornament and institution, have
" generally in other princes been the effect
" of politick wisdom, which the gods, judges
" of their real springs, don't always reward:
" But with our queen all these things have
" been the result of virtue, and have had
" no other principles but a love of her duty,
" and a view to the publick felicity. Far
" from regarding the sovereign power as a
" means to indulge her passions, it has been
" a rule to her to make the tranquillity of
" the state the ease of her own mind, and
" a standing maxim, that patience and affa-
" bility could alone make her the ruler of
" the hearts of men. Vengeance never so
" much as enter'd into her thoughts, but
" abandoning to those beneath her the shame
" of embracing every opportunity of exer-
" cising their hatred, she, like the gods, par-
" don'd, when she had the power of punish-
" ing. She curb'd the rebellious, not so
" much because they oppos'd her will, as in
" consideration that they were an obstacle
" to her good designs. She submitted her
" judgment to the counsel of the wise, and
" every order of men in her kingdom to the
" equity of its laws. She subdu'd her ene-
" mies

" mies from without by her courage, and a
" ſtrict obſervation of her ingagements, and
" her domeſtick enemies by her fortitude,
" and the happy ſucceſs of her undertakings.
" She never ſuffer'd a ſecret, or a falſity, to
" proceed out of her mouth; and that diſſi-
" mulation, which is ſo inſeparable from
" ſovereignty, in her never extended beyond
" ſilence. She never gave way to the im-
" portunity of the ambitious; nor did the
" aſſiduities of paraſites ever run away with
" the rewards due to the ſervices of the abſent.
" Diſtinguiſh'd favourites were unknown in
" her reign; even that friendſhip which ſhe
" practis'd and cultivated, had never with
" her the aſcendant over merit, tho' often
" leſs affectionate and leſs engaging. She
" beſtow'd favours upon her friends, and
" gave the moſt important employs to thoſe
" who beſt were able to diſcharge them.
" She heap'd honours upon the great, with-
" out exempting them from duty; and eas'd
" the burden of her people, without taking
" away that neceſſity which was a ſpur to
" their induſtry. She has not, by creating
" new offices, given an opportunity to others
" to take part with the prince, and unequal-
" ly for him, of the publick revenue; and
" the meaneſt of the people have paid the
" taxes rated and levy'd upon them, with-
" out any regret, becauſe they have not
" ſerv'd to render their equals more opulent,
" haughty,

" haughty, or wicked. Convinc'd, as ſhe " was, that the providence of heaven was " not excluſive of the vigilance of man, ſhe " prevented publick miſery by a regular and " timely proviſion; and thus rendring every " year equal, her wiſdom, in ſome meaſure, " over-rul'd the ſeaſons and elements. By " her favourable reception of all thoſe whom " the fame of her prudent government drew " from other the moſt remote countries, ſhe " facilitated negociations, maintain'd peace, " and rais'd her kingdom to its higheſt pitch " of opulency and glory; and at the ſame " time enforc'd, by her example, that ho- " ſpitality, which till then was not enough " cultivated among the Egyptians. When " any of the great maxims of government " were to be put in practice, and it was " neceſſary to purſue the publick good, tho' " attended with private inconveniencies, with " what a generous indifferency has ſhe not " endur'd the murmurings of a populace, " blind, and perhaps ſtirr'd up by the ſecret " calumnies of thoſe who, tho' they knew " better, might not find their private ad- " vantage in the publick felicity? Putting " frequently her own glory to ſtake for the " intereſt of an ungrateful people, ſhe has " waited the event of time for her own juſti- " fication; and tho' ſnatch'd away in the " very beginning of her courſe, the purity " of her intention, the juſtneſs of her views,

" and her assiduity in the execution of them, " have procur'd her the advantage of a glorious memory, and an universal regret. " To be in the better capacity of watching " over the whole of the kingdom, she confided the several under-branches of management to able ministers, who were oblig'd to depute subalterns, and these others, " for whose conduct she could be no ways " answerable, as well because of their remoteness, as their number: I dare therefore affirm before you her judges, and before those of her subjects, who now hear " me, that if, among such a number of inhabitants as this city of Memphis, and the " other five thousand * cities of this dynasty " are known to contain, it may appear, that, " contrary to her intention, any one has " been oppress'd, the queen is not only excusable in regard of the impossibility of " providing for all, but is praise-worthy, in " that, knowing the bounds of human understanding, she has kept to the center of " publick business, and has fix'd her whole " attention upon the first causes and motions " of things. Unhappy those princes with " whom some particular subjects only have " cause to be pleas'd, when the publick has " reason to complain! and tho' private per-

* There were in Egypt 20,000 cities, Plin. l. 5. c. 9. & Pomp. Mela. But Theocritus Idyl. 17. reckons 33,339 under Ptolom. Philad.

" sons

" ſons may ſometimes ſuffer, they have no
" right to blame their princes, when the body
" of the ſtate is ſound, and the principles of
" government ſalutary. However, as irre-
" proachable as the queen has appear'd to us,
" with regard to men, with reſpect to you,
" ye juſt gods, ſhe builds her hopes of re-
" poſe and bliſs upon your clemency alone.

As ſoon as the high-prieſt had finiſh'd his diſcourſe, he cover'd his head and face with a veil, and proſtrated himſelf on the chariot where he ſtood, in expectation of judgment. The judges immediately enter'd into conſultation in the middle of the place; and after having conferr'd ſome few minutes, retook their ſeats. The preſident of the tribunal then ask'd the whole aſſembly with a loud voice, If any one had any thing to lay to the charge of the queen's memory? Some of thoſe who had been prejudiced in their private affairs, by ſome regulations of great advantage to the publick, had prepar'd complaints, more juſtifiable on their parts, than of validity againſt the queen: But the laſt plea, made by the high-prieſt of Memphis in her defence, had put a ſtop to their intentions, and they were the moſt zealous of that numerous aſſembly in promoting, by their applauſes, her entrance into the manſions of the bleſſed. When (as in the caſe before us) no charge is enter'd againſt a deceas'd monarch, the urn is of no uſe, but he is admitted by general aſſent. The preſident of the tribunal having therefore look'd round upon all the judges, and receiv'd from each of them the ſign of their conſent, ſaid, "Sacred prieſt of Memphis, ariſe; the gods "approve the teſtimony you have born con- "cerning your queen, and are going to con- "fer upon her the reward due to good kings. "May her ſucceſſors walk in her footſteps, "and, by rendring their people happy, trea- "ſure up greater bleſſings for themſelves." He then commanded the chief officer of the ſecond order to touch the queen with his wand, of which our poets have made Mercury's Caduceus: At the ſame time turning to Amedes, the chief of the two judges appointed by the nome of Memphis, who ſate at his right-hand, he ſaid: "Wiſe "miniſter of your queen, you, whoſe pru- "dent counſels have had ſo great part in the "actions which bring her this day to glory, "accompany the holy prieſt, who conducted "her hither; help to convey her into the "bark, and from thence into that temple, "the gates of which are ſhut againſt the "wicked, be they living or dead: We haſten "to open theſe gates to her, and to receive "her ourſelves." The judges immediately aroſe, and enter'd the temple of the infernal deities by a private way. The dead, who were oblig'd to enter the ſubterranean gate,

had

had no other paſſage to come at it, but by croſſing the lake, the breadth of which was in that part about a quarter of a league, and upon which no other bark was admitted but that of Charon. The officers having looſen'd the cords with which the queen was faſten'd to her throne, and laid her in the ſame coffin which had brought the high-prieſt, ſhe was convey'd into the bark, and the high-prieſt, together with Amedes, having firſt paid the uſual tribute to Charon, accompany'd her. They were no ſooner arriv'd at the gates of the labyrinth, but the people, who follow'd them with their eyes, heard a noiſe as of thunder, which they believ'd to be real, and look'd upon it as a miracle which always happen'd when the temple of the infernal deities was open'd: But in reality it was no more than the hollow ſound of the brazen gates at the entrance, which was redoubled by the repercuſſion of the vaults, and by the neighbouring echo's.

THE corpſe was no ſooner entered into the labyrinth, than a joy ſucceeded as general as that of the preceding mourning; and as ſudden as that of a perſon, ſeeing his deareſt friend riſen from the dead. This joy proceeded from the idea they conceived of the happineſs their ſovereign enjoy'd in the manſions of the bleſſed. Even thoſe, who could not ſo ſoon overcome their grief, were oblig'd to conceal it under the moſt viſible demonſtrations of joy. The populace, in whom nothing is more eaſy than a tranſition from one extreme of paſſion to another, and to whom beſides every opportunity for merriment is acceptable, omitted in their return no frolick or jollity to which Egypt could adminiſter on ſuch a pilgrimage. Perſons of the greateſt diſtinction took pleaſure in joining with the commonalty, as well on the road, as in the ſeveral cities they paſs'd through: but they were eaſily diſcover'd by the magnificence of their habits, which they had brought with them in the baggage-waggons, that clos'd the proceſſion; and they put on theſe habits, either in the neighbouring cities, or under coſtly tents which were erected on every ſide. As the Egyptians in general think themſelves noble, the peaſants, men and women, being neatly attir'd, mix'd even with princes and princeſſes, not only at the ſame dances, and ſports, but at the ſame tables under tents in the meadows, or in the middle of the open places in cities. The profuſion of wines and proviſions which are expended on this occaſion is inexpreſſible; and nothing can give a more adequate idea of the plenty of Egypt, and of the riches of its inhabitants. All familiarity was allow'd in diſcourſe, and every thing was matter of joy. Not a ſingle inſtance was ever known of any quarrel amidſt this

agree-

agreeable confusion; because nothing was transacted with an intent to offend or prejudice. Even the great, as they were of easy access, and affable to persons of all conditions, drew upon themselves, by so much the more, those obsequious regards, which politeness inspires. All such as excell'd in exercises of strength or ingenuity resorted thither in companies, and diverted the spectators with amusing sports on the land and upon the canals. Troops of satyrs and nymphs, an idea of whom the worship of the god Pan had cultivated in Egypt, long before it pass'd into Greece, were seen sallying out of the thickets, or rushing into the waters.

† THE nights were more dazzling than the days, occasion'd by the illuminations in the cities, which at a distance, and in the fields, made a more glorious appearance, than in the cities themselves. Nor is it possible for painting to represent, or words to express their lustre; especially on the banks of the lake Moeris, that sea of sweet water, the work of mens hands, which, according to our best authors, * was one hundred and fifty leagues in circumference, and where those illuminations were doubly represented by their reflections in the waters. An infinite number of gallies, richly adorn'd, and illu-

* Diodorus reckons it 3600 stadia in circumference; 24 stadia making a league of 3000 paces.

minated like palaces, cruis'd upon the lake, or row'd from port to port, at the will of those who possess'd them, sure always of meeting with some agreeable amusement which ever way they directed their course. The prodigious concourse of people, the perpetual sound of musical instruments, and the frequent shouts of joy, left no room for complaint in this affluence of all manner of diversions, except it were for want of silence and sleep. In a word, the feast of Diana at Bubastes, or the nocturnal festivals of Minerva at Sais, which are yet celebrated annually, though with less pomp than licentiousness, are but faint images of these festivals on the return from the labyrinth, the ceremony of which drew together the most considerable part of Egypt.

* THE temperature of the climate in this country is exceeding favourable to these sorts of festivals. But more particularly in spring (which was the season at that time) the serenity of the days is as certain as the coolness of the nights; and what is more, winter there differs very little from summer. It is true, the four months of the rise and fall of the Nile, compar'd with the remainder of the year, make a very different appearance. For in these four months, or

* *Vid.* Paul Lucas's Egypt corrected and amended by M. l'Abbe Banier.

there-

thereabouts, the whole country being overflowed, makes the cities appear like ſo many iſlands of different bigneſs, which ſeem to ariſe out of the waters: and during the whole remainder of the year, where theſe waters were, are gardens cover'd with every ſpecies of flowers of the ſpring; or fields fill'd with all the fruits of the earth in autumn. Theſe gardens or fields are ſurrounded with little canals, which flow out of others which are larger, as theſe again do from others yet larger, even to thoſe which proceed immediately from the Nile, and which are like unto rivers, being intended to encompaſs large provinces, and to diſtribute themſelves ſucceſſively, till they ſerve as incloſures to the poſſeſſions of private perſons, Funerals were never perform'd during the time of the inundations, nor never deferr'd, but on that account. The feſtivals of return from the labyrinth laſted always twice as long as the march of the proceſſion thither: So that the king of Memphis had not an account in form of the accompliſhment of the queen's obſequies, till the one-and-thirtieth day after the departure of the proceſſion.

End of the FIRST BOOK.

THE

LIFE

OF

SETHOS.

BOOK II.

IF Daluca closely besieg'd the king even when she could not flatter herself with any approaching hopes; it is easy to believe, that she redoubled her officiousness after the death of Nephte, who, by the indolence of this prince, left the government vacant; for as Amedes had not held that part which he had in the administration, immediately from Osoroth, he had laid down all his employs, even before he departed to attend the queen's obsequies, at which he was to assist as a judge. The king, whom Daluca never quitted, and who

who in the firſt days of mourning had had more opportunities of being alone with her, was wont to communicate to her ſuch concerns as he could not avoid knowing, and to confide in her for the execution of what they had concerted together. This weak prince, who had enjoy'd that tranquillity, which the wiſdom of Nephte had procur'd him, as a perſon enjoys health, without knowing the value of it, look'd upon a peaceable government as a thing eaſy in itſelf, and which any one was capable of ſupporting: or, if he imagin'd that any particular talent was neceſſary, he was tempted to believe, that Daluca's courage and vivacity ſupply'd to advantage the want of Nephte's modeſt and ſober virtues. So that whereas conſiderations of conveniency only had made him diſcharge the burden of the government upon the late queen; it was by a kind of choice that he ſolemnly reſign'd it to Daluca, who had no title to pretend to it. He adviſ'd her however, in particular, to conſult with Amedes upon any emergency. Daluca anſwer'd him, That the deceas'd queen having intruſted Amedes with the education of the young prince, this employ was ſufficient to take up his whole time; and ſhe maliciouſly added, that ſhe would have the aſſiſtance of miniſters yet more devoted to the king's will than he was.

THE

THE new regent, when ſhe took the helm of ſtate into her hands, behaved with that preſumption which is common in perſons of no worth, when ſucceeding thoſe of the moſt diſtinguiſh'd merit. However, the averſion of the publick plainly ſhewn with regard to her, and the honourable mention continually made of the deceas'd queen, gall'd her to the ſoul; and ſhe could never have perſuaded herſelf that the entrance into ſovereign power could have been ſo diſagreeable. This poſſeſs'd her mind, from the very beginning of her adminiſtration, with ſuch aſperity, as could not but prove fatal to her in the ſequel: and this lady, who, in the earlieſt hopes of her future grandeur, was wont ſometimes to diſtribute her chimerical benevolence to thoſe who were in her intimacy, without ever propoſing to do any good to the publick, as ſoon as ever ſhe had attained her wiſhes, thought no more of doing ſervice to any one. The hatred which thereby became deeply rooted in the hearts as well of the courtiers as the people, made her reflect more ſeriouſly upon the project ſhe had before conceiv'd of eſpouſing the king, and attaining to the royal dignity. This indeed was the ſecret inclination of the prince; but till then it had not been a practice in Egypt for kings to marry below their rank; and ſo ſcrupulous had they been

on

on this head, that they took their own ſiſters to wife, if ſuitable princeſſes were not to be found in the neighbouring courts. This cuſtom had taken footing among them independant of this pretext; and the Ptolemies, though originally Grecians, comply'd with it.

NOTWITHSTANDING the care the king took to abſent himſelf from all affairs of ſtate, and to be unacquainted with what was tranſacted in the heart of his kingdom; he could not, however, be ignorant, that the choice he had made of Daluca, to confide his authority in, had given uneaſineſs to his ſubjects. But the ambition of this lady, who thought the power ſhe had over him uncontroulable, prompted her to make uſe of that very argument for her aſcending the throne, which ought to have mov'd him to deprive her of the adminiſtration. She took a proper time to inform Oſoroth, with tears in her eyes, that the favours he had honour'd her with, and her intire devotion to him, had excited envy againſt her. She obſerv'd, that her zeal for the king's perſon began at a time when ſhe could not be ſuſpected of any future views. Even now, added ſhe, that my enemies apprehend it is time I ſhould receive ſome reward for my diſintereſted affection, I abandon all, and conſent that my fidelity become unprofitable to me for your ſervice. I accepted of the adminiſtration, only

only that it might not devolve into the hands of ſome ſecret enemies to that abſolute power inherent in you: but you may, if you think proper, give yourſelf up to them. I will even acknowledge, continued ſhe, in a more reſolute tone, that I ſet too high a rate upon the continuance of my adminiſtration. But as the reformers of government have dared to bring their complaints even to you, either you muſt allow them juſt, and baniſh me from your court, or confound their preſumption, by heaping new honours upon me. Without abandoning my affection for you, which is an impoſſibility, I, from this moment, renounce all the functions you have conſtrain'd me to accept of, unleſs attended with the ſupream dignity, which alone was the eaſe and glory of the late queen's adminiſtration: Such a reſolution, hitherto without example, will convince the world you dare exert your authority. The king, who till then had ſtruggled with the conſideration of his own honour, and his ſon's intereſt, gave way to his natural weakneſs, upon falſe principles of courage; and by a very improper marriage confirm'd that power, which he had unſeaſonably conferr'd upon a woman, who was about to cruſh his age with care and troubles: acting in this reſpect, like other weak princes, who inſtead of remedying the errors they have already enter'd into, endeavour to ſupport them by the commiſſion of ſtill greater evils.

OSOROTH, however, conſcious of the irregularity of his choice, and Daluca of the inferiority of her birth, did not preſume to convert the publick diſcontent into matter of rejoicings. The nuptials and coronation were both celebrated with very little ceremony: and it was not without pain, the queen could at firſt behave in a ſplendor ſo much ſuperior to her former condition. Her pride however ſoon recover'd upon the birth of a ſon, for whoſe advancement ſhe became immediately ſollicitous. But as ſhe could no ways carry her views to the height her ambition ſuggeſted to her, but to the prejudice of young Sethos, ſhe perceiv'd the difficulties ſhe had to encounter with, in attempting that injuſtice, and purſuing ſuch crimes as ſhe foreſaw would be neceſſary for attaining her end, ſo long as that ſpirit of equity, reaſon and order, which had been eſtabliſh'd for ſeveral reigns, was predominant at court, and amongſt the chief men of the kingdom. Her firſt attempt then was to corrupt the morals of the court; hoping, with reaſon, that ſhe ſhould then find ſuch perſons to fill up all the great offices, as would be baſe enough not to contradict, or wicked enough to further her deſigns. But as a mark of her more refin'd policy and capacity for perpetrating miſchief, ſhe concluded, that the moſt unſuſpected, and at the ſame time ſure and ſpeedy means of corrupting the court,

court, was to introduce, as much as poſſible, a relaxation of manners, and levity of mind. She knew by particular experience, that thoſe men who are enemies to all application and buſineſs, and wholly given up to their imaginations and pleaſures; tho' they might at firſt be endu'd with that common probity, which coſts nothing, were no proof againſt thoſe vices which offered them any advantage. Virtue never takes root in a mind poſſeſſed with vanity; and opportunity either finds or renders ſuch a one capable of every crime.

Daluca judg'd then, that to put this her deſign in practice, ſhe muſt begin by breaking off gradually thoſe aſſemblies and converſations which were uſually held in the palace towards evening, among men of ſenſe and diſcretion, that idle diſcourſes might ſupply their place; and that above all, it would be neceſſary to ſupplant the uſual exerciſes of the young Egyptian nobility, and ſubſtitute vain amuſements in their room. But before I proceed to the method ſhe took to introduce this firſt depravity, which was to be the ſource of all the reſt, I believe it may be very proper to give an idea of the manners of this nation, with regard to the intercourſe of wit and ſcience which flouriſhed in it; and the care that was taken to enforce whatever could ennoble the heart, cultivate the mind, and

and invigorate the body *. This account will at the ſame time ſerve as a general plan of the education of young Sethos, which we ſhall ſpeak more particularly of hereafter.

THE Greeks were as yet a barbarous nation, with regard to their cuſtom of locking up their wives, the ſavage rather than warlike education of their children, and the preference they gave to bodily force, beyond the virtues of the mind; when the Egyptians, under the happineſs of an uniform and wiſe government, had attain'd to politeneſs, which conſiſted more in the great principles of mildneſs and diſcretion, than in tireſome ceremonies. Human learning was the true ſource of this politeneſs: and as the ſciences were very ancient in Egypt, the manners of that nation were early form'd. It has been a true obſervation, that good breeding never made its way into any nation but by means of learning. The Romans were an uncivilīz'd people, till they learnt the ſciences of the Greeks; as the Greeks themſelves were, till they became acquainted with the knowledge of the Egyptians. And tho' learned men are not always the moſt civiliz'd, it is nevertheleſs, to their writings, in philoſophy,

* Theſe very expreſſions are found in Boſſuet, ſpeaking of the Egyptians, in his diſcourſe upon univerſal hiſtory.

history, morality, and even poetry, that their fellow-citizens are indebted for the true foundation of their accomplishments.

THE king's palace at Memphis, which was situate on one side of a large square, opposite to the temple of the three deities, was the theatre of the arts and sciences. We have already observ'd, that the ancient kings of Egypt chose rather to shew their magnificence in the edifices they were to inhabit after their death, than in those they dwelt in while living. Pursuant to this principle their palaces made no appearance, either in themselves, or in those ornaments which regard only pageantry and luxury. But in recompence, nothing was omitted in them that contributed to the cultivation of the sciences; Witness the gardens of the king of Memphis, which contain'd every sort and species of known plants which Egypt had ever produc'd, and even all those peculiar plants which travellers had brought from the most distant climates, especially after the conquests of Sesostris. And besides, all the advantages which the due ordering and ranging of this immense variety of plants could possibly afford to the eye by beautiful views and prospects, was nicely observ'd. An elegant choice of the most agreeable flowers, which are singly planted in our modern parterres, cannot afford a sight equal to that of many

large

large compartments, in which were ſeen in ſeparate borders all the flowers ſimple or compound; which blew in the form of roſes, pinks or lillies; or whoſe leaves took the ſhape of a vaſe, an umbrella, or a tuff; or in ſhort, whoſe colours were either ſimple or mix'd.

ON the wings of the parterre were planted the twenty ſpecies or kinds of palm-trees, in one ſingle row on each ſide; one of flower- or male-palms, and the other of fruit- or female-palms. They thought this correſpondence neceſſary to render the females fruitful, by the duſt of the flowers which the wind convey'd to them from the males. A diſtinction of ſex, which, tho' more perceptible in palm-trees, may perhaps be the ſame in many other plants. The parterre had no other ſhelter but theſe two rows of palms; but there were two other ſhady walks under arch'd terraſſes, to the very bottom of the garden. At the end of the parterre were two great woods ſeparated by the continuation of the main walk, which were travers'd by an infinity of other leſſer walks, that the ſun never pierced. Theſe two woods conſiſted of every ſpecies of thoſe trees which are called barren, from the humble broom to the haughty cedar, aſcending gradually from that ſide towards the parterre with their tops joining, which from the windows of the palace reſembled a talus or glacis, and by the favour of the climate were ever green. Behind these woods were all sorts of plants, roots and pulse necessary in a kitchen-garden. And on the sides continued downwards, were planted every sort of wall- and other fruit-trees. But as they were design'd for no other use but to shew the extent of botany, there were no more than what might be sufficient to exhibit the several kinds or species.

THE priests, who were the orderers and managers of this garden, had a passage to it thro' a gallery at the top of a colonnade, which reached from their college behind the temple, and, bordering one side of the square by the river side, run along by the north wing of the palace, and so descended on the same side into the parterre. They had caus'd to be drawn and painted in natural colours, all the trees and plants of the whole garden; and all these figures were to be seen in one of those galleries of the palace, which were always open to the curious, even to strangers. These figures were more in number than the plants of the garden, because they represented a great many others which were not transplantable from the soil where they grew: Tho' there was nothing wanting that could possibly be procured, not even coral, madrepores, lithophyton, and other marine petrifying plants. In short, every thing was there

in

in the most exact order, according to their kinds and species: Plants as yet unknown, had in some manner their places assign'd them; and botany seem'd here to be compleat, independent of its parts, which in all appearance will never be so.

BUT as the curiosity of the Egyptians was not limited to this article alone, they had in the same gallery samples of all the productions of nature, treasured up in repositories, with grates before them of that metal call'd electrum, a mixture of gold and silver, ranged under classes in such excellent order, as rais'd curiosity in the most indifferent. Even nature herself may be said to have been honour'd in this collection by the multiplicity and variety of her own gifts, and her riches thus assorted, under the proper names and inscriptions which distinguish'd them, seem'd to exceed in number those same productions, when dispers'd in her own extensive field, and frequently unknown. In this collection were comprehended all such substances, as are gather'd from the surface, or taken out of the entrails of the earth, in their natural form, and but barely cleans'd and purify'd: Such were not only all manner of concretions, congelations and crystallisations, but all sorts of fossils, minerals and metals, and that in the several progressions and degrees from whence they receive different appellations. Hence they took their notions of all thoſe juices and gums which proceed from plants or other bodies by exſudation, the greater part of which were either precious aromaticks, or ſovereign antidotes: An immenſe treaſure of delights in health, and of remedies in ſickneſs. To conclude; Here was that grotto of Mercury, in which, as Orpheus ſays, was treaſured up a collection of every good thing, and from whence no one ever return'd with the infirmities he brought.

FROM this gallery, ſet apart for natural hiſtory, was a paſſage into that deſtin'd for Chymiſtry. * Some believe this ſcience took its name from Egypt, formerly call'd Chemia; but that it took its riſe there is certain. The renown'd Mercury of Thebes, whom the Egyptians look'd upon as the author of all their knowledge, gave name to that liquid metal which he found the method of extracting out of Cinnober, and which is found to be exactly the ſame with the Quickſilver which runs in the mines, the object of ſo many chymical experiments, and the miracle of nature, by the variety of colours which it aſſumes in its precipitation, and from whence it has likewiſe the name of Proteus. Mercury it was who taught

* With regard to this article our reader may conſult the works of Olaus Borrichius, in which he defends the antiquity of chymiſtry againſt Conringius.

them

them to reduce bodies by decompoſition into their three principles, ſalt, ſulphur and ſpirit; the latter of which, as the moſt ſublime, has retain'd in our authors the name of Mercury. Several kings of Egypt follow'd his example in the ſtudy of chymiſtry; and Theophraſtus tells us we are indebted to one of them for the artificial azure. The Egyptians, by an imitation of almoſt all compound bodies, had form'd, as it were by art, a ſecond nature; and chymiſtry furniſh'd them with nitres, vitriols and ſalts, always more beautiful, and ſometimes more efficacious than thoſe of nature. Seneca the philoſopher aſſures us, * that Democritus had learnt of them the art of ſoftening ivory, and to give to flints the colour and luſtre of emeralds. We have at leaſt a recent and inconteſtable proof of the efficacy of their diſſolvents, in that pearl of ineſtimable value and uncommon ſize, which Cleopatra took from her ear, and liquify'd in an inſtant in prepar'd vinegar, that Mark Anthony might ſwallow it: And it is certain, that this vinegar was no corroſive diſſolvent, becauſe it was drunk without danger.

THE teſtimonies of antiquity have gone yet farther with regard to the Egyptians; and we are plainly told, that Mercury, or

* Ep. 90.

Hermes Trifmegiftus, taught them the fecret of transforming all metals into gold, call'd for that reafon the Hermetical philofophy. As a proof of which they alledge the vaft extent of their riches, which, fay they, one fingle mine of gold, the only one they knew, could never have furnifh'd. Witnefs the fhip of cedar, of four hundred and twenty foot long, which Sefoftris caus'd to be plated on the infide with filver, and to be cover'd with gold without; the aftronomical circle of maffive gold in the tomb of Ifmandes, which by the account Diodorus gives, was of the thicknefs of a cubit, or a foot and a half, and in circumference three hundred fixty five cubits; a great number of temples of gold dedicated, according to the fame author, by Ofiris to Jupiter, Juno, and other gods; temples fo large, that priefts were appointed to officiate in them; and to conclude, fo many other works, which, tho' but of marble or ftone, coft more than the former. Notwithftanding all which, the opinion I am of, that the integral parts of all bodies are determin'd to their nature from the formation of the earth, would alone hinder my granting, to any one whomever, the power of tranfmuting them; or at leaft allowing that their change can be effected by operations fo imperfect and fo fhort as are thofe of mankind, in comparifon with the fubtlety and extreme length of thofe of nature. Befides, wife men don't doubt but

this

this true philosopher's stone, of which Mercury or Hermes was the inventor, was the commerce which this first king of Thebes establish'd in Egypt. And in reality, it is not the quantity of matter, either gold or silver, be it taken from the mines, or the laboratories of the chymists, that renders a nation opulent. The mines of Norway, Germany, Spain and Africa, don't make the inhabitants of those countries one jot the richer. The continual circulation of a moderate quantity of this matter, and a perpetual commerce, with the productions of a soil, and the fruits of industry, have rais'd nations to extreme plenty, who have no mines either of gold or silver. We must however grant, that the Egyptians closely pursu'd this secret of Hermes, taken in its literal sense; and we may even conjecture, that the real knowledge they attain'd to in the art of physick, was owing to their vain labours in quest of the philosophical gold.

THIS chymical gallery led to another appropriated to anatomy. The dissections were always perform'd in the priests college; but they brought into the palace entire and natural demonstrations, consisting of the bones, muscles, arteries and veins of most animals, either of the air, earth, or water: And their entrails, shewn separately, were made more discernable by being laid open, or by injections. Pliny relates, that the ancient kings of Egypt did not think it beneath them to aſſiſt themſelves at diſſections. It is certain at leaſt, that Æſculapius, king of Memphis, being the firſt author of phyſick, was likewiſe the inventor of anatomy. But Egypt having ſince embrac'd a more regular form of government, the ſeveral functions were better diſtributed, and the particular profeſſions of the ſciences devolv'd upon the prieſts, or their ſubalterns. The practice of embalming human bodies, and even thoſe of animals, moſt of which were ſacred with them, in one city or other, had render'd them extremely knowing in the outward and inward conſtruction of all living bodies. The ſeveral devaſtations in Egypt which have robb'd their catacombs of an infinity of mummies and bones, are even to this day of great help to the ſtudy of this ſcience; And the famous Galen, phyſician to our auguſt Emperours Marcus Aurelius and Lucius Verus, excludes from the profound knowledge of anatomy thoſe who did not come for inſtruction from theſe objects to the academies of Alexandria, tho' now held by the Greeks.

THE knowledge the Egyptians had in anatomy, was a conſequence of their curioſity in living creatures. I don't ſpeak of the cuſtom yet in practice in Egypt of hatching the eggs of fowls deſtin'd for the nouriſhment of mankind, in furnaces made for that purpoſe,

purpose, which prodigiously increases their number. But the kings of Memphis had, besides the garden I have above describ'd, a large inclosure, with a park and proper conveniencies for four-footed beasts, canals and basons for fish and amphibious creatures, and aviaries for birds. And here were frequently represented sundry sports of these animals, tam'd and train'd up to surprizing exercises. * Crocodiles were seen floating upon the surface of the canals and basons with men on their backs, who made them perform all sorts of evolutions, or walking on dry land, led by chains, and often obedient to their master's voice alone. The same evolutions were perform'd by the Hippopotamus, or River-Horse, whose aspect alone was so hideous, that it was believ'd fire proceeded out of his nostrils. The bones of this animal are shewn in several cities of Greece for the bones of giants. We have seen, even in the days of the Ptolomies, when the sciences began to decline in Egypt, Cynocephali, a sort of apes, of which they made their hieroglyphical Anubis, that were taught to play regularly on the guitar and the flute. †

BUT we must allow, that the curiosity or ingenuity of the Egyptians, in what was

* Plut. c. de solertia anim.

† Ælian. de natura animal. l. 6. c. 10.

com-

commendable, does no ways excuſe the ſcandalous and ſuperſtitious abuſes they are fallen into with reſpect to animals. Many cities in Egypt have borrow'd their names from thoſe monſters they paid adoration to, as Crocodilopolis and others. The Hippopotamus is worſhipp'd at Pampremis, tho' this city don't bear its name. The moſt excuſable among them ſeem to be thoſe who worſhip the animals that are of uſe to mankind. The * Heracleoti offer'd incenſe to the Icneumon, a ſort of rat as big as a little dog, which deſtroy'd the crocodile in a very ſingular manner: This little animal, after having daub'd itſelf all over with a ſort of thick ſlime, which when dry'd ſerv'd it as a coat of mail, jump'd into the jaws of the crocodile, and ſo kill'd it. The ancients ſay, this is the only animal that ſecures itſelf with defenſive armour. All Egypt ador'd the bird Ibis, a ſort of ſtork, that freed their cities from the little wing'd ſerpents, which the African wind was wont to bring them; but this bird was itſelf very troubleſome, by reaſon of its voracity and filth. It is related, that Cambyſes being upon the point of giving battle to Pſammenitus the ſon of Amaſis at Paluſa, on the confines of Egypt, rang'd a row of theſe birds before his avant-guard, and that the Egyptians choſe rather to ſub-

* Cic. de natura, Deor. l. 1.

mit without oppoſition, than to draw their arrows againſt them. The Greeks with reaſon reproach'd the Egyptians for the ſingularity of their religion. But they pretend to juſtify themſelves with regard to their worſhip of crocodiles, and other ſuch hideous animals; by alledging, that they defended their country, and render'd the acceſs to it dangerous to the pirates of Arabia, and the ſcouts of Libya. They even retort the ſame reproach upon the Greeks, * and ſay, that the Theſſalonians worſhipp'd a ſtork, and the Bœotians a weaſel. It is indeed a common thing for men to deride with great haughtineſs the ſuperſtition of others, when they are blind to their own folly, tho' often of the ſame kind.

AFTER having gone thro' what regards experimental ſciences, the next gallery was the firſt of thoſe deſtin'd for the ſciences of computation. The peculiar neceſſity incumbent upon the inhabitants of this country, of adjuſting the bounds of their lands after an inundation of the waters of the Nile, had put them upon the ſtudy of geometry ſooner than other nations: But they had carry'd their contemplations much farther than this

* Clem. Alex. admon. ad gentes. This father even adds, that it is leſs ignominious to worſhip animals, incapable of crime, than gods, vitious and unjuſt, as were thoſe of the Greeks.

neceſ-

neceſſity oblig'd them; And had attain'd to thoſe ſciences, of which the ſimple meaſuring of their lands, or geometry properly ſo call'd, was but a very ſmall part. The canals and other bounds, which in courſe of time ſeparated the eſtates of private perſons, made them ſufficiently known. But geometry became the knowledge of every kind of proportion repreſented by lines.

THE firſt elements of the mathematicks are very ancient. It is related, that Mercury, the firſt king of Thebes, whom we have ſo often mention'd, being concern'd at the changes, which an univerſal deluge then recent had caus'd upon the ſurface of the earth, and for the want of all human ſcience, which that terrible cataſtrophe had ſo totally effac'd, thought of an expedient that might prevent ſo great a loſs, if the diſaſter ſhould ever happen again. * He caus'd ſubterranean and winding paſſages to be dug in the neighbourhood of Thebes, the remains of which are yet to be ſeen, and go by the name of the Syringes. Theſe he fill'd with ſquare and pyramidal columns, upon the ſurfaces of which were carv'd the principles of every ſcience; but in hieroglyphical ſymbols, that if even the art of writing ſhould be loſt, they might be explain'd by conjecture; and that if any of

* Ammian. Marcel. l. 22. vid. Marſh. p. 39. & 41.

the race of man ſhould eſcape, they might at leaſt have this aid, and not be reduc'd, as they had then juſt been, to labours that requir'd ſo great a length of time as a new invention of all things. It is added, that Mercury himſelf had enjoy'd the ſame advantage from ſome columns anterior to the deluge, which had been erected by the hero-kings or demi-gods, his predeceſſors.

IN the mathematical gallery at Memphis were plac'd columns of the height of a cubit, but which had all the proportions of thoſe columns of the Syringes, which contain'd the principles of this ſcience. The proprieties of numbers were engraven on the firſt of them; foraſmuch as their proportions being perceptible by operation alone, they ſerve as elements and a model for all mathematical proportions. * Pythagoras, who, as the ancients ſay, receiv'd great inſtruction by Mercury's columns, thence took his idea of numbers. He likewiſe carry'd it as far as any of the Greeks before our celebrated Diophantes; and he was the firſt amongſt them who made uſe of them for the muſical diviſions of the monochord: But he afterwards made allegorical applications of them, which may have been of ſome moral uſe, but were of no advantage to arithme-

* Jamb. de Myſt. Ægypt. l. 1.

tick itſelf. Upon other columns were the elementary propoſitions of geometry, with their figures, under each of which was the name of him who firſt demonſtrated them, and the date thereof; but not the demonſtrations themſelves. Theſe monuments formed a very curious hiſtory of the ſteps and progreſs of human underſtanding. The ſciences were pointed out, and the degree they had attain'd to in each age known; but there were other meaſures to be taken before they could be attain'd to. Thales had obſerv'd there, that an angle taken in the circumference of a circle, and carry'd to the two extremities of the diameter, was always rectangular: And it was from the demonſtration he found of it after his return to Greece, that he gather'd all the other proprieties of the circle, and all the trigonometrical reſolutions, or thoſe which give the meaſure of inacceſſible diſtances. There it was that Pythagoras found out the famous propoſition upon the hypothenuſe of the rectangular triangle, compar'd to the two other ſides. * And it was not without reaſon he ſacrific'd a hecatomb in thanks to the gods for having at laſt diſcover'd it; ſince this propoſition, and that which eſtabliſhes the analogy of the ſides of ſuch triangles, are the two axles

* See Olaus Borrichius, Hermetis ſapientia, where he ſpeaks in general of the ſciences of the Egyptians, c. 8.

upon

upon which the whole ſcience of geometry turns.

NEXT to the elementary propoſitions, which reſpect only figures terminated by direct or circular lines, were all thoſe parts of geometry, which require no other aſſiſtance. Upon this baſis alone were rais'd all the mathematicks employ'd for the uſe of man, the convenience of cities, and the ornament of all Egypt; in a word, all practical geometry. The principles of this geometry carved upon columns, tho' they were not all copy'd from thoſe of Mercury, and the date of the greater part ſhew'd that the invention was more modern, took up one ſide of this ſpacious gallery. The other was adorn'd with diſcoveries made in compound geometry, or that part which treats of curvilineal figures. Theſe diſcoveries being owing to the prieſts alone, after they had form'd a peculiar ſociety in Egypt, were not upon columns, but carv'd with proper figures upon tables of white marble, higher and larger than the columns. Eſtabliſh'd theorems, and problems reſolv'd, * were only expreſs'd,

* Thoſe prieſts who apply'd themſelves to the moſt abſtruſe ſpeculations in geometry, were call'd Arſepedonaptes, or Arpedonaptes. See on theſe two words the notes of S. Clem. of Alex. in Potter's Edition, p. 357. The reader will find in the text, that Democritus boaſted of having learnt of theſe men as much of geometry as they themſelves could know.

as thoſe in ſimple geometry, without any demonſtration.

BUT of all the curioſities in theſe galleries, nothing came up to the beauty of the aſtronomical inſtruments. The Chaldeans have been accounted the inventors of this ſcience: But they themſelves were but a colony of the Egyptians, led into Babylon by Belus, who, according to Diodorus, was born in Egypt. The very climate of this country favour'd their aſtronomical obſervations, not only on account of a continual ſerene sky, but becauſe, being near the equator, it diſcovers the greateſt part of the firmament, whoſe revolutions over it are almoſt direct. It was by this advantage of ſituation, that the ſhepherds, who ſpent their nights in the open fields, were the firſt aſtronomers: they could not but remark the different elevations of the ſtars in different hours of the night, the ſucceſſive riſe of thoſe which abſented themſelves from the rays of the ſun, during the courſe of the year, and the particular courſe of the planets, generally oppoſite to the diurnal motion of the whole firmament. But no ſooner did the more curious and penetrating part of mankind begin to cultivate theſe objects, than they converted them into the moſt noble of all human ſciences, and the only one which can render a prophet infallible. The ſituation of Egypt made it ſo famous

famous for aſtronomy, that, ſince the foundation of Alexandria, all the great aſtronomers of Greece have been either born, or have acquir'd their knowledge and fame in that city. Such as, Timocharis, Denis the aſtronomer, Eratoſthenes, the famous Hipparchus, Poſſidonius, Soſigenes; and, to conclude, Ptolomy, the laſt and the greateſt of them all. The Egyptians were the firſt who made ſpheres according to the two different ſyſtems of the univerſe; upon a ſuppoſition, either that all the heavenly bodies have their revolution about the earth, or that the earth takes its circuit round the ſun as a planet. Tho' the Greeks now follow the viſible and apparent ſyſtem of the diurnal revolution of the ſun about us, a ſyſtem to which our Ptolomy has added great luſtre; we can't be ignorant that our antient philoſophers, ſuch as Thales and Pythagoras, believed all the planets, and the earth itſelf, had their motions round the ſun. And as both of them learnt the ſciences in Egypt, it is a certain proof, independant of my memoirs, that this laſt ſyſtem took its riſe there. The motion of the earth has been even admitted by Greeks of a pretty modern date; and Philolaus has lent his name to the Philolaick aſtronomy, which has this hypotheſis for its baſis. Theſe two ſyſtems are equally ſatisfactory as to the periodical revolutions of the ſtars. But if the Ptolomean ſyſtem be in ſome manner better adapted to the ſenſes, and may ſerve for aſtronomers who only obſerve the celeſtial appearances; that of Philolaus, being infinitely plainer in itſelf, of conſequence comes nearer nature, and is more agreeable to philoſophy. I ſhall ſay nothing here of the Egyptian aſtrology, becauſe it was only taught to initiates, in the inmoſt receſſes of their temples. But as a ſearch after the philoſopher's ſtone has been the parent of chymiſtry, ſo we may ſay that the vain ſcience of aſtrology, with which all the nations of the world are infatuated, has produc'd excellent diſcoveries in aſtronomy. A general knowledge of this great art was common to all the prieſts in Egypt; but we muſt allow that thoſe of Thebes ſurpaſſed in this article * all their brethren. I ſhall therefore defer ſome other obſervations on this ſcience, till I ſhall have occaſion in another place to ſpeak of this famous metropolis of the upper Egypt.

BUT what attracted the attention of a greater number of people in the palace of Memphis, were the models of all the machines which had been made uſe of to level the ſoil in Egypt, to water every part of it, to raiſe thoſe waters to conſiderable heights, and to keep them within bounds. It was after a view of theſe

* Diodor. l. 1.

wonder-

wonderful machines, of which ſome were yet in being in the days of Archimedes, that this famous prince of Syracuſa invented at Alexandria the hydraulick ſcrew or engine which bears his * name. In this gallery was likewiſe ſhewn the models of thoſe multiplied powers, by the means of which they had been able to hoiſt out of their quarries, to tranſport, and to raiſe to the very clouds, ſtones of ſo prodigious a ſize, as perpetuate the labours of Egypt. To conclude, whatever invention had furniſh'd for the ſervice of war, by land or ſea, was there carefully treaſur'd up. Aſtronomy, added to the active genius of the Egyptians, had made them very expert in navigation; and the models of veſſels of every form, and of inſtruments proper to build and work them, were not the leaſt among the curioſities we have been deſcribeing.

THIS extraordinary collection was indeed but a mute object, or ſpoke only by means of the inſcriptions which were affix'd to each article. We muſt likewiſe allow that foreigners had hardly any other inſtructions to expect, but what they could draw from theſe kinds of objects, which were in ſome of the cities of Egypt, before Cambyſes, the ſon of Cyrus, the moſt ſavage

* Diodor. l. 5. p. 217. Ed. Hen.

and inconſiderate of all conquerors, had laid them waſte. Thales and Pythagoras were the laſt of the Greek philoſophers, who had the advantage of ſeeing them before their deſtruction. They both reſided in Egypt a great number of years; and had contracted an intimate friendſhip with ſome of the Egyptian prieſts: They were both initiated, and Pythagoras in particular *, deſirous of being ſo, at Heliopolis, where the prieſts were accounted the moſt expert at divination, purchas'd it at the expence of being circumciſed. Notwithſtanding which, their travels and labours had been of little profit to them, if they had not, as great inventers themſelves, drawn large conſequences from the little which was communicated to them †. The prieſts thought themſelves indeed oblig'd to be liberal of their inſtructions to foreign initiates, with regard to certain myſteries of their religion, but were very ſparing in the ſecrets of their ſciences. In favour of their own nation however, there were commonly attending, in other galleries of the palace of Memphis, the greateſt maſters of thoſe ſciences, of which the principles and inſtruments had been expos'd to view in thoſe already deſcrib'd. Renown'd Athens never produc'd

* Clem. Alex. Strom. l. 1.

† Philoſtrates in the life of Apollonius, l. 1. c. 1. ſays, that Pythagoras, as an excellent painter, had embelliſh'd with colours what the Egyptian prieſts had only sketch'd with the pencil.

ſo many ſchools, nor them more frequented; tho' in theſe of Egypt none were admitted but natives *. Beſides the hours ſet apart for regular lectures, the prieſts, who were the only teachers in theſe ſeveral academies, were ready every moment of the day to anſwer all queſtions that might be propos'd to them by any perſons whomſoever. But their chymical preparations, anatomical diſſections, and even aſtronomical obſervations, were always in private; that they might in ſome meaſure conceal, even from the Egyptians themſelves, the means by which they attain'd to their knowledge.

THO' the Egyptians gave preference, among the labours of the mind, to natural philoſophy, as more directly conducive to the advantage of the publick; they were not, however, negligent in thoſe which are the objects of erudition. Their conſultations on this head were held in a vaſt library, which they increas'd daily. Upon the gate of this library was written in letters of gold, FOOD FOR THE MIND. An inſcription of greater extent than that of the library of Thebes, plac'd there by Iſmandes the founder:

* Monuments of antiquity give ſo often an idea of theſe academies, that F. Laffiteau, in the life of John de Brienne, l. 2. p. 145. having had occaſion to ſpeak of Philippus Auguſtus, ſaid; That he had made the univerſity of Paris as famous as thoſe of Athens and Memphis had been, in their greateſt ſplendour.

viz. PHYSICK FOR THE MIND *. It is not in the power of a king to collect the curiosities of nature and art, which one learned man may have describ'd and explain'd in his writings; but no private person can make so ample a collection of books as a king may. The library of 700,000 volumes collected under the care of Ptolomeus Philadelphus, and burnt against the will of the conqueror, when Julius Cæsar enter'd Alexandria, was a wonder of Egypt, greater than any of those which now go by the name. At Memphis, and in other cities, the priests kept in their own possession all the books, which contain'd the mysteries of their religion, and even the histories of the heroick times, or those which preceded Menes. They communicated them only to initiates, to whom they expounded them in private. Having establish'd it as a maxim, to deprive the laity of all means of becoming arbiters in points of religion; the people, and especially the women, knew no more of it than what the priests taught them by word of mouth. But all histories from the time of Menes, and even those of foreign countries, which they had collected with as much assiduity as the curiosities of nature, were preserved in the royal libraries, and shewn to all Egyptians who desir'd it.

* Diodor. Description of the Memnonium, l. 1. §. 2.

* THE priests in Egypt were the only judges in point of civil right: But if they themselves had any matter of dispute with private persons, and by so much the more if with the king, it was decided by the assembly of initiates: So that the priests and initiates might have kept the knowledge of the law wholly within themselves. However, as they thought it reasonable that every one who was cast should judge of the equity of their judgments; and besides, it was requisite for private persons to know the laws they were to live up to; the priests taught this science publickly in a hall of the palace: and that was the only school into which strangers were admitted. The Egyptians had right to boast that Solon and Lycurgus borrow'd from them the best of those laws which they establish'd, one of them in Athens, and the other in Sparta. † Among these was one very remarkable, which oblig'd all the commoners of Egypt to declare to the judges every year what profession they propos'd to follow for a livelihood, and they were forbidden, at least for that time, following any other upon pain of death. This made them assiduous every one in his way. And that activity yet so visible in our city of Alexandria, made the

* Ælian. var. hist. l. 14.
† Herodotus, l. 2. Diodor. l. 1.

emperor Adrian ſay, * there was not a man in that great city who was not diſtinguiſhed by ſome or other profeſſion or trade. Even the blind, added he, have their work. None are exempt, no not the gouty, if they have either hands or feet free from the diſtemper. This is but one inſtance, among an infinite number of excellent laws, which from the Egyptians were propagated among the wiſeſt nations, and of which ſome are eaſily diſtinguiſh'd in the Roman laws ||.

THE kings of Egypt had always been promoters of theſe academies, being convinc'd, that a love of the ſciences, and the tranquility they requir'd, were alone ſufficient to ſuppreſs all thoughts of revolt and ſedition. The ſciences not only employ and adorn the mind, but endue it with a certain ſolidity and uprightneſs, which generally prevent men not only from being vain, but from being wicked. This truth had been experienc'd by many kings, in the great miniſters, magiſtrates, and even great commanders, which theſe ſchools had furniſh'd: For the exerciſes of the body were here as little neglected as thoſe of the mind.

* Fl. Vopiſcus in Saturnino.

|| Solon ſententiis adjutus ſacerdotum Ægypti, latis juſtâ moderatione legibus, Romano quoque juri maximum addidit firmamentum. Amm. Marc. lib. 22. See likewiſe Nicolai de Synedrio Ægyptiorum, where he compares the 14 chief laws of Egypt to thoſe of other nations.

mind. I don't mean only ſuch as wreſtling, ſwimming, running, riding, and walking a ſingle rope, which latter they ſuppos'd render'd the eyes, and footſteps ſure; all exerciſes of great uſe in the art of war, whether in battles or at ſieges; but every article belonging to the military art which requires ſtudy and ſcience. Here young noblemen, emulating one another, were employed in taking the diſtances of inacceſſible places, and delineating every ſpecies of fortification. They diligently followed the moſt famous architects in the execution of their immenſe undertakings, to learn of them the proportions which the foundations of walls bear to their height; the power of thoſe vaults which tho' ſolid were light; the different ſorts of timber, and the degrees of force it attain'd from different poſitions.

EVEN queens, and the ladies that attended them, were endued with this noble emulation. The ſet races, and other exerciſes of theſe young noblemen, on their feſtivals, and days of publick rejoicings, furniſh'd them with very agreeable entertainments, and they took a ſingular pleaſure in diſcourſing in the circles which were form'd about them at court towards evening, thereby to be inſtructed, and render'd worthy of that ſociety they were neceſſarily to be engag'd in with the moſt learned men: For, according to a cuſtom

custom as antient in Egypt as monarchy itself, the priests, as austere as they were in their sacerdotal functions, frequented the assemblies at court. The first design of this custom was to keep up a spirit of religion in their kings, and a decorum in courts, where, contrary to the custom of other nations, the women were allowed freedom of conversation with the men. The priests themselves had this advantage by it, that in return for their sciences they learned politeness from the courtiers: and both together made up that mixture, which perhaps alone deserves the name of good company; that is, of persons of distinction join'd with men of wit and learning. Rules for conversation were needless among persons whose minds were so form'd: and as no one presum'd to speak beyond the measure of his genius and knowledge, every person at court, tho' in different degrees of learning, render'd himself almost equally valued. It was even a maxim with the Egyptians, that a refin'd wit was not the greatest qualification a man could have, not only with respect to the affairs of state and war, which of course were preferably put into the hands of men of deep knowledge and experience; but even with regard to the common intercourses of life, and the agreeableness of conversation: so that profess'd wits were no otherwise esteem'd than as they render'd themselves agreeable by their affability, modesty, and other qualities common to men of honour. In short, in a nation where every subject, animated by a reciprocal emulation, discharg'd his function or employ equally well, that real esteem they had one for the other added a harmony to society, now hardly any where known.

THIS solidity of mind, which appear'd in the employments, and even conversations of the Egyptians, extended to matters of mere entertainment. They were admirers of elegant writing in prose and verse: but having in general a more favourable opinion of men of a common genius who render'd themselves useful by their knowledge, than of those fine wits, who only supply'd the publick with vain amusements, they reconcil'd both by this unquestionable maxim, that the great man in point of learning was he who cultivated a profuseness of wit with as large a degree of knowledge. In consequence of this maxim, universally received, there appear'd very few authors who had not treasur'd up a stock of reading sufficient to be the guide and support of their own reflections. Hence it was that the readers found a great deal of instruction even in those books, which seem'd to be written only for pleasure and diversion. And thus those who presided over learning prevented, as well in authors as readers, that taste for trifles which is the ſtumbling-block of polite nations, and ſoon becomes a greater hinderance to noble undertakings, than ſimplicity and impoliteneſs. As for poets, they were very ſevere in examining their notions of virtue and vice; and undeceiv'd them in the opinion they almoſt all fell into, that morality was an innate knowledge, which required no ſtudy to attain to. But poetry was abſolutely forbid to perſons convicted of diſſolute and irregular morals. By this they ſecured themſelves from a publick evil, always found among the Greeks; which was, that whenever authors became ſcandalous in their perſons, they were the firſt who took upon them to reform mankind by ſatire, almoſt always levell'd at perſons of ſuch merit, whom a juſt reputation plac'd above them. The antient Lacedemonians, in imitation of the Egyptians, forbad every vicious man even to mention a moral maxim. And in effect what are poets, who, as we have frequent inſtances among the Greeks, undertaking to repreſent the characters of virtuous men in their poems, but who having themſelves no idea or knowledge of virtue, never ſet it in a juſt light: or, which is yet more pernicious, give an advantageous turn to vice conceal'd under the larve of falſe heroiſm?

IN the palace of Memphis were two peculiar galleries, which not only ſerv'd as ſchools

for

for ſculptors and painters, but for the learned were the richeſt monument they could deſire for the hiſtory of theſe two arts. At the entrance into one of theſe galleries were on the right and on the left columns of wood or ſtone, roughly hewn, about the height and thickneſs of a man. The name of the god, or hero, which was deſign'd to be repreſented, was written upon ſome of them; and that was all the ſculpture of the firſt times. Advancing farther, human form began to unfold itſelf more and more: but the two legs were as yet join'd together, and the two arms glued to the body at their full length. By degrees the members were looſen'd from the trunk, and plac'd in the poſtures of action. From thence they came to elegant attitudes, and ſoon to miracles of art. For as ſoon as man has found out the good in any art whatſoever, he riſes with a prodigious rapidity to the excellent. The Grecian ſculpture paſs'd thro' the ſame degrees; and Plutarch relates, that the Spartiates call'd all thoſe figures they had of the Dioſcuri, or the two brothers Caſtor and Pollux, Docanes. They were two beams * plac'd upright, and join'd together at top by a croſs piece of timber. Dædalus was the firſt who brought out of Egypt into Greece the art of putting the arms of ſtatues in an acting, and the legs in a

* *Docos* in Greek ſignifies a beam.

walk-

walking poſture. The Greeks were ſo ſurpriz'd at this new attitude, that they chain'd down their ſtatues made in this manner, for fear they ſhould run away; and Plato obſerves, that ſtatues which were faſten'd to pedeſtals yielded a greater price than others; as ſlaves who were not addicted to elopement. There is even ſomething more in it: for tho', on the teſtimony of the Greeks, who had ſeen the ſtatues of Dædalus, they were, with reſpect to the ſculpture, not brought to that pitch of perfection, to which Phidias and Praxiteles brought theirs; he had given them, by means of ſome inward ſprings, a real motion. Ariſtotle himſelf, quoting Philip the comick writer, aſſures us, that Dædalus had carv'd a ſtatue of Venus in wood, which mov'd by means of quickſilver he had pour'd into the inſide of it. Be it as it will with regard to the truth or circumſtances of this fact; theſe allegations will ſuffice to make us take the deſcription Homer gives us of the moveing figures in Achilles's buckler in a literal ſenſe, notwithſtanding thoſe interpreters who will reduce the deſcription of it to that of a common picture or baſſo-relievo, the figures of which are repreſented as moving, tho' they are in reality motionleſs. And it is eaſy to diſcover, that Homer, in his deſcription of this buckler, had in view this art of Dædalus, more famous in his days than in ours. But nothing is of greater honour to the

the Egyptian ſculpture, than that piece of hiſtory with which the firſt book of Diodorus Siculus concludes. The moſt famous ſculptors of Greece, ſays this author, were train'd up in the ſchools of Egypt. Such are Telecles and Theodorus, the ſons of Roecus, who made the ſtatue of Apollo Pythius, now at Samos; in ſuch manner that Telecles having made one half of it at Samos, while his brother Theodorus made the other half at Epheſus, the two pieces fitted ſo exactly, that the whole figure ſeem'd to be by one hand. This peculiar art, which is but little known, continues he, to the Grecian ſculptors, is very much cultivated by the Egyptians: for theſe don't judge of a figure, as the Greeks, barely by the eye; but meaſuring all the parts one by the other, they carve the ſtones which are to form a ſtatue ſeparately, and with the utmoſt accuracy. For this end they divided a human body into 21 parts and $\frac{1}{4}$. So when the workmen had once agreed among themſelves upon the height of the figure, every one made that part which fell to his ſhare, and they join'd in ſuch manner as was aſtoniſhing to thoſe who were not acquainted with this art. But the two pieces of Apollo of Samos join according to the height of the body; and tho' the arms are ſtretch'd out, as in action, and the legs are in the poſture of a man walking, it is every where correſpondent,

 and

and the whole figure is in the most exact equilibrity. In short, this piece of workmanship, which is finish'd according to the Egyptian method, is very little inferior to the most accomplish'd pieces of Egypt itself.

THE other gallery was appropriated to painting. The first that appear'd in view were boards whited over, upon which the objects, generally describ'd in black, were so ill drawn, that the painter thought himself oblig'd to write on the side of each, This is a man; This is a horse; This is a tree. Advancing farther, were draughts which seem'd to have been mark'd out round the shadow of an object set in the sun. In the following pictures the perfection of draught and variety of colours increas'd visibly. The Egyptians, as the Greeks, had for a long time only four: and we know that Zeuxis, Polygnotus, and Timanthes made use of no more. Echion, Nicomachus, Protogenes, and finally Apelles, were those, who, with their different compound colours, found out all the shadowings of nature. There are yet to be seen, in a grotto not far from Thebes, paintings which are remaining from the times of the antient kings of that dynasty, the colours of which are as lively as if but just laid on *. But the

* Paul Luc. t. 6. p. 69.

more modern Egyptians did not fall into the fault with which Denis of Halicarnaſſus reproaches the modern Greek painters; that they endeavour'd to cover the neglect of deſign by the variety and livelineſs of their colours. The Egyptians compar'd thoſe who preferr'd colours to deſign in painting, to thoſe who in eloquence and poetry preferr'd bright thoughts to thoſe which are juſt. Cicero, the maſter and pattern of latin eloquence, applying his reflection to oratory, ſays, That we ſoon grow weary of thoſe pictures which at firſt ſight attract us by force of colours; whereas we are conſtant in our admiration of thoſe that excel in the beauty of deſign, which is the true character of antiquity *.

To conclude; the muſick-gallery, where, on certain days, were held concerts of voices and inſtruments, was likewiſe a treaſure for the antiquities of this art. Here 'twas found that the ſhalm, the ſhepherd's flute, and other wind inſtruments, were the firſt invented; and here was even ſhewn the flute of ſeveral pipes of unequal lengths, that was in uſe before Oſiris invented the ſingle flute, which expreſs'd all the tones of the former. This hero had thoſe hymns which he ſung in honour to the gods accompany'd by it; and the

* See, on the two foregoing articles, Junius de pictura veterum.

verſes, according to Plutarch, contain'd thoſe precepts which he gave to the people, whom he had got together, and was deſirous to civilize. The ſame Oſiris in time invented the trumpet and kettle-drums, to animate the ſoldiers he made uſe of in his conqueſts. Mercury afterwards invented the harp; which leaves the muſician the liberty of adding his voice and words to the ſound of his inſtrument. In ſome ancient monuments this god is deſcrib'd with a harp of ſeven ſtrings; the two extremes of which, as they pretended, being ſtruck together, from'd the diapazon or octave, even before the laſt ſtring but one, which renders it compleat, was introduc'd into the diatonick ſyſtem *. Next to the harps, they ſhew'd in this gallery at Memphis, the firſt tables, or the firſt bodies of inſtruments, that are of ſo much ſervice to ſtrengthen the ſounds, which are too weak in a ſingle circumference of ſolid wood, as that which ſupports the ſtrings of the harp. They came at laſt to the inſtruments with necks, or which were touch'd at a diſtance; in which the fingers forming the ſounds, find, upon a leſſer number of ſtrings, a greater number of tetra-chords, and even of octaves, can paſs indifferently thro' all the moods, and have full ſcope to perform whatever the imagination of the boldeſt compoſer

* See that excellent treatiſe of the muſick of the antients, aſcrib'd to M. l'Abbe de Chateauneuf.

can produce. Diodorus was but ill inform'd of the fact, when he said, the Egyptians did not cultivate musick. On the contrary, it was of them Pythagoras got such a taste of it, as to admit of harmony in the skies, and apply the proportions of it to the general constitution of the universe. The Egyptians encourag'd their young men and maidens to learn and perform every species of musick, to render them more polite and more agreeable: And, in imitation of them it was, that the Greeks plac'd musick in the number of those things necessary to the education of youth.

WE see by this faint sketch, that however valuable private education may be, it never can have the advantages of this publick education of the Egyptians: But what seems to be the most valuable in it, is, that youth is not abandon'd, as in our modern educations, as soon as they come out of their infancy; that is, at a time when their judgments being better form'd, are susceptible of knowledge, either more abstruse in itself, or of more service to the publick, and when they have most need of help to suppress the first flights of youth: So we see that this Stage, which is the most propitious to the female sex, because they are more carefully guarded than in any other, is the most extravagant in the male, who are abandon'd to their own passions, not eaſily govern'd, if they be not endow'd with excellent natural talents. Levity of mind, an averſion to duty, and a neglect of time, now ſo faſhionable among the Greek and Roman youths, would have been a blemiſh upon their honour in Egypt, even in the eyes of the ladies, who had any concern for them; and, as the only mark of a court truly polite, there were no advances to their favour but by merit and wiſdom. But above all I muſt not forget to obſerve, that the exerciſes, and even the labours of the Egyptian youth ſecured them from that fatal wearineſs of mind, that general diſtaſte which accompanies ours even in the very height of their debauchery.

THERE were, indeed, at that time, ſome young men more ſollicitous for preſent pleaſure than future merit, who thought theſe ſtudies and converſations a burden: And ladies, who qualify'd only to diſcourſe of their conſtitutions, taſte and dreſs, were uneaſy that they could not carry theſe their only objects of entertainment into the palace, and make them general. And by ſuch Daluca was ſoon ſeconded in her reſolution of bringing into evil repute theſe learned ſchools, the fountains of that merit ſhe had moſt to fear, and to break off thoſe inſtructive conferences of all kinds, in which the rules of a moſt refin'd moral were frequently the ſub-

ject.

ject. The method ſhe pitch'd on, as moſt expedient for her deſign, was, to give the privilege of keeping aſſemblies, and the ſole empire of converſation, to ſuch ladies of the court as ſhe had obſerv'd the moſt vain, and who had the faculty of talking loud and long upon nothing, when they found it was countenanc'd. The queen, under pretext of being extreamly taken up with the affairs of ſtate, appear'd very ſeldom in theſe aſſemblies herſelf, and prevented the king from going to them, by amuſing him as much as poſſible with other private diverſions: But having before confer'd the chief offices at court upon ladies of the character I have juſt deſcrib'd, ſhe deputed them to perform the honours of the palace in her room, and to preſide in her name at the converſation of thoſe circles which were form'd in her abſence. Theſe ladies, like the queen, had all paſs'd their meridian, and having made no proviſion to ſupply the loſs of exterior beauties, by the more valuable qualities of the mind, were but juſt before bewailing their abandon'd ſtate: But being now rais'd by an exceſs of favours, which the queen ſeem'd to heap upon them, were extreamly ſubſervient to her deſign, without ſo much as knowing it. They were always ready to interrupt any diſcourſe that might but ſavour of learning or ingenuity; but they were not often put to the trouble:

for their own perpetual talk was ſo vain, and ſo little approv'd, that no man of ſenſe could find room, or thought it worth while, to put in a word. It was obſerv'd, that they were continually whiſpering to one another in theſe aſſemblies, and ridiculing certain perſons, who in the preceding adminiſtration had been greatly reſpected, tho' in the preſent they were not thought neceſſary. By theſe odious freedoms they drew upon themſelves a contempt, which waited only for an opportunity of diſplaying itſelf, and which already very ſenſibly leſſen'd the regard otherwiſe had to them and the whole ſex. In the mean time, all perſons of good ſenſe and merit by degrees abſented from theſe aſſemblies, where they perceiv'd their company was a burden: And thus the court, which was wont to be the center of good taſte in all manner of ſubjects, and the model of purity for the Egyptian tongue, was become the abode of ignorance, or of indifferency to every thing that was the object of good ſenſe and reaſon. The language itſelf being corrupted with improper terms, and a neglected pronunciation, became a jargon of the fancy; which being without rule, was ty'd down to none. The writings of thoſe who formerly frequented the court were known by a juſt and natural elegancy, in a great meaſure owing to their intercourſe with ladies of the moſt polite parts, in whom it it eminently abounded: But the modern wits, who ſucceeded them, forgetting that language muſt always have the ſanction of the publick, introduc'd, of their own private authority, an infinite number of fantaſtick terms and expreſſions, which ſo far from being adapted by cuſtom, were carefully avoided by all correct authors.

On the other hand, the young nobility, ſeeing that probity and good breeding was as little required in the men, as prudence and behaviour in the women, and that every thing depended on favour, abandon'd all thoſe exerciſes of mind and body which they had till then purſued, that they might devote themſelves to theſe new creatures of the queen. The grand art was to perſuade them, by force of flattery, to believe they were poſſeſs'd of thoſe charms which they themſelves had given over for loſt; and they began to hope, that Daluca having brought their age into faſhion, youth would be no more regarded. The beauties of the court of Memphis had always had their admirers; accompliſh'd merit on both ſides was generally the origin of the paſſions they excited. A deſire only of gaining the eſteem of a charming perſon, produc'd ſuch endeavours after virtue and valour, as was admir'd by the publick, without knowing their firſt cauſe;

But as for the modern intrigues *, they were owing to a mutual conformity of bad taste and bad choice; their beginning was debauchery, and a communication of vices between the pretended lovers were the fruits of them. It was an observation in former times, that those who had been singled out, and train'd up by certain ladies of the court, became the most accomplish'd men: But for these, the beauties of the mind, or a total want of them, were qualities they had no discernment of, and were equally indifferent to; and they entertain'd no hopes of making any advantage by persons of a too distinguish'd probity. In times past, the most discerning had no other way of discovering a passion between two persons, but by a greater circumspection in the one, and a more irreproachable behaviour in the other. But now the new favourite of each of these ladies was immediately known to every one; and they were sooner put out of countenance, when complimented upon that account, than their mistresses themselves.

THE queen, who at a distance saw this progress, began already to gather the fruits of

* The author seems here to have in view the licentiousness of the court of the empress Faustina, the wife of Marcus Aurelius. See the history of the Roman empresses, by M. de Servies.

her

her endeavours, by the contempt, hatred and jealoufy which was fomented among the courtiers. Both men and women, as fhe had forefeen, were totally loft to all good manners, by a diffipation and levity of mind. There was not one among them who had not taken a fteady refolution to facrifice virtue, honour and duty to the leaft fmile of fortune; and nothing lefs than adverfity, or the moft terrible events, were capable of awaking them from this infatuation: Even the minifters of ftate, who till then had every moment of their time fo taken up, either in their different employs, or in recreating themfelves in their families, that they never ftir'd out of their clofets, but to council, or to give audience to the publick, thought themfelves now under an obligation of making their court to thefe ladies in authority; and all the affiduity they formerly employ'd in the affairs of ftate, was now neceffary to keep them in their places: To continue in their favour, it was not enough to comply with their fantaftick humours, to adminifter to their ruinous pleafures, to provide immenfe entertainments for them; they infifted, that all their recommendations fhould take place, tho' they were ever in favour of fome unjuft caufe, or unworthy object; and that their counfels, tho' moft pernicious to their prince, fhould be approv'd, in confideration of a fmall gain to them. Thus, tho' the deceas'd queen had

had left all things in ſo excellent an order, that they might have ſubſiſted, and even held out againſt mal-adminiſtration for a long time, yet the ſtate was ruſhing on very faſt towards its ruin. Peace, which, eſpecially in dominions of ſo ſmall extent as thoſe of Egypt, is not to be preſerv'd but by ſecret ſprings of the cabinet, and by a regard ſhewn, at leaſt in appearance, to neighbouring princes, ſoon was ſhaken by a neglect of cultivating their friendſhip, by the little ſatisfaction given to their ambaſſadors, and by the infringement of ſeveral laws, which concern'd the tranquillity of all Egypt, and its ſecurity againſt enemies from abroad. And thus Daluca, with a view only of prejudicing Sethos, expos'd the welfare of the kingdom and her own ſafety to all the ill conſequences of ſo pernicious a conduct.

BUT while this unworthy queen was thus fomenting diſorders, the wiſe Amedes was aſſiduous in the education of the young prince, whoſe fate had deſtin'd him to be firſt the victim, and afterwards the repairer of them. He did not, in expreſs terms, diſcover to him the diſgrace he perceiv'd he was already fall'n into; a condition not eaſy to be conceiv'd by a child of eight or nine years of age, eſpecially when diſguis'd under thoſe profeſſions of kindneſs and flattering careſſes which Daluca hitherto continued to ſhew to Sethos.

But the chief aim of Amedes was to inſpire him with the principles of every virtue, which he might ſtand in need of to ſupport him in the moſt adverſe fortune. He put him in mind of his illuſtrious birth, to make him ſenſible not of the reſpect due to him from others, but of what he owed to himſelf. He gave him lively ideas, not of a prince ſurrounded by his obſequious ſubjects and ſlaviſh courtiers, but of a prince dethron'd by uſurpers, and reſiding among foreigners, where he would have no other grandeur but that of his own mind, and his perſonal courage. The queſtions he propos'd to him, either to diſcover his ſentiments, or to exerciſe his talents, were generally upon perilous and intricate circumſtances, which a prince could not extricate himſelf from without the greateſt courage, nor ſuſtain without the higheſt pitch of probity. He did not, however, at any time, wholly bereave him of the hopes of peaceably enjoying the kingdom to which he was the lawful heir: but he inſtructed him, that the principles of thoſe morals fitting to be practis'd in danger or adverſity, or rather, that danger and adverſity themſelves naturally lead a prince to a regular and advantageous enjoyment of peace and happineſs. With regard to the religion of his anceſtors, Amedes inſtructed him therein, in a conciſe, plain and conſiſtent manner with regard to facts, but laid

laid great ſtreſs upon the examples and moral precepts he drew from them.

IT is common to give princes only general ideas of the ſciences; and, indeed, it is ſufficient, if they be but acquainted with as much as will make them friends and protectors of them. But Amedes was deſirous, that whatever might be his fate, his pupil ſhould attain to all the merit of a private perſon. He alſo concluded, that Sethos being yet too young to comprehend the great maxims of government, politicks and war, could not better employ the firſt years of his tuition, than by initiating him early into all the Egyptian ſciences. Youth has this peculiar advantage, that men never arrive to perfection in any arts or ſciences, if they don't overcome the main difficulties of them while they are young: And to give a diſadvantageous inſtance as to my own part alone, I muſt confeſs I have, in different ſtages of my life, endeavour'd to acquire thoſe ſciences which are eſteem'd among the Greeks, but have never been able to attain to more than reading and writing in ſuch a manner as I am ſatisfy'd with, they being the only arts that became eaſy to me in the days of my youth. However, as human knowledge is of ſo vaſt an extent, that not youth alone, but life itſelf is hardly ſufficient to attain it; this

great

great maſter inform'd his pupil, that he ſhould make him acquainted only with the firſt rudiments of the ſciences; and that thoſe who reſt ſatisfy'd with that part they have gone thro' in this firſt ſtage of life, ought modeſtly to confeſs their ignorance.

AMEDES perceiv'd that this young prince gave every day new ſigns of an admirable genius. He had form'd no deciſive judgment upon that agreeableneſs, that vivacity and wit which he frequently obſerv'd in him during his mother's life, when he was ſurrounded with the flattering ſmiles of fortune: ſuch indications are not always to be depended upon, becauſe thoſe repartees which we think ſo witty in children, are often but an effect of the liberty allow'd them, and generally beſtow'd upon trivial occaſions; and conſequently no concluſion can be drawn from thence applicable to that period of time in which they are to employ their thoughts upon ſolid and ſerious ſubjects. But in natural philoſophy, our maſter could hardly keep pace with the docility of his ſcholar; and in hiſtory he had much ado to ſatisfy his unbounded curioſity: So for his own eaſe, and the more readily to accuſtom young Sethos to be his own inſtructor, he exercis'd him in the former, by putting him upon experiments and the ſolution of difficulties; and in the latter, by making him read the moſt celebrated authors

authors from the beginning to the end; and afterwards obliging him to give coherent abridgments of every hiſtory. He made him acquainted in the firſt, with the progreſs of human underſtanding, and the advancement of the ſciences from one century to another; and in the ſecond, with the great men and the beſt writers of all the ages paſt.

HE likewiſe carry'd him every day, at certain hours, into the ſchools we have mention'd above, which were not now ſo crowded as in former times; but then they were ſure of meeting there the flower of the youth of Memphis, and all thoſe who had not been yet corrupted by the preſent taſte of the court. Our own application muſt render us maſters of the ſciences; but the knowledge of applying them rightly is only to be acquir'd by converſing with men of underſtanding and merit. Beſides, Amedes, without affecting at an improper time to oppoſe the queen's meaſures, was deſirous of making Sethos known to the youth of the kingdom, who were growing up with him. The hiſtory of the infancy of Seſoſtris was yet recent in his memory. This prince was no ſooner born, than his father Amenophis caus'd all the infants of his kingdom, who were born on the ſame day with his ſon, to be brought before him; he provided them with nurſes, appointed tutors for them, and gave them all the ſame education;

tion; being persuaded, that children who had been brought up in a familiarity with their prince from their most tender years, would the more firmly adhere to him in the course of his life, and would serve him best in his wars. Amedes was moreover desirous that Sethos should converse in the publick assemblies with those foreigners, whom the fame of Egypt drew thither from all the parts of the world, where knowledge and good manners were cultivated. Men of attention gather new knowledge in the conversation even of such as have less than themselves; and the Egyptians, at the same time they communicated their instructions to others, became more learned themselves. Besides, as the greater number of those who came into Egypt, were led thither, either to obtain the initiation, or to perfect themselves in the sciences, and sometimes for both, they were generally the greatest men of every nation. These strangers, it is natural to conceive, apply'd themselves with a great deal of care to the learning of the Egyptian tongue: And the most curious among the Egyptians studied those of other nations. The priests divided all the languages of the known world among themselves, that they might be able to give satisfaction to all those who apply'd to them for advice from every quarter. To this end they sent the most expert among them, disguised like merchants, into the most distant states.

states. The laity, who were destined to the war, or to trade, generally confin'd themselves to the Phenician, the Greek, and the Punick tongues. The first gave them access at the chief courts of Asia, the second to those of Europe, and the third in Africa: But the Egyptian tongue was in some degree the common source of these three; for the Phenicians, Greeks and Carthaginians were Egyptian colonies. A knowledge of the Egyptian tongue was therefore in a great measure a key to the others. Amedes, however, let Sethos learn the first rudiments of the latter, but he left him to acquire a perfection in them by practice, and the frequent conversation he procur'd him with such strangers, as appear'd to him the most knowing.

THE education of Sethos was not confin'd to the improvement of his mind; Amedes put him also upon exercises of the body: He even took advantage of the neglect which he saw this young prince suffer'd from a father, who was govern'd by a second wife, to make him submit to those, which he render'd more laborious or more perilous in proportion as he advanc'd in years. This is a sort of trial which the best of parents are but too backward in putting their children to; and to which Amedes himself had, perhaps, not expos'd an undoubted heir to the crown: But he look'd upon his pupil as one, who, like

a private

a private perſon, was to make his own fortune.

HE made him walk on foot to all the places near Memphis, with a double view; firſt to inure him to hardſhip, and then to make him take notice of every thing that was remarkable in his own country, which is often more neglected than foreign curioſities: Above all, he carry'd him more than once to the Pyramids. In his time there were a hundred, but of very different ſizes, all together in one place, at about four miles diſtant from Memphis, towards Libya. In all Egypt there were none but at this place, and about Thebes: the kings of which two cities, in imitation of one another, had been curious in giving this form to their tombs, or of leaving theſe monuments of their own grandeur and power. Amedes was willing to exhauſt this ſubject, that his pupil might draw advantages from it of ſeveral kinds. Sethos had often heard talk of theſe enormous piles; and Amedes expected they would at firſt ſight make the ſame impreſſion upon this young prince, as they do upon travellers who come to ſee this wonder of the world, from the remoteſt parts of it: that is, they always find them leſs than they expected. Amedes did not neglect this opportunity of making Sethos obſerve, that the eye of man is never abſolutely contented with the bigneſs of things artificial, unless they be carry'd to a distance as far as the sight can reach: but it is not so with respect to things which are determin'd by nature; as animals or trees, which we don't love to see represented beyond their usual proportion: Hence it is, said he, that this bust of a sphinx or woman fix'd on the ground among the pyramids, which is forty feet high, seems of a monstrous bulk to you; whereas the great pyramid which takes up more than a furlong every way, appears too little in your eye. Another reason for this is, because its height not being quite equal to the length of one side of its basis, it must of course look squat and low. So, added he, with regard to buildings, we can never justify ourselves, if the proportion of their dimensions be not graceful, and according to the rules of art. Notwithstanding all which, continued he, observe the pyramids more nearly, they are not less wonderful, and you'll soon see just cause to admire them. Make a trial yourself, in the first place, by the surest methods you have been taught in the academies of Memphis, to take the four cardinal points; see how exactly the four sides answer with the winds*. And besides, as large as the most beautiful temples of Memphis may seem to you, there is not one of them whose dimensions come near

* See the elogium of M. de Chaselles, by M. de Fontenelle, in his memoirs of the academy of sciences. Ann. 1710.

to those of the great pyramid; tho' the form of our temples has something more agreeable and engaging.

* IN reality, the basis of the first and largest pyramid, the surface of which is to this day entire, is in every square 704 feet; and † its perpendicular height 630. The whole pyramid is compos'd of courses or lays of bricks, which grow narrower in proportion as they ascend to the top, where there is a platform of twelve feet square. The borders of these courses, which gradually decrease towards the top, serve as steps to ascend to it. Of all those who used to accompany Sethos and Amedes to see the pyramids, only some few of the most venturesome attempted to go up to this platform; but none durst come down again otherwise than backwards, as well to have the assistance of their hands, as for fear the height and vast extent of the prospect might make them giddy. Sethos, who before had gone thro' many hazardous exercises, could not comprehend why Amedes should not indulge him in this, of which he was in

* This whole description is taken from de Bruyen's travels in folio, and the notes added to them in the quarto edition.

† That is five feet or a pace more than the olympick furlong determin'd by Hercules, who ran 125 paces, or 625 feet in one breath. This is the common computation, saving the interpretations of the learned; for this distance seems no such great matter for Hercules.

 no

no wiſe fearful. Amedes at laſt told him, that the concern he had for his life and honour, wou'd not ſuffer him to expoſe him to this trial, till he was able to deſcend the pyramid with his face toward the plain. It is not becoming, continu'd he, a prince, as you are, to ſhew the leaſt ſign of fear upon any account whatſoever. Amedes had hardly done ſpeaking, when the prince, running to the pyramid, and placing his hands upon the lowermoſt ſtep, which is four feet high, he aſcended from one to another with wonderful agility and eaſe, till he came to thoſe of but one foot high, which he walk'd up like common ſtairs, and was ſoon at top of the platform. As ſoon as he had recover'd breath, he turn'd toward the ſpectators, who were in great numbers at the foot of the pyramid, and came down with as little concern as if it had been a cover'd ſtair-caſe of equal and eaſy ſteps. His example render'd the enterprize more common; and ſeven or eight young lords, who from that time devoted themſelves more particularly to his ſervice, always attended him, as much as poſſible, as well in his exerciſes as his expeditions. It had likewiſe been an error eſtabliſh'd either by the timorouſneſs which was apt to ſeize people at top of the pyramid, or by an idea conceiv'd from the vaſt extent of the baſis, that it was impoſſible to ſhoot an arrow from the top to fall beyond the lowermoſt

ſtep

ſtep at bottom. This error prevails yet among us; and all travellers, who are too apt to enlarge upon things, mention the impoſſibility of it. The prince, even before he made the trial, was ſenſible of this error: Being well aſſur'd of the length of the four equal ſides of the baſis, he boldly engag'd to ſhoot an arrow from the middle of the platform, which ſhould fall not only beyond one of the faces, but even beyond one of the angles of the pyramid, being directed in a diagonal line; which, according to the exact calculation he had made of it, could not be 500 feet, and hardly above half the diſtance an arrow will fly when diſcharg'd by an able archer.

WE have hitherto only ſpoken of the ſurface of the pyramid; but Sethos was continually urging Amedes to let him ſee the inſide of it. If the king who erected it had been interr'd in it, the prophane, ſuch as Sethos yet was, would not have been permited to enter: but it being an empty tomb, every one who had the patience and reſolution, was allow'd to go in. As there were ſeveral deep and dark paſſages, Amedes was perſuaded, that this trial would be an excellent remedy againſt thoſe panick fears, which are apt to ſeize many people in the dark, and againſt the apprehenſion of bugbears, with which common reports then fill'd all uninhabited places, as it does now: But this view was nothing to a far greater design which he had conceiv'd upon this occasion, and which was to be the crown of Sethos's education.

AMEDES, therefore, returning one evening with him alone, and directing his discourse to him, said, My prince, to view the inside of the pyramid in such a manner as will be necessary for you, is an enterprize very different from what you think it to be: The secret passages of it lead those men, who are favour'd by the gods, to a point I dare not so much as name; for which the gods must create a desire in you. The entrance into the pyramid is open to every body; but I pity those, who coming out by the same way they went in, have only satisfy'd a very imperfect curiosity, and seen no more than what they are allow'd to relate. A discourse so uncommon as this was to the young prince, fill'd him with an impatience, which made him resolve instantly to unriddle this mystery, by deceiving even his governor's vigilance, if he refus'd to accompany him. Amedes, who read this resolution in his looks, did not give him time to answer, but continu'd; Sir, I will conduct you myself to this enterprize, which it is almost impossible to begin alone, tho' it must be finish'd alone: But I must not expose you to the dangers that attend it, *till* opportunities,

tunities, which may offer hereafter, have given me ſufficient proofs of your valour, and eſpecially of your prudence. I have reaſon to be ſatisfy'd with the marks you have already given me of both. The age you are now approaching to, will demand greater of you, and will ſoon furniſh you with means of ſhewing them. Don't give way then to your impatience, but place your confidence in me; and begin, by keeping, as a ſecret, that little I have now reveal'd to you, to accuſtom your ſelf to greater. The young prince, who could not yet fix an idea to the ſenſe of theſe words, told Amedes, that, without diving farther into the myſtery in queſtion, the firſt mark he would give of the prudence his tutor wiſh'd to ſee in him, ſhould be to confide entirely in his conduct.

THE

LIFE

OF

SETHOS.

BOOK III.

THE war with which the king of Memphis was threaten'd, particularly on the part of Thebes, fill'd Sethos with a secret joy; for he concluded, that war only would furnish him with means of making those experiments which Amedes expected from him. This wise governor, who perceiv'd it, told him one day, that tho' in the enterprize he had

had mention'd to him, on occaſion of the pyramid, there were no blows nor combating with armed enemies requir'd; he could not enough commend the good there was in the confus'd ſentiment which had inclin'd him to war; but, added he, I ſhould ill perform the function I have the honour of exerciſing in the ſervice of a prince born to the throne, if I did not inform him, that a king, who loves his ſubjects, always looks upon war as a misfortune: and, in order to prevent it, uſes all efforts that do not derogate either from his eſtabliſh'd rights, or his due honour. From this maxim, deeply engraven in the heart of a king, reſults a principle of true bravery, the more ardent in the defence of his own property, as it is leſs inclin'd to invade that of others. Moſt princes, who upon every occaſion are taking up arms, ſpend their days in a continual alternative of good or bad ſucceſs, which makes their enemies fear them but little, and value them leſs; Whereas on the contrary, a prince who is ſtedfaſt in his juſt pretenſions, and gives no ſubject of complaint to his neighbours, is reſpected: Remember therefore, my lord, never to make war from a fancy or inclination to it; but when you are compell'd to it, do it in ſuch a manner as may take away that pleaſure and inclination in your enemy. Sethos anſwer'd, that he was ſenſible of the importance of this advice to a prince actually upon

upon the throne; but, continu'd he, the war I am inclin'd to, is a war in which I have no part, and in which all I have to do is, to fight for the king my father, without enquiring, as I take it I have no right to do, into the merits of the cause. You say true, my lord, reply'd Amedes; and a young prince ought even to set a great value upon every lawful occasion offer'd by which he can give proof of his valour; that whenever he comes to have the care of the tranquillity and happiness of a whole nation, he may avoid a war without being apprehensive of any reflections on that account to the prejudice of his person. However, that your wishes may not be continued for a war, in all appearance so fatal, as that which is kindled against the kingdom, I have laid hold of an opportunity which the gods seem to have thrown into my way, to exercise both your prudence and valour at the same time, and to advantage.

THE frontier-towns of the kingdom of Memphis on the side of Libya, as Plinthinus, Taposiris, Scyatis, Oasis the lesser, and several others, have acquainted me, by a private deputation, that they have been sorely afflicted by a hideous serpent in their neighbourhood; which, as they believe, has his retreat in a den of mount Aspis, and ravages all the plain, call'd the little Catabathmus; where they

they are oblig'd to seek their sustenance. They at first thought of desiring the assistance of the king's huntsmen; but then they imagin'd, that the queen, being taken up with affairs which she would think of greater importance, would be little concern'd at a misfortune which could not penetrate to the royal mansions; and especially as she had already let the nomarchs or governors know, that she requir'd no other care of them, with regard to their provinces, than to levy the imposts, and to prevent revolts. Besides, added he, it is very well known, that the court has no taste for fatiguing and hazardous exercises; and that of all those who now compose it, not one would be ready to undertake an expedition, where no other advantage is to be hop'd but the welfare of the people. They therefore apply to me in the conclusion, as to the governor of a prince, in whose virtuous inclination the hopes of the whole kingdom center, and whose example animates the flower of the youth of Memphis to the most noble exercises of body and mind: Adding, That if this prince would, under my care, be their leader in the expedition, they would receive him in every place he should pass thro' with all the marks of respect and gratitude due to his rank and worth. I immediately undertook for you, and for some other young lords, your academical companions, who would be proud of the 'he honour of accompanying you. But I old the deputy, that to avoid all appearance of affectation, we would appoint a hunting-match; that for the ſame reaſon we would make no ſtop, either in going or returning, at any city of note; and that they ſhould, upon no account, make any preparations to receive you that could have the appearance of ceremony: it was with the ſame view, that I diſpatch'd this deputy as privately as he came, without allowing him ſo much as to wait on you. Sethos was pleas'd with all theſe precautions on his part, and thank'd him as well for his zeal as his care. Amedes immediately interrupting him, ſaid, that ſince he approv'd of all the meaſures he had taken, he adviſed him to depart early the next morning, to prevent any obſtacle that might hinder their journey. That he ſhould therefore employ the remainder of the day in ſelecting, with all the prudence of an able chief, ſuch of the young noblemen his companions, as beſt deſerv'd to be confided in, becauſe they would find upon the ſpot all the men they ſhould want to make up a number: And finally, that he ſhould recommend to them all to ſpeak no otherwiſe of their expedition, than of a cuſtomary hunting of wild beaſts.

SETHOS having given notice to his eight companions, whom we have already mention'd, tion'd, they all took horſe the next morning, attended only by ſome ſlaves, and rode along the north ſide of the lake Moeris. Amedes, for their greater encouragement, told them, during their journey, that great hunting-matches were by the antient heroes look'd upon as an apprenticeſhip to war; not only on account of the long courſes they were oblig'd to run, the inconveniencies they were liable to, and, in a word, all the bodily fatigues this exerciſe demanded of them; but far more by reaſon of the judgment, nice obſervation, and exact knowledge of the hills, valleys, and by-ways, which a hunter was oblig'd to acquire: But, added he, the hunting you are now going about is a real war: Its motive, in the firſt place, is the only one which in general can render war lawful; that is, the defence of the people. For whereas hunting with moſt great men is but a ſavage paſſion, which puts them upon deſtroying the innocent animals of the woods and fields, and often ſpoiling the lands thro' which they paſs; you are going to deliver a whole people from a monſter that deſtroys their harveſt, and devours their ſheep and ſhepherds: nay, you have the reſolution to go in ſearch of a dreadful ſerpent, which, according to report, is of an enormous ſize and length, cover'd all over with ſcales, that are proof, as I am inform'd, againſt all darts.

darts. Shall we then confine ourselves to shut him up in his den, if we can discover the entrance? But tho' it should have no more than one outlet, it will be easy for him in time to force a way thro'. Shall we be contented to drive him out of the plain of Catabathmus, and beyond the mountains of Libya, by force of our numbers and cries? But as soon as we are departed, he may return again: And besides, it would not be generous to throw upon our neighbours, tho' our enemies, a desolation from which we may have just deliver'd our own country. I dare propose to you, my lords, a project more worthy of you. Let us endeavour to take this monster alive, and carry him in triumph into the king's park. Thereby you will accustom yourselves to an advantageous practice in almost all the incidents of life, which is to prefer skill to force. The youth were all charm'd at this proposal of Amedes, and promis'd him faithfully to obey his orders in the execution of this design. He answer'd them, That prince Sethos, who however should never be out of his sight, must be their leader in this expedition. That by commanding them, he would learn to make an advantageous use, not only of the valour, but of the advice of his officers; and that consequently, as in a well-disciplin'd army, and a war duly concerted, every one would have

have a ſhare in the glory of the ſucceſs, in proportion not only to his valour, but to his knowledge.

AFTER ſix days march, our warriors having diſcover'd the neareſt point of mount Aſpis, imagin'd that the monſter made his retreat thither to be the nearer to the inhabited and fertile plains. They had already obſerv'd his tracks by means of ſlime he had left upon the corn and hedges, which he had laid even with the ground. But, as yet, they had not ſeen any perſon who could tell them where he was; becauſe the very noiſe of his ſcales, which was to be heard at a great diſtance, made all the inhabitants of the plain fly before him; after he had devour'd ſome perſons, who, thinking themſelves out of his reach, ſtopp'd to view him. They only remark'd, that he made a very ſhort ſtay in places at a little diſtance from the mountain; and that he return'd thither as ſoon as he had made prey of any cattle in the meadows. Our noble hunters, that they might be more ſure of their game, continu'd their way toward mount Aſpis. They were not above half a league from it, when they diſcover'd between them and the mountain a large moraſs, and behind it a ſort of hillock, which look'd as if cover'd over with leaves of iſingglaſs, that glitter'd in the ſun. Fixing their eyes upon this object, they ſoon perceiv'd

ſome

ſome motion. They immediately ſtopp'd to obſerve it with the greater attention : And it appear'd to be the monſter roll'd about itſelf, that chang'd its poſture without ſhifting its place. Sethos, who now began to exerciſe his office of commander, addreſs'd himſelf to the company, and ſaid, My dear companions, as our deſign is to take this monſter alive, I preſume, the firſt thing neceſſary will be to know exactly his length and bulk, that we may be the better acquainted with the enemy we are to encounter ; and the rather, ſince without doubt we ſhall be oblig'd to convey him away, like other ſavage creatures, in an iron cage, into which we muſt find means to put him : 'Tis of importance therefore now to know his dimenſions, that we may, as ſoon as poſſible, order one to be made in the neareſt town. In order to this, it is my opinion, that we all march ſlowly on one ſide of this animal, like a caravan purſuing its way, without making the leaſt ſign of attacking him. It is the nature of all ſavage animals to avoid mankind, eſpecially when they march in companies, unleſs they are excited by wrath or hunger. The preſent tranquil ſtate of this monſter gives us no reaſon to think he is diſturb'd by either, ſo that I fancy he will retire as ſoon as he ſees us. Then let us endeavour to obſerve at a diſtance ſuch objects, as trees or large ſtones, which when he ſtretches out to his full

length,

length, he may reach with the two extremities of his body; and when we are on the other ſide of the moraſs, we will meaſure the diſtances. Sethos appointed ſome of them, whoſe peculiar buſineſs it ſhould be to make theſe obſervations: Others he nam'd to remark the bulk of the ſerpent, by comparing it with the height of any thing he might paſs by; and with the reſt, among whom was Amedes, he undertook to keep the monſter always in ſight, and even to advance near enough to diſcover, if poſſible, the entrance into his den. Amedes ſhew'd by his punctual obedience, his approbation of what his pupil had propos'd.

WHAT Sethos foreſaw, actually happen'd. As ſoon as the ſerpent perceiv'd at a diſtance this troop of horſemen, together with the ſlaves of about twenty perſons, he began to unfold himſelf: His triangular head riſing as it were out of the baſis of the cone, which was form'd by all the Revolvings of his body, he at firſt erected, by eaſy degrees, to the height of two men; but he immediately popp'd it down again, and made off towards the mountain: With the middle of his body he form'd a ring or circle; the diameter of which was equal to the height he had lifted his head to: The lower part of this circle towards the tail ſerv'd as a reſt, by means of which he puſh'd himſelf forward without any rebound, and very ſlowly. However, the length of each of theſe motions ſoon brought him to the foot of the mountain, and left the place entirely free for them to take meaſure of his track. Upon an exact calculation, they found his length to be near 45 feet, and the thickeſt part of his body, which was his head, about 6 feet in diameter, or about 18 or 19 in circumference. While moſt of theſe young huntſmen were buſied in making this calculation, Sethos, Amedes, and three or four more follow'd the monſter: They kept as much as poſſible out of his ſight, by going the moſt round-about or by-ways which the ſituation of the place would admit of, for fear he ſhould ſeek to conceal the place of his retreat, as is common for ſome animals when they find they are diſcover'd. He compaſs'd the baſis of the firſt peak of the mountain, till he got almoſt over-againſt the moraſs from whence he came: Here the baſis of the ſecond peak began, and betwixt both was a pretty long and narrow avenue to the ſerpent's den. Our obſervers had the pleaſure to ſee him enter at a gap or paſſage, that he almoſt fill'd up, and through which he dragg'd his body with difficulty, becauſe he could not form it into a circle as in the open field.

AFTER theſe obſervations, which were made the firſt evening they arriv'd, Sethos conducted

conducted his troop to the place where he propos'd to reside till the conclusion of their expedition; which was in the neighbourhood of Scyathis.

As they were conversing together upon what they had seen, Sethos observ'd to them, that this serpent being by nature much like an adder, its activity lay only in his head, and in the part that might be call'd his tail; which was about twelve feet to the first joint, where his body began to form a circle when he roll'd along. The first degree of valour, added he, and indeed the only one we shall want upon this occasion, is, to know the just extent of the danger, and not to be terrify'd with the approach of it, when in reality we are out of its reach: And even supposing that the rage of the creature should make him more nimble and formidable than it seems to be, yet I judge by his unweildiness, we need only keep at eight or ten feet from him to be secure from all manner of danger.

THE next morning Sethos, accompany'd by Amedes, who had entirely approv'd his project, and by three of their companions, to whom he afterwards open'd it, took their way towards the den. Their design was to enter it when the monster was absent, to see if there was any possibility of laying snares there to entrap him. The first of those centinels, whom he had detach'd to observe the monster's motions, had given information that he had quitted his den a little before day, and made directly towards the morass, into which he plung'd; and that afterward, crawling toward the north-side of the plain, his comrades, before they follow'd him, had agreed, that as fast as one advanc'd, the others behind should be within call of one another, that they might successively give notice one to the other of the monster's return. Sethos being thereby safe from a surprize, enter'd first into the den: They had all provided themselves with light iron boots, a precaution common among the Egyptians, when they only walk'd in the fields, to secure them against those stinging insects which come with the African winds in some seasons of the year. On the left, they found a natural arch, where, at intervals, drops of water trickled down a stony sloaping soil; and on the right, a bed of clay, which by several marks seem'd to be the place where the serpent lay: At the end of this cavern was another opening, thro' which they might have gone farther: But as they were not led there by a motive of curiosity, they did not go near to it. It was enough for Sethos, that he found the inside of the cave was capacious enough to hold a cage, contriv'd in such a manner as might serve not only to contain the animal,

mal, when taken, but as a trap to catch him. So having made all the obſervations neceſſary for this deſign, he left the cave, and haſten'd to Scyathis, where, with his four companions, he apply'd himſelf immediately to the chief magiſtrates, and demanded of them for his atchievement 3000 men of the militia of their province, but not of thoſe appointed for the military ſervice of the year: He told them, that tho' he believ'd theſe ſoldiers capable of expoſing themſelves to the greateſt perils in caſe of neceſſity, he would be anſwerable for every danger, if they punctually obey'd the orders of the young lords he ſhould appoint to be their captains. He order'd the troops to be ready in three days at Scyathis, arm'd with bucklers, ſwords and quivers of arrows, without forgetting their trumpets and kettle-drums. And to conclude, he deſir'd an order might be ſent to all the ſmiths in the town to apply themſelves immediately to the making of a machine according to the plan he ſhould give them.

THIS young prince having obtain'd his demands, with great acknowledgements from thoſe who granted them, he order'd the ſmiths to make a cage of eight feet ſquare, and fifty long: The ſides were to be of bars of iron, ſo contriv'd as to be taken out, and ſet in again with eaſe. The maſter bars, which were to receive the extremities of the others, were likewiſe to be rivetted in one another, and the whole to be plac'd upon low wheels, at ten feet diſtance: At the entrance into this cage were to be plac'd ſpikes of iron, in ſuch manner that they might give way to the monſter at going in; but if he ſhould endeavour to come out, might faſten in his ſcales and ſtop him. The reaſon for ordering it in ſeveral pieces, was not only that ſeveral ſmiths might work at it at the ſame time, but that it might be tranſported in ſeveral parts with eaſe to the place where it was to be employ'd. The whole was undertaken, and perform'd in three days; and the troops being aſſembled at the ſame time, Sethos appointed the fourth day in the morning for the execution of the enterprize.

HAVING plac'd centinels the evening before, as he did the firſt time, to obſerve which way the monſter took at leaving his den in the morning, he caus'd all the pieces of the cage to be tranſported thither in carts by day-break. It was put together in leſs than three hours, and ſtopp'd at the end, and on both ſides, by pieces of the rock which they found in the cavern. The mouth of the cage being a little wider than the entrance into the den, it would not be perceiv'd by the monſter, eſpecially in the diſturbance which Sethos propos'd to give him. He next order'd a detachment of his troops to file

file off one by one, with the greateſt ſilence, toward the place where they knew the ſerpent then was, and to get beyond him to the other ſide of the entrance into the cave; while another detachment beſet his haunt. At this firſt motion, the monſter, who did not yet perceive he was purſu'd, made the beſt of his way, as he had done before, towards his cave: but diſcovering a long train of people at a diſtance, he ſtopp'd, and ſoon after began to hiſs in a horrible manner. Sethos's companions then gave orders for the troops to join, and to cloſe their ranks by degrees: At the ſame time he caus'd them to ſound all their trumpets, and beat their kettledrums, while one part of the ſoldiers, as they had agreed, claſh'd their ſwords upon their bucklers; and a greater number, gall'd him with thouſands of arrows. The monſter perceiving he had reſolute enemies to encounter with, who notwithſtanding his motions and furious menaces, baffled him, by drawing near to, and retiring from him, and who beſides had ſhut up all retreat but to his den, haſten'd thither faſter than he had done before. The noiſe of the military inſtruments, the ſhouts of the ſoldiers, and the ſtorm of arrows, purſu'd him more and more. It was obſerv'd, that ſoon after he had got his head into the cage, he made an attempt to ſlip back again; but being ſtopp'd by the ſpikes of the bars, and finding himſelf more cloſely pursu'd, he chose to take refuge in his prison. He push'd forwards with all the activity he was capable of, deceiv'd, perhaps, by the hopes of getting out at the other end, and escaping by those out-lets which he knew were in his cavern. He was immediately follow'd by those who were order'd to put in the bars at the entrance into the cage; who having likewise widen'd the entrance into the den, with the help of tools they had convey'd thither for that purpose, they drew the cage out with a long team of horses. The inhabitants of the neighbouring towns and villages, who were there in throngs to be eye-witnesses of this expedition, saw the monster stretch'd out at his length, and turning his eyes sometimes on one side and sometimes on the other, without any marks of fury. Sethos disbanded his troops on the spot, without returning to the town, that he might avoid all the ceremonies of thanks. He commended their exact obedience to the least signs given to them by their commanders, in which they were exercised perfectly. The monster was drawn in his cage backwards, that all objects which might present to his view in the passage, might the less disturb him: And thus he was conducted to the lake Moeris; where Sethos, for the greater ease, put him on board a vessel to be convey'd by water. Sethos and his companions accompany'd him to Memphis; but he would not allow any food to be given him during the whole passage, well knowing that serpents would live much longer without eating.

DIODORUS * relates the hunting and taking of a serpent of as monstrous a size as this; And our own travellers pretend to have seen some of above 100 feet long; but no one ever question'd the truth of Diodorus's relation of that monster he mention'd in the place quoted. It was brought out of Ethiopia to Alexandria in the reign of Ptolomy Philadelphus. The generosity of this prince, which was to none more extensive, than to those who presented him with curiosities, was a motive to some bold men to make him a present of this kind. Some of them lost their lives at the first onset; but at last, they tam'd the monster by expedients not very different from those I have related from my authors, under the name of Sethos. Diodorus adds, that by fasting they made him as tame as other domestick animals.

THO' Osoroth was not so taken with the wonders of nature, or the industry of men, as Ptolomy has since been, he receiv'd his son, and the young noblemen his companions, with great encomiums. The queen, for her part, was secretly disturb'd at this first

* Lib. 3.

exploit of Sethos; and Amedes thinking to overcome evil with good, from this time haſtned to render Sethos more worthy of her jealouſy. He thought he might now rely ſecurely enough upon his pupil's prudence and courage, to execute the ſcheme he had form'd for his advantage: but it would oblige him to be abſent three or four months from court; however, he did not think it would be difficult to obtain leave. The queen ſeldom allow'd Sethos to ſee the king, who, conformable to his character, as ſeldom aſk'd after him; and the vanity and corruption of the court made the courtiers have no great regard for the young prince.

IN eight years which had now paſs'd ſince the death of Nephté, Daluca had been deliver'd of two ſons, who, with their elder brother are confounded in the common annals, by the name of the three Anonymous of the iſſue of Oſoroth; but the private memoirs I have before me, call the firſt Beon, and the ſecond Pemphos. As ſoon as they were of an age fitting to appear before a father, who thought of nothing but his diverſion, the mother brought them continually into his preſence, to accuſtom him, if poſſible, to own them, and them only, for his ſons: She even affected to give to the firſt all the prerogative of primogeniture, tho' neither one nor the other had any right on that ac-

count

count. Sethos residing in the palace, began now to be an eye-sore to her: Till then she had born it patiently, that it might not be said the king had no issue; but purposing for the future to heap all favours upon her own, she sought to supplant an elder brother, whose birth-right, and what could already be call'd merit, excited in her so tormenting a jealousy. Amedes, for the sake of Sethos, taking advantage of this disposition, which he plainly saw in the queen, addres'd himself to her, to obtain the king's consent to let him visit some of the chief temples of Egypt. He added at the same time, to remove all suspicion from her mind, that in the course of this journey, which would be for three or four months, the prince should lodge with none but the priests. Daluca, tho' she thought very meanly of the design, gave her full consent to it, and engaged to procure that of the king immediately. She left Amedes with a great deal of satisfaction, believing he had inspired the prince with a fit of devotion, which would take him off from all views of ambition and policy: and in a few moments she sent him the king's sign manual; letting him know by the bearer, she did not think it necessary, that for so short an absence the prince should take leave of the king, or any one else. This was just what Amedes wanted; who speaking to Sethos of the inside of the pyramid, which he had been

desirous

desirous of visiting, and of the disposition he was now in to accompany him thither, did not, however, yet discover his whole design to him: but he had taken care to make the high priest of Memphis (the same who had conducted the late queen to the labyrinth) acquainted with it.

SETHOS and Amedes left the palace on foot, telling the chief officer of the prince's apartment, that they might perhaps not return in some time, and that the queen was inform'd of their journey. Being provided with a lamp, and whatever was necessary to light it when it went out, they arriv'd by that time it was night at the pyramid: Amedes order'd it so, that he might go alone with Sethos into that dark building. They ascended together to the sixteenth step on the north-side, where there is a square window always open: But this entrance, which was but three feet every way, led to a passage of the same dimensions, where they were oblig'd to crawl upon their bellies. Sethos went foremost, which was an honour that Amedes did not envy him, nor the trouble of carrying the lamp: and besides, he never gave him any previous knowledge of the length of each passage, nor of what he was to meet at the end of it; tho' every one had its peculiar difficulties: But not to detain my readers with all the particulars, I shall at once bring Sethos to the place, where, guided by

Amedes,

Amedes, he perceiv'd a large well, crusted on every side with a black pitchy scum as smooth as glass. The bare mouth of this well by lamp-light was a frightful object: The depth of it seem'd to have no bounds; and there was no sign either of wheel, pully or rope to descend it, or to sound the bottom. Here it was likewise, that all those who were not acquainted with the secret; or who if they were, had not the courage to pursue it, put a stop to their enquiries. Amedes leaning with his elbows on the brink of the well, and holding the lamp, waited in silence the effect of Sethos's curiosity; till being satisfy'd of his resolution by his impatience, he arose, and placing the lamp, the bottom of which was made hollow for the purpose, in the form of a helmet, upon his head, he set himself astride upon the brink of the well, on the same side where he had been the whole time. He immediately put his foot upon a step of iron of about six inches long, which the shaddow had conceal'd from the sight of Sethos, and the more because it was very narrow. Amedes then getting entirely on the inside of the well, put his other foot on another such step about a foot lower; and so, without saying any thing, continued to descend, and Sethos soon follow'd him: Being gone down sixty steps, they met with a stop, tho' they were not near the bottom of the well; on the side they perceiv'd a window, which

which was the entrance into a pretty easy passage, hollow'd out of the natural rock, by which there is a gradual winding descent for 124 feet.

HITHERTO the inside of the pyramid is such as I have just given a small description of; excepting that the bottom of the well is fill'd with rubbish for a considerable height: But this winding passage led to a grate with two folding doors of brass, which open'd with the least push, and without any noise; but with the fall in shutting again, by a contrivance in the hinges, made a very great sound, which echo'd till it lost itself a good way off in a vast edifice. They were then at the bottom of the well, which is in all 150 feet deep. Opposite to this gate, which was on the north-side, there was another on the south-side, shut with iron grates, each bar of which was as thick as a man's arm. Thro' these grates Sethos saw a long walk, to which he could perceive no end: On the east-side of it was a long row of arches or vaults, from which proceeded a great light of lamps and torches; and from the bottom of these vaults he heard the voices of men and women, which made very harmonious musick. Amedes inform'd Sethos, That the walk he saw thro' the grates was a series of the bottom of the other pyramids, which were real tombs; and that the arches led to a subterranean temple,

where the prieſt and prieſteſſes, whoſe voices he had heard, perform'd every night different ſorts of ſacrifices and ceremonies; which he could not yet reveal to him, becauſe he was not initiated. It is eaſy to imagine, that a young man of a warm diſpoſition, whoſe curioſity alſo was excited by ſo many circumſtances, long'd to be initiated; and he inſtantly deſir'd Amedes to procure it for him. My ſon, ſaid Amedes, that courage which has led you hither, and which if you purſue, will conduct you farther, is a preparatory ſtep to this prerogative. From this moment I ſuppoſe your youth at an end, and that from the deſire you have juſt teſtify'd for the initiation, you this day begin to be a perfect man. The initiation, to which we are not allowed to invite any one whomſoever in direct terms, is the enterprize of which I ſpoke ambiguouſly to you, and for which I requir'd particular proofs of your prudence and valour. Father, ſaid Sethos, I then conceiv'd a faint idea of it, but I never would preſume to mention it, fearing you would reject with anger a propoſal which ſeem'd to me to be too raſh at my age, and which even now I ſhould not have preſum'd to make you, were it not in this place. It is with reaſon, ſon, reply'd Amedes, that you now look upon this demand as very bold. The preparations which will be requir'd of you, with regard to the body, are painful and perilous,
but

but they are very trivial in regard to those of the mind. The priests, who are accountable to nobody, either as for their choice or refusal, are extremely rigorous, especially with regard to those who are destin'd to the throne, and desire to partake of the mysteries of the priesthood. They will examine you on topicks of the most sublime moral, by questions which you can't foresee, and to which you can't answer but by filling your mind with copious and enlightned principles, from whence all your replies must naturally flow. Oh! my father, reply'd Sethos, how much time I have hitherto lost, and what treasures I have squander'd in the lessons you have already given me! I consider my attention to your precepts till now only as my duty; whereas I ought to have look'd on them as the only way by which I could attain to real riches. Son, answer'd Amedes, as yet, nothing is lost: Your youth has been duly employ'd in making you acquainted with the condition of mankind; and you must not expect the gifts of heaven before their time. You will, on proper occasions, recal to your mind a great number of those principles you now think forgotten: And besides, the priests themselves will instruct you for three months previous to your examination. But it is time for us to repose ourselves, whatever resolution we take, whether it be to return by the way we came, or to go on. They therefore

therefore ſate down upon a ſtone bench, which went all round the bottom of the well.

THEN it was that Sethos, ſtruck with the grandeur of thoſe ſubterraneous works, unknown to the greater part of the Egyptians themſelves, indulg'd his aſtoniſhment, and extoll'd the magnificency of the kings his forefathers, who had brought ſuch vaſt undertakings to perfection. Amedes told him, that theſe works, conſider'd in themſelves, were truly worthy of his higheſt admiration; but, added he, do you make no reflection on the hardſhip thoſe have undergone, who have executed them with their own hands? I perceive, ſaid Sethos, I have been guilty of a fault in judgment, by praiſing theſe enterprizes, and have begun the new way of thinking I propos'd to myſelf by an error. You need not doubt of it, ſon, ſaid Amedes, you here ſee the blood and ſubſtance of an infinite number of wretches, whoſe eſtates and perſons have been employ'd in theſe immenſe labours: Millions of men have even periſh'd by the ſudden falling in of the earth. Seſoſtris, that hero, to whom Egypt is oblig'd, on other accounts, for great part of its glory, has, in vain, caus'd to be engraven on the ſtately monuments erected by his command at Thebes, that he had employ'd none but foreign ſlaves in the building of them; that alone would be no juſtification: For tho' it be the fate of ſlaves to ſerve, we ought always to remember they are men, and never to expoſe them to unreaſonable labours, or evident dangers, except upon extraordinary and preſſing occaſions. And as to captives taken in war, it is yet a barbarous cuſtom, in all nations, to reduce perſons free-born, and often of the higheſt birth, taken in battle, or at a ſiege, to the ſtate of ſlavery: So that neither I nor you are ſecure, in the firſt battle we may be engaged in againſt a foreign enemy, from being liable to the meaneſt of ſervitude, and the moſt unworthy treatment. Let me inſiſt upon your giving the world a contrary example in the firſt victory you may obtain over any nation, capable of ſociety, and worthy of your alliance: We ſhall find in the ſequel that this advice was not unprofitable. But, continu'd Amedes, with regard to the enormous works you now ſee, I muſt inform you, that Cheobus, the eighth king of Memphis, and founder of the great pyramid, on which they are all dependant, was, on his own judgment, depriv'd of ſepulture in the tomb he had built for himſelf; and puniſh'd for the vanity of his tyrannical undertaking, by the ſhame of having his deſign fruſtrated. The other pyramids are neither ſo large, nor have they ſuch works on the inſide as this of Cheobus; and even their ſubterraneous paſſages, which you ſaw through the grates, are the work of Cheobus. His ſucceſſor, whoſe conduct was

not

not ſo much diſlik'd as his was, took advantage of his folly to order their tombs in a place already deſtin'd for that uſe. For, in ſhort, tho' we ought moſt certainly to condemn all thoſe undertakings of princes which are a burden to their ſubjects, their ſuperfluous wealth may be employ'd in giving evidences of their magnificency. It is actually very praiſe-worthy in them to incourage the induſtrious, and to cut out work for thoſe who want it. So tho' the vain extravagance of a king brings his ſubjects to beggary, expences prudently laid out are preſervatives againſt it. Among the latter, the wiſeſt beyond compariſon are thoſe which have a view to the general advantage of the ſtate. The kings of Egypt have render'd their names immortal by their works on account of the Nile; and one might ſay, they look'd upon all Egypt as a manſion of pleaſure, which it was their duty to improve, adorn and maintain. However, to put an end to this ſubject, the uſe you perceiv'd to be made of one part of theſe ſubterraneous edifices for the ſervice of the gods, obliges me to aſk you, Whether you don't approve of ſuch undertakings, however expenſive and perillous they may be, when they have an object ſo noble and ſo ſacred? But before you anſwer me; ſuppoſe the prieſts themſelves are putting you to a trial by this queſtion. Sethos having reflected upon it with greater attention than he otherwise would have done, answer'd thus; I can't think it allowable to be cruel to men, under pretence of serving the gods; and am persuaded, 'tis the forming a wrong idea of the authors and benefactors of mankind to offer them such victims. Human sacrifices have been abolish'd by a more enlighten'd religion; and I think our late kings seem'd to have abandon'd these dangerous, and at the same time, too laborious undertakings of subterraneous edifices, which are all very antient: But I think, at the same time, we can't better repair the errors of our fore-fathers, than by employing the monuments of their tyranny in the worship of the gods, as I see it is a practice in these times. Son, answer'd Amedes, such answers as this will extremely facilitate your initiation.

THIS their discourse was overheard, tho' Sethos knew nothing of it; for the priests having notice given them by the noise of the folding doors, immediately repair'd thither, to spy thro' private openings in the wall who were come to the bottom of the well, that they might prepare every thing for their reception, if they ventur'd farther. Sethos and Amedes having rested, and discours'd thus for the space of an hour; Amedes first arose, and said to Sethos; Son, you see on the north-side the gate by which we enter'd, and thro' which

which we may return; or here, on the east-side, you see another gate, which will lead you to a way parallel to the extremities of the arches, from which you are as yet excluded. This passage was six feet broad, very even, running in a strait line, and vaulted in an arch of a semi-circle upon a moulding which run on both sides at six feet from the earth. Sethos being about to enter, could not avoid turning his eye to an inscription engraven in black letters upon a very white marble, which was plac'd in the nature of a pediment upon the mouldings of the arch thro' which was the entrance into this passage: He there read these words; *Whoever goes thro' this passage alone, and without looking behind him, shall be purify'd by fire, by water, and by air; and if he can vanquish the fears of death, he shall return from the bowels of the earth, he shall see light again, and he shall be intitled to the privilege of preparing his mind for the revelation of the mysteries of the great goddess* Isis.

THE bare reading of this inscription frighted away almost all who had the courage to descend to the bottom of the well. Some, tho' but few, went thither of themselves, on no other motive but a most hazardous curiosity. But when any one went to demand the initiation, the priests, who seem'd to grant it without any difficulty, only requir'd him to write down his name and petition, and then immediately appointed him an initiate to inform him of the trials he was to paſs thro'. This guide attended him into the pyramid, and led him to the mouth of the well, ſhew'd him the ſteps, and went down firſt himſelf, as Amedes had done with Sethos. But the prieſts were pretty ſure, that the conditions enjoin'd by the inſcription would be accepted by none but men of a more than common intrepidity. And as courage alone was not all the merit they requir'd in their initiates, theſe terrible trials ſerv'd only to admit thoſe who aſpir'd to it to a very ſevere examination upon all the other virtues. Some were of opinion, they were to deſcend alive into hell, and not to return without the moſt frightful labours; Others imagin'd, that all the initiates ſubmitted to a real death; and tho' they ſaw them afterwards riſe again, they fear'd the agonies: They alſo knew, that ſome who were eſteem'd men of ſingular valour, never return'd at all. The initiates, who were tied down to an inviolable ſecrecy, allow'd the liberty of theſe different interpretations to thoſe who had either heard of this inſcription, or who had been ſatisfy'd with the reading of it. However, as the initiates were in extraordinary repute among the people, for the great virtues they had given proofs of, and eſpecially for the incorruptible juſtice, which was their characteriſtick; as they were reſpected by the kings themſelves, who look'd upon

upon them not only as men intrepid in battle, but as the moſt experienc'd miniſters they could be ſerv'd with, and often as their mediators between them and the prieſts, whoſe influence they were ſometimes afraid of: To conclude, as nothing could be more agreeable to a private perſon, than to enjoy almoſt all the privileges of the prieſthood, without being tied down to their ſubjections and diſciplines; there were always ſome who had reſolution enough to expoſe themſelves to any dangers for the ſake of the initiation.

SETHOS was too young to be led by any remote views; his high birth had left little room in his mind for that ambition to riſe, ſo common in other men. Amedes reflected more than he upon the ineſtimable advantage it would be for a king of Egypt to be initiated. This young prince therefore being in reality puſh'd on by no other motive than a violent curioſity, and arguing, that he might as well come out again in ſafety as others had done, ſnatch'd the lamp out of the hands of Amedes, who yielded it to him with a caution once for all, to add prudence to his courage. However he follow'd him at a diſtance without his knowledge. This was an eſtabliſh'd cuſtom; becauſe, if the courage of the candidate ſhould happen to fail him before he had gone thro' the firſt trial, his guide, who was always near him, brought him back out of the well, by the way he came, to the window of the pyramid thro' which he enter'd: There he advis'd him, for his own honour, not to divulge an undertaking in which he had no succefs, and warn'd him never to attempt obtaining the initiation, either at Memphis, or at any other of the twelve temples of Egypt where it was conferr'd. But the firſt matter of aſtoniſhment to thoſe who perſiſted in their deſign, was the length of the way, for they were oblig'd to walk more than a league in this ſubterraneous paſſage, without ſeeing any thing new. At laſt they obſerv'd in the wall on the right hand, or on the ſouth-ſide, a ſmall iron-door ſhut, and two paces beyond it three men having helmets on, upon which was the head of Anubis. This gave occaſion to Orpheus to make of theſe three men the three heads of the dog Cerberus, which admitted perſons into hell, but ſuffer'd none to come out again. One of theſe three men ſaid to the candidate; We are are not poſted here to ſtop your paſſage; Go on, if the gods have given you the courage: but if you be ſo unfortunate as to return, we ſhall then ſtop your paſſage: As yet you may go back, but from this moment you'll never get out of this place, unleſs you go on, without turning or looking back. If the candidate was not ſhock'd at theſe words, he was ſuffer'd to paſs, and the three men follow'd him at a diſtance; but his firſt guide abandon'd don'd him, and enter'd the little door: A moment afterwards, the candidate perceiv'd at the end of this paſſage the light of a very white but lively flame, juſt kindled: Sethos mended his pace to come at it. At the end of this paſſage was a vaulted room of above 100 feet ſquare. At the entrance into it were, on the right, and on the left, two piles of wood, or rather pales of wood planted in the ground upright, and very near to one another, twin'd about in the nature of vines, with branches of Arabian palm, Egyptian thorn and tamarind, three ſorts of wood very pliant, fragrant and cumbuſtible; the ſmoke went out thro' long pipes made for that purpoſe: But this flame, which eaſily reach'd to the top of the vault, and bore down again in waves, gave the ſpace it poſſeſs'd all the reſemblance of a burning furnace: But what was yet more terrible, Sethos obſerv'd upon the ground, between the two piles, a grate of red-hot iron, eight feet broad and thirty feet long. This grate was form'd of bars, which were ſo cloſe to one another, that there was only room for a man to ſet one foot between them. He perceiv'd there was no other paſſage but this, and he went thro' it with as much agility as circumſpection. Moſt fiery trials, of which hiſtory makes mention, were no other than theſe: But hiſtorians, who don't know the truth of the matter, and who love to exaggerate their miracles, ſay, that ſuch a one paſs'd thro'

thro' flames of fire, inſtead of ſaying he paſs'd thro' two lanes of flames, and that he walk'd over red-hot bars, inſtead of ſaying that he walk'd between them.

SETHOS having with joy paſs'd this trial, ſaw at ſome paces diſtance a canal of more than fifty feet broad, which came in on one ſide of this ſubterraneous room thro' grates of iron, and went out again in the ſame manner on the other ſide. This canal, which came out of the Nile, before it enter'd thro' the grates, made a great noiſe, as of a water-fall, which Sethos miſtook for the noiſe of the flames he had juſt eſcap'd: By the light of theſe flames, tho' they were conſiderably lower'd, he perceiv'd on the other ſide of the canal an arch, in the inſide of which were ſteps; the higheſt whereof were involv'd in darkneſs. Sethos imagin'd there was the gate thro' which he was to paſs into the open air, and the rather, becauſe the paſſage was mark'd out in the canal by two baluſtrades of iron, which aroſe from the bottom of the water on the right and on the left. Being apprehenſive that the light of the flames might fail him before he reach'd the other ſide, he made uſe of one of the firebrands to light up his lamp, which the rarefaction of the air had extinguiſh'd amidſt the flames. He undreſs'd himſelf, put his cloaths upon his head, and ty'd them with a girdle, which paſs'd under his arms, acroſs his breaſt:

In this manner he ſwam croſs the canal, holding his lamp burning in one hand. He quickly got his cloaths on again; and aſcending the ſteps of the arch which was before him, he came to a landing-place of ſix feet long and three broad. The bottom was a draw-bridge, which hung by very ſtrong irons to rings faſtned in the uppermoſt ſtep of the arch; ſo that this draw-bridge ſeem'd to be let down to receive him. The walls on each ſide of him were of braſs, and ſerv'd as ſupporters for the naves of two great wheels of the ſame metal, one on the right, and the other on the left: The lower half of them went down behind the walls; and on the upper parts, which were in ſight, lay a great iron chain: The top or roof of the landing-place diſcover'd, at the height of fifteen feet, three dark concavities, which reſembled the inſide of three large hollow ſtatues, look'd into from below: Before him was a door cover'd all over with the whiteſt ivory, adorn'd in the middle with two mouldings of gold; which ſhew'd that this door, that had no ſcutcheons on the outſide, open'd inwards with two leaves. Sethos having ſet his lamp on the floor, try'd twice or thrice in vain to puſh open this door, which had reſiſted the force of much ſtronger men than he: But to the lintel of the door, which was rais'd about ſeven feet above the threſhold, and to which the ends of the draw-bridge ſeem'd to be

ſuſpended

ſuſpended by two ſtrong chains, were faſten'd two great rings of poliſh'd ſteel, which by the light of the lamp ſhone like the fineſt diamond. The candidate could not avoid laying hold of them to try if by this means he might open the door: and here he began his laſt trial, the moſt difficult for an aſtoniſh'd imagination; for the very firſt motion which he gave to theſe rings, rais'd the triggers of the two wheels, which being turn'd by a prodigious weight hanging to their chains, produc'd ſeveral very frightful effects. The draw-bridge began to raiſe itſelf at that end which was neareſt the door; ſo that the candidate was oblig'd either to recover the ſteps, and ſo turn back again, contrary to the law preſcrib'd him, or to hold faſt by the rings: but the very lintel of the door was likewiſe rais'd up with the candidate hanging at it. The lamp which ſlid upon the draw-bridge was ſoon overſet, and left him in the dark, in the midſt of a horrid noiſe made by the two wheels, ſuch, that the moſt courageous would hardly forbear thinking that a hundred machines of iron and braſs were breaking in pieces about his ears. This motion, which laſted almoſt a minute, rais'd the candidate to the height of a quarter of a circle: but leſt the lintel, which was then looſen'd from the great wheels, might fall again with too great violence, being born downwards by its own weight, and that of the candidate, it was faſtned with ropes, which

which went thro' ſeveral pullies, to another wheel made up of flies or fanes of iron plates, which broke the fall, and prevented the candidate from being hurt. But at the ſame time this wheel, which was plac'd oppoſite to him in a large open place above the ivory doors, by its motion made him feel a violent agitation of the air. The candidate being in this manner let down again to the place from whence the machine had lifted him up, the two leaves of the ivory door open'd by the motion of the lowermoſt trigger, and preſented to his view a place where it was broad day, or if in the night-time, was illuminated with lamps, which caus'd a light equal to it.

SETHOS, who came thither about ſun-riſing, perceiving the Ox Apis thro' the bars of his ſtable, which was oppoſite to the ſanctuary of the temple of the three deities at Memphis, found, to his great ſurprize, that he was come out from under the great hollow pedeſtal of the triple ſtatue of Oſiris, Iſis and Horus, before which ſo many ſupplications had been offer'd for the late queen's recovery. He was receiv'd by the prieſts, who made a lane for him behind the ſanctuary. The high-prieſt embracing him immediately, extoll'd his valour, and congratulated him upon the happy ſucceſs of his trials. He then preſented him a cup fill'd fill'd with the water of the canal he had just pass'd. Whilst he was drinking, the high-priest said, Let this water be a draught of lethe or forgetfulness with regard to all the false maxims which you have heard from the mouths of prophane men *. After this, making him turn toward the triple statue, he order'd him to prostrate himself before it, and then said these words over him: Isis, great goddess of the Egyptians, pour down thy spirit upon thy new votary, who has gone thro' so many perils and laborious trials to come before thee: Make him victorious also over his passions, by rendring him tractable to thy laws, that he may be worthy to be admitted to thy mysteries. All the priests having repeated the first words of this Invocation: Isis, *great goddess of the* Egyptians; they rais'd Sethos up, and the high-priest presented him a compound liquor, by the Greeks call'd Cyceon; saying, May this be a draught of Mnemosyne or memory for the lessons, † which will now be given you by wisdom. These were all the ceremonies of the first day. The high-priest restor'd Sethos to Amedes, who standing behind him, led him to the apartment prepar'd for him in the college of the priests, which was

* See the manners of the savages; by father Laffiteau, t. 1. p. 313, 314. where he mentions these customs of the antients.

† Arnob. l. 5.

provided

provided with all neceſſaries, he being not to ſtir from thoſe holy places till the ceremonies of his initiation were perform'd.

As much as Sethos was overjoy'd for having form'd a right judgment of what he had to do in trials which required as much preſence of mind as reſolution; yet greater was the joy of Amedes, who having ſo precious a truſt committed to his care, had prevail'd upon himſelf to hazard the life of this young prince to obtain the initiation for him. As he was apprehenſive that Sethos would ſoon be oblig'd to quit Memphis on account of the queen's jealouſy, and that conſequently he ſhould never have the like time or opportunity to procure him this advantage for the future; he put him to theſe trials as ſoon as he thought his tender age capable of going thro' them. Had it not been for theſe preſſing reaſons, Amedes would never have expos'd a youth at ſixteen years to ſuch dangers and uncertainties as had perplex'd men of the greateſt valour and prudence, not to mention thoſe raſh perſons whoſe hearts or heads had fail'd them in the enterprize. For as ſoon as any candidate had paſs'd the little door that was ſhut, and got a ſight of the flames, if he offer'd to return, the three men, who were officers of the ſecond rank, ſeiz'd him, and made him enter thro' this door into the ſubterraneous temples, where he was for ever confin'd, confin'd, that he might not divulge the nature of the trials. Juſt ſo it was with reſpect to the canal; if any came thither after paſſing thro' the flames, and was deterr'd from croſſing the water, either by ſwimming or holding by one of the two balluſtrades, which appear'd above the ſurface: for theſe officers were ready to help all that ran the riſque of burning or drowning; but it was in order to confine them. Their impriſonment was however not very rigid. They were made, if they deſir'd it, officers of the ſecond order in theſe ſubterraneous temples, and were allow'd to marry the daughters of ſuch officers: But they were oblig'd, in the firſt place, to give an account of their condition to their families by a note written and ſign'd with their own hands, in the following terms: "For attempting a raſh undertaking, the juſt and merciful gods confine me to a perpetual but favourable priſon; fear the gods, and love them." This form made them look'd upon as dead, and diſcharg'd their families from all ties with regard to them. They were in reality ſecur'd from ever ſpeaking to any of thoſe they call'd prophane. The other officers of the ſecond order, who were the children of theſe, had the freedom, not of changing their condition, which otherwiſe was not allow'd to any Egyptian, but to officiate in their turns in the ſuperior temples, and even, like the prieſts themſelves, to converſe with every

every body, becauſe they were bound to keep the ſecret by an oath; which they did not vouchſafe to thoſe who had fail'd in the trials, and had therefore, ſaid they, forfeited their engagements to themſelves.

As for the latter of theſe trials, the noiſe of the wheels, and darkneſs of the place, made it really look like the chambers of death: But this noiſe ſerv'd likewiſe to give warning to the prieſts, who waited the candidate's arrival in the ſanctuary, to let down curtains immediately before all the crannies thro' which the people might look in: So that the populace, if there were any in the temple, knowing nothing of the ſecret, imagin'd it to be thunder, which warn'd the prieſts of the approaching preſence of a deity, who came to unfold ſome myſtery to them. It was at this trial that Orpheus, who was then in Egypt, had fail'd: however, the prieſts had granted him the initiation ſome months before, as a peculiar favour they thought due to his merit, on another account.

THIS famous Greek, who had obtain'd of the gods the gift of poetry, and playing on the harp, in ſo eminent a degree, that in thoſe fabulous days he paſs'd for the ſon of Apollo and Calliope, was born in Thrace. But that being ſomewhat a ſavage country, and its fierce inhabitants more addicted to war than the sciences, he came to settle in Thessalia, among a more civiliz'd people, and in a country render'd delightful by the course of the river Peneus, and the delicious vale of Tempe. There it was he espous'd the fair Eurydice; yet more famous for the love she bore to her husband, than for her beauty. The concourse of people from all parts of Greece, which the charms of the place, and the curiosity of hearing Orpheus, had drawn into Thessalia, soon made him acquainted with the fame of the Egyptians. As superior talents generally suppose a loftiness of mind and sentiments, Orpheus resolv'd to go into Egypt to obtain the initiation, persuaded that his poetry would become more sublime, when he had gain'd a thorow knowledge of theology, morality, and nature, of which he had been inform'd the Egyptians were the true and only masters. He began from that time to learn the Egyptian tongue: but there was one great obstacle to his design, which was the absenting himself for a time from Eurydice. All he could say to her of the charms of her country in which he left her, and of the esteem she was in at the Thessalian court, could not ease that grief she entertain'd upon his first mention of it; it had a quite contrary effect upon her. It was some time before that Aristeus came to reside at this court. He pretended to be the son of Apollo, and the nymph Cyrene, the daughter of king Peneus, grand-

father

father to the king then upon the throne. It is ſaid, that Apollo, falling in love with this princeſs, carry'd her into Africa, where ſhe gave name to the province of Cyrenia; ſo that Ariſteus eſteem'd Theſſalia as the country of his anceſtors. He no ſooner came to this court, than he fix'd his eyes upon Eurydice, and made fruitleſs addreſſes to her, which ſhe was ſo diſcreet as to conceal from her huſband. But now ſhe imagin'd her reſidence at this court, which Orpheus had offer'd as an argument of conſolation, might prove moſt fatal in his abſence; and not being able to diſſuade him from his deſign, ſhe declar'd ſhe would follow him where-ever he went.

THEY therefore embark'd together; and, after all the labours and dangers of a tedious voyage, arriv'd at the port of Canope in the Delta, and thro' the Heracleotick canal at one of the harbours of Memphis. As it was late, they reſolv'd to lie the firſt night without the city. In the ſhort way from the ſhore to the inn they were directed to, Eurydice felt a little ſmart in her heel, which ſhe did not think of conſequence enough to mention to her huſband; but ſhe was no ſooner enter'd into her chamber, than ſhe was ſeiz'd with a great heavineſs to ſleep, which made her re-fuſe all refreſhment: However, as ſhe had eaten more than once with the company on board, her huſband did not apprehend any thing from a drowsiness which seem'd to him to proceed from a cause very common and natural. She even remov'd all his uneasinesses, by telling him, she wanted nothing but rest. About half an hour afterwards, hearing her fetch her breath with great difficulty and irregularity, he ran to her; and being surpriz'd to find her face swell'd, and livid, and above all, that he could not awake her, he call'd out to his host; who no sooner saw her, but he told him, it was caus'd by the sting of some venomous insect that lay in her way, and that he would certainly find the mark of it in her foot: Having soon discover'd it to be as he said; Stranger, continu'd the host, if you desire it, I will fetch a physician, but he will find your wife dead. It is a great misfortune that you have never heard, or, if you have heard it, have never given attention to it, that there is no such thing as walking in Egypt, without having a preservative balsam about one, to apply immediately to the place stung: 'tis an infallible remedy; but a few moments delay render the evil incurable. Oh! cry'd Orpheus, I have the remedy, but my wife, my cruel wife, conceal'd this accident from me. Alas! my lord, answer'd the host, as he was retreating, I find, to her misfortune, the sting was hardly perceivable, as it often happens to the Egyptians themselves, if they are not very careful.

THUS

THUS Orpheus, after having in vain implor'd all the deities of Greece and Egypt, loſt the moſt tender and the moſt faithful of wives. She was interr'd in the ſepulchre of foreigners, without any ceremony, becauſe Orpheus was ſo overwhelm'd with grief that he had not diſcover'd himſelf to any one. This burial-place was without the walls of Memphis, on the ſame ſide as the pyramids, and the ſame place where the tombs of the natives were. They were the catacombs of the mummies, which ſubſiſt to this day; but ſtrangers were let down by a ſeparate opening. At the entrance into theſe catacombs was the lake Acheruſia; on the brink of which the Egyptians, when dead, were brought before their judges, as the kings were to the labyrinth: But to ſtrangers this ceremony was not obſerv'd, and they were interr'd without embalming. Orpheus, in the mean time, as yet unknown, walking every day in the neighbourhood of the catacombs, where Eurydice was interr'd, met one evening with ſome Egyptians, who were diſcourſing among themſelves, that there was a ſubterraneous communication between the catacombs and the pyramids, and that the ſouls of the dead had all that ſpace to walk in. They added, that ſome who had had the reſolution to enter into theſe pyramids by the opening which was viſible on one ſide of the greateſt, had there heard the voices and ſongs of the bleſſed ſpirits. Orpheus remembered theſe words; and as true lovers, eſpecially thoſe who never were in love before, look upon their paſſion as eternal, and carry their ideas of conſtancy even beyond the grave: ſo Orpheus giving himſelf up to this illuſion, and depending upon the ſame ſentiment in the ghoſt of his Eurydice, hop'd to meet her in theſe tombs, or to intice her to him by the ſound of his voice and harp. Being return'd to Memphis, and having attentively conſider'd the anſwers of all thoſe whom he interrogated concerning what he had heard, he was confirm'd in his deſign; and taking a lamp fit for his purpoſe, and his lyre, which had lain unſtrung for a long time, he went the next day in the evening to the firſt pyramid. As ſoon as it was night, he enter'd alone, and made its long echoing vaults ring with the name of his Eurydice. Having paſs'd frightful windings and turnings, he came to the mouth of the well; and the fervent deſire he had to meet either with Eurydice, or his death, made him reſolved to deſcend. It was ſome conſolation to him to hear thro' the grates of the iron gate a compleat muſick, in which he diſtinguiſh'd the voices of women, and even fancy'd he heard that of his Eurydice: But his ſatisfaction was yet greater, at reading the inſcription. He ſaw he was at the very gate of the initiation, which had been

the

the occasion of his voyage, though the loss of his wife had made him forget it: But then joining both ideas, and giving up his imagination to his desires, he believ'd that the initiation itself would lead him to the mansion of the souls of the blessed, and that, perhaps, he might bring back Eurydice from thence. He enter'd the narrow way, and with great resolution went thro' the trials of fire and water. But at the noise of the wheels, and the motion of the landing-place or draw-bridge, he had not the presence of mind to hold fast by the rings; so was forc'd to retreat, and was thrown against his will upon the steps of the arch. He perceiv'd his mistake even before the noise ceas'd; and as soon as he saw from the top of the steps, where he had kept his ground, that the door of the pedestal was open'd, he took his lyre, and, being resolv'd to die, comforted himself with the hopes of meeting his Eurydice. In the mean time he advanc'd slowly towards the sanctuary, singing verses fill'd with the names of the gods, and of Eurydice, and sung, in concert with his lyre, such just, such melodious, and such tender strains, that all the priests who surrounded him, were charm'd with it. After a short space he gave over singing, and fell on his knees, as if in expectation of his sentence. The high-priest, after having conferr'd a few moments with his companions, made him rise, and thus accosted him; Virtuous stranger, who can be no other than the renown'd Orpheus, we know by the piety of your verses, and the excellency of your talents, that you reverence the gods, and are dear to them. Our goddess is equitable; she considers what is due to your resolution in entring this abyss, and to the progress you have made in it without advice and without assistance: your judgment, indeed, fail'd you in the last of your trials; but she pardons this mistake, in consideration of the grief you labour under for your late loss. Your only consolation will be in that virtue, of which our goddess, by our means, will explain to you the true principles. But as an atonement for your fault, she expects, that after your initiation, you introduce her worship into Greece, your country, the fame of which has been long since known to us. Orpheus made no other answer to this discourse but by tears of gratitude and joy; the high-priest went through the ceremonies of that day with him, and admitted him to the exercises of those that follow'd.

IT is not difficult to trace all the customs of the Egyptians in the greek mythology, of which Orpheus was the principal author. We have elsewhere shewn what the obsequies for the dead had furnish'd him with. What he has taken from the initiation is something more disguis'd; but in the three trials of fire,

water,

water, and air, are plainly diſcover'd the three purifications the ſouls of men were to go thro' before they return'd to life; which the greateſt of the latin poets borrow'd from him, in the ſixth book of his Æneid; *Infectum eluitur ſcelus, aut exuritur igni:* not to omit the circumſtance of ſuſpenſion in the agitated air, or in the winds: *Suſpenſæ ad ventos.* The waters of forgetfulneſs, and the gate of ivory have their places there. Hercules returning with Alceſte out of hell, and Theſeus condemn'd to ſit there for ever, are the two different ſymbols of thoſe, who either paſs'd thro', or fail'd in their trials. But farther, Orpheus gave a ſymbolical or diſguis'd hiſtory of his initiation: when connecting what had paſs'd in his mind, with what actually happen'd to him at his laſt trial, he ſuppos'd, that he had infallibly brought Eurydice back again from hell, if he had not, contrary to the law preſcrib'd him, look'd back before he recover'd the light of the day.

EVEN theſe allegories are nothing in compariſon with the myſteries of Ceres, which he actually inſtituted at Eleuſina, after the model of thoſe of Iſis; and which he divided into greater and leſſer myſteries, in the ſame view as the greater and leſſer initiations were diſtinguiſh'd in Egypt. The firſt was only beſtow'd upon natives of the country; and the

the ſecond only to foreigners. Both one and the other, as well at Eleuſina as at Egypt, were oblig'd to a ſecrecy which had never been violated but at the expence of the life of him who reveal'd any of theſe myſteries, either by a formal ſentence, or by other means, in whatever part of the world he might happen to be; and then they never fail'd of altering, at leaſt in part, ſuch of their practice as had been reveal'd. This is the reaſon why we know ſo little of the antient ceremonies. What I am acquainted with myſelf came to my knowledge only by means of ſome uncommon documents very difficult to be decypher'd; which, in the confuſion of the wars, had been taken out of the archives where they were treaſur'd up, and which the poſſeſſors of them very carefully conceal'd. And tho' to this day initiations are in practice, both in Egypt and in Greece, they are not ſo rigid, nor are the myſteries to which they are introductory ſo ſecret. Perſons of diſtinction are admitted without any probation. Even children are frequently conſecrated to Iſis, or to Ceres, which in the main are but one and the ſame goddeſs, without any condition, and merely by the devotion of their parents.

BUT to return to Sethos; the whole firſt day and night following were, as cuſtomary, allow'd him for reſt. His table was ſerv'd in in the ſame manner as at the palace; and inſtead of his ordinary domeſticks, he was attended by a good number of officers of the ſecond order; but he was not allow'd to ſtir out of his apartment all that day; and his confinement there would have been longer, if there had been any other candidate in the prieſts houſe before him; for then he muſt have waited till they had gone thro' their exerciſes.

THE next morning, ſome hours after ſunriſe, the prieſts came to inform Sethos, that he muſt begin a faſt of fourſcore and one days in different degrees of auſterity: During the whole time he was to drink nothing but water: In the firſt two months he was to eat as much bread as he pleas'd; and for his meals fruits, either raw or only dry'd in the ſun. But this courſe of diet was more tolerable in Egypt than in any other country. The following twenty-one days were divided into two parts; the firſt twelve days he was to have as much bread as he wou'd, but only eight ounces of fruit every day; and the laſt nine days the faſt was to be very ſevere, for he was to have only eighteen ounces of bread with water. During the ſeventy-two firſt days, he was to eat his meals alone, and at ſuch hours as he liked beſt. He was to lie in a bed without curtains, on girths of Papyrus ſtretch'd tight, with only a bolſter, and

two

two ſheets of linnen; of which the uppermoſt might be doubled into as many folds as he pleas'd. He was allow'd to lie but ſix hours, and at noon he might take an hour's nap ſitting. This was all that related to the purification of the body, or the firſt of the three parts of initiation. The two others were the purification of the mind, and the manifeſtation.

THE purification of the mind conſiſted of two parts, * invocation and inſtruction. The invocation was only aſſiſting an hour every morning and evening at the ſacrifices which were offer'd in ſight of all the people, but the candidate was ſo plac'd that he could neither ſee them nor be ſeen. The inſtruction conſiſted of more particulars: The candidate was firſt of all acquainted, that it chiefly concern'd the duties incumbent on him in the condition of life he was in, and that his examination would be only on that head. Mean time the prieſts held every day two conferences on this account, at which he was oblig'd to be preſent. In the morning-confe-

* Beſides the treatiſe of Meurſius, call'd Eleuſina, the reader may conſult what father Laffiteau, in his cuſtoms of the ſavages, t. 1. p. 221. and fol. ſays of the initiations of the antients. He begins by theſe words: The initiations to the myſteries were a practical ſchool of religion and virtue, inſtituted by the antients to inſtruct men how to live up to the principles of reaſon and prudence. And this is in effect the idea Cicero gives us of them; De leg. 2. &c.

rence

rence one of them ſpent an hour in explaining the general principles of the Egyptian religion. He * inculcated the notion of one only God, who by his knowledge conceiv'd the world, before he form'd it by his will. But to comply with the frailty of mankind, they were allow'd to adore the different attributes of his eſſence, and the different effects of his goodneſs, under the ſymbols of the ſtars, as the ſun and the planets; of renown'd perſonages, as Oſiris, Jupiter, Mercury; and even of terreſtrial bodies, as animals and plants †. He added, that the ſubaltern deities were likewiſe ſpirits, whoſe miniſtry the ſupreme God thought expedient to employ in the government of the univerſe. He did not forget that ſpirit, who was the tempter of men, and the diſturber of nature, repreſented by Typhon, by the evil genius's, and by pernicious animals and poiſonous plants. From thence he proceeded to explain the ceremonies they put in practice to win the favour of the beneficent deities, or to avert the anger of the miſchievous. The Egyptians by this confus'd idea of unity in the divine being, and of multiplicity in his ſymbols, are the firſt authors of what has

* Lactant. l. 1.

† The Ab. Banier obſerves very juſtly, that the firſt fathers of the church demonſtrated to the Pagans, that this interpretation did not clear them from idolatry. Origin of fables. p. 2. p. 266.

been the most sublime in philosophical opinions, and the most gross in popular superstitions. Besides this, the physical and historical origins of the denominations of these secondary deities, and of the varieties of the worship paid to them, were expounded in a manner so learned and so curious, that Sethos sometimes envy'd these men, who being freed from all the incumbrances of life, could devote themselves wholly to such satisfactory enquiries.

THE evening conference lasted an hour and half. The only subject was morality. One of the priests began, by laying down general maxims of it, which he afterwards apply'd to such cases or instances as best suited the circumstances of the candidate. Then other priests made objections; which were answer'd by the first. In these conferences the candidate was not allow'd to speak; but in the familiar conversations, which the priests held twice a day among themselves, he was free to speak his mind, not on religion but on morals; in which they endeavour'd to satisfy all his questions or objections. Besides which, all the priests, whose business it was to teach their divinity, were oblig'd to receive him into their closets whenever he came during the intervals of his exercises. This freedom, which he enjoy'd forty-two days, gave the candidate an opportunity of unfolding the most inward recesses of his

his mind, and even of relating ſuch actions of his life, as he could ſuppoſe might tend to his honour : and the prieſts, on their parts, gave great attention to him, in order to diſcover his character and inclinations. For whereas in other ſchools, one ſingle maſter was the inſtructor of many diſciples, here the whole college of prieſts was employ'd to inſtruct one candidate. Their wives, who in compliment were ſtil'd prieſteſſes, tho' in Egypt they had no ſacerdotal functions, at leaſt in the ſuperior temples, dwelt with them under the ſame roof: But the four ſtories of this houſe being double, the prieſt's apartments look'd towards the gardens, and thoſe of the prieſteſſes forwards. Of theſe two ſides, which were ſeparated by a gallery, that deſtin'd for the women was call'd, likewiſe by favour, the ſacerdotal palace; whereas the other ſide was only ſtil'd the prieſt's houſe. The prieſteſſes had the liberty of their huſbands apartments, but not of their cloſets. They never went into the halls, or common offices of the houſe; but they had the freedom of the galleries, and of thoſe paſſages alone which led to the galleries of the temple, and into the gardens. The candidate was forbid to ſpeak to them, or ſo much as to ſalute them, where-ever he met them, though he generally knew them, and had ſeen them, perhaps, in the apartments of the king and queen, whither they went

at

at certain hours, as other ladies did. By this the candidate was taught, that he muſt know how to deny himſelf ſometimes thoſe things which were lawful in themſelves, tho' within his reach. But that which will appear, without doubt, mortifying to well-bred gentlemen, theſe ladies, who were moſt of them of ſingular beauty, never paſs'd by him without paying him their reſpect; and he was not ſuffer'd to make the leaſt ſhew of a return. By this he was put to a trial of that fortitude with which every virtuous man ought to reſiſt the charms of the ſex when they appear in competition with his duty.

ON the evening of the forty-ſecond day, the candidate was inform'd, that the next day he muſt commence a ſilence of eighteen days complete; during which he muſt not utter one ſingle word, nor even make any ſign to expreſs his thoughts, on any account whatſoever; only in caſe of illneſs, he might demonſtrate it by laying his hand to his heart: but if he did not give this ſign, ſuch of the prieſts as were phyſicians, could eaſily perceive it; and in this caſe, all his exerciſes were ſuſpended, and he was look'd after with a great deal of care: But after his recovery, whatever day of the three months the purification of his mind was interrupted, he was oblig'd to begin again. The candidate was offer'd at the ſame time a certain number

of

of proper books, tables to write on, and a ſtylus or iron pen to write with, if he had not thought to aſk for them before. But Sethos had this foreſight the very ſecond day of his retirement. He conceiv'd, that the frequent viſits he was allow'd to make to the prieſts, and the queſtions he might be continually aſking them, would not conduce ſo much to his inſtruction, as recollection and reading. He had already copy'd all that he was able to remember of their moral conferences, and had endeavour'd, by meditation, to go back to the grounds of every particular queſtion. By this means his mind was ſtor'd beforehand with all the anſwers which he heard given by the prieſt, who held the conference, to all the queſtions and objections ſtarted to him by the others: And in, their private converſations, they all admir'd the accuracy and modeſty of his deciſions. But theſe converſations were now to be ſuſpended: His other exerciſes remain'd the ſame, and the two conferences were continu'd during the whole eighteen days. However, he was not call'd to theſe exerciſes as before, but was oblig'd to repair punctually thither at the common ſignal. In a word, he had no other notice given him, but by being awak'd mornings and afternoons. He had the liberty of the gardens, but he was not to take notice of any perſon, either man or woman; ſo that he was all alone as it were, in the midſt of a houſe full of people. On the other hand, nobody, either man or woman, ſeem'd to take any notice of him; nor was any manner of attendance given him, excepting that his food was brought once a day into his apartments when he was abſent. The prieſt, who inform'd him of this new regulation, acquainted him, that he was enjoin'd to the moſt rigid obſervance of it: that they excuſed ſome ſmall inadvertencies which he had been guilty of during the forty-two preceding days; but that the leaſt violation of the rules now preſcrib'd him would forfeit his liberty for the remainder of his life. Upon this the prieſt, without ſtaying for any anſwer from Sethos, led away Amedes, who not having quitted this young prince hitherto, left him, as it may be imagin'd, overwhelm'd with grief. It was not that they ever deſign'd to put their threats in execution, but they did it to put the candidates to a trial under this ſituation of mind, in order to give them an opportunity of exerting their courage; for they wink'd at any ſmall failures in thoſe whom they judg'd worthy of the initiation in other reſpects.

NOTHING could more ſenſibly affect Sethos than to be ſeparated from his governour, whom he eſteem'd as a father. The ſolitude he was now left in, which was but as a trial or exerciſe, made him reflect upon

the

the real ſituation of his fortune, to which he had, properly ſpeaking, as yet not open'd his eyes. He recall'd to his mind the loſs of a mother, and the ſucceſſion to the throne, with the loſs of which he was threatned; and nature prevailing, either over the unſettledneſs of his youth, which he had hardly quitted, or over the heroick fortitude which was viſibly growing up in him, he ſhed a torrent of tears. But conſidering at laſt the vanity and weakneſs of ſuch a conſolation, he arm'd himſelf with reſolution and conſtancy, and had the courage to promiſe within himſelf, that, what ever ſtate of life he might fall into, he would never ſeek comfort in tears, but would look upon virtue as a man's only good and ſupport.

THE next morning, ſoon after he roſe, he ſaw three prieſts with very auſtere countenances, enter his chamber. It was very ſhocking for the candidate to ſee theſe men, who before had ſhewn him all marks of friendſhip and complacency, approach him with the appearance of ſevere judges. They came to reproach him, not for the ſmall faults he might have been guilty of ſince the commencement of his preparation, which were only failings for that time and place, but for the defective or vicious diſpoſitions they had obſerv'd, either in his converſation or manners. But they did not ſtop there;

for, as the resolution which is necessary in a person to expose himself to the trials of the initiation is hardly to be met with but in persons of note, the priests knew pretty well, either from their own intelligence, or publick fame, all their perfections or defects. Besides, as it was common for people to come for advice or prediction to the priests, whom they suppos'd to have a profound knowledge in futurity and hidden causes; they spared no diligence to get information under hand of all the secrets as well of princes as of private persons; to which, the industry of their wives, and the officers of the second order, who went abroad, did not a little contribute. And after a candidate was shut up amongst them, they employ'd their utmost care to gather all possible circumstances of his life. Thus they put him to a strange surprize, by recalling to his mind such of his past actions as might merit censure, and by reprimanding him in proportion to the heinousness of the case, without so much as allowing him to open his mouth: They even forbid him losing any time to justify himself in writing; but then they took all imaginable precaution not to lay any thing to his charge but what was strictly true. This vexatious exercise was shorter or longer every time, and was continued more or fewer days, according to the nature of the subject; and they insinuated to many, that they knew more than they would ſay. But, with reſpect to Sethos, whom the prieſts had nothing to reproach with, they only reprov'd him for the tears he had ſhed the foregoing evening, and which he ſuppos'd had been ſeen by none: They repeated to him the very ſame reflections he had made himſelf; after which they retir'd, and came no more.

TOWARD the evening of the laſt day of ſilence, the three prieſts came into the candidate's apartment with a ſerene countenance. They told him, that one of the wholſomeſt inſtructions a wiſe man could receive, was that which he drew from his own faults. That he muſt not fail to correct and amend them; but that he ought not to conceive ſuch a ſhame for them as might be diſcouraging and unprofitable. They added, that they had admitted guilty perſons to the initiation, but that their hiſtory did not furniſh a ſingle example of the meaneſt of the Egyptian initiates, who after admiſſion had abandon'd the paths of the nobleſt virtue. That he was going to be incorporated with a body of men, which merit alone had form'd, and which, tho' it had no pre-eminence of itſelf, poſſeſs'd, however, the firſt place in the eſteem of all men. They went ſo far as to tell him, that though initiation was but a participation of the prieſthood, it was their birth made them prieſts; whereas initiates were choſen men, who only attain'd to that dignity by a merit that had been ſeverely try'd. They then inform'd him, that beginning at the following day, in which he would be allow'd to reſume the uſe of his ſpeech, they would give him twelve days to recollect in writing, or in his memory, what he had learn'd in the conferences he had heard, or from his lectures; in order to prepare him to anſwer to three queſtions in morality, which they ſhould propoſe to him at the expiration of this term. It was for this end that the conferences now ceas'd, that he might not be perplex'd with new ſubjects for application. That they would only hold one diſcourſe a day, to ſpend their leiſure time, and that it ſhould be upon a ſubject a little differing from the former; to which he might only give ſuch attention as he ſhould judge proper. That his attendance at prayers and ſacrifices ſhould be no longer than his piety and inclination ſhould direct. To conclude, that he ſhould have the ſame liberty as before to converſe with all the prieſts either in publick or private; and that he even might ſalute the prieſteſſes, but he was deſir'd however not to ſpeak to them.

SETHOS, who had before made great advances, as well in virtue as knowledge, had gain'd extraordinary advantage during his retreat and ſilence with regard to both theſe views: ſo that at the beginning of this third month, he ſeem'd, in ſome meaſure, to be equal to the prieſts; and from thenceforth they behav'd to him as great men are wont to do to one another. He had ſo much reſolution and preſence of mind the firſt day not to aſk again for Amedes, who was out of ſight; and the prieſts, who did not ſuſpect him of indifferency, perceiv'd he was ready himſelf to meet every trial they were willing to ſubject his mind to. However, he was reſtor'd to him the ſame evening: But the politeneſs, which was natural to him, having prompted him to take advantage of the freedom which was allow'd him with reſpect to the prieſteſſes, he was not a little ſurpriz'd, that the firſt time he ſaluted two or three of them, whom he met together in a walk of the garden, they did not return him the compliment. He was, in ſome meaſure, aſham'd that he had not preſuppos'd ſome ſuch reſerve in a place like that: and turning this trifle to advantage, he imagin'd they would thereby inure him to comply with the cuſtoms of every place, tho' never ſo ſingular or trivial.

THE diſcourſes or conferences of the two preceding months had been held by prieſts of the greateſt ability and experience in the ſubjects they had treated. But if in the whole claſs of ſacred literature there was one man superior in genius and eloquence: it was he who was employ'd to hold the twelve last discourses at the beginning of this last month. For his general subject he chose the GENIUS OF A TRUE INITIATE. An initiate, said he, is a new man, in whom the love of virtue and his duty has taken place of all those passions which were before the motives of all his actions. In every juncture, what he will do is infallibly visible in what he ought to do. Life is of no account to him. It is neither example, nor opportunity, nor a transitory passion which engages him to expose it. These circumstances are necessary to the man of passion: but the man of principle, such as an initiate, holds, as it were, his life in his hand; and if he has not put it to stake, it is because his duty has not yet requir'd it. Glory is generally inseparable from those eminent virtues which we see practis'd by initiates; but 'tis neither their motive nor their aim. It is requisite to preserve the idea and name of glory among men, especially with respect to those who, being high born, are seldom animated by any other sensible interest. But in the main, glory is a spur only to the weak, and to novices. The motive of an initiate is the voice of his duty, and his aim the discharge of it. From hence it comes, said he, that many of our initiates had rather do private services to their prince or country in obscurity, than be distin-

distinguish'd by the most shining dignities, Ambition has prompted most candidates to submit to the trials of the body; but the trials of the mind have eradicated that ambition. In whatever rank an initiate finds himself plac'd, either by his birth or fortune, he believes himself to be establish'd in it for no other end, but for the benefit of his country, and even, if possible, for the whole race of mankind. So consequently, this man, not being to be biass'd by any desire, or any fear of his own, is taken up with all the desires, and all the fears of those whom he is to make happy, as their master, or to serve, as their fellow-citizen. On this occasion he alledg'd the several great things, which the first heroes of Egypt, who instituted the worship of the gods, and the initiation, had done for the world; the security, happiness and glory which they had at first procur'd for Egypt itself: But, added he, their magnanimous valour not being to be confin'd within bounds so streight, they carry'd their profitable arts to nations as uncultivated as their lands; they purg'd the country of robbers, and the seas of pyrates; or they transform'd them into a civiliz'd people by the laws they subjected them to, the sciences they taught them, and above all, by the heroick virtues of which they set them examples: It is to them, in short, the world owes that form we now see it in. He afterwards mention'd mention'd the names of the moſt famous initiates of the following ages, and related thoſe paſſages of their lives, which were as affecting by the ſingularity of the incidents, as the generoſity of their actions. He finiſh'd his relation of theſe wonders by ſaying, that the ſoul of an initiate, that ſoul ſo couragious and ſo ſublime, was humble, gentle, and indulgent. This man, who centers all the virtues in himſelf, eſteems, and praiſes the leaſt footſteps of them which appear in others. He places them above him, who deſpair ever to come up to him. He can witneſs for the ſincerity of his intention, but he miſtruſts his own thoughts and his views. He perceives he is uncapable of committing an injuſtice or a crime; but he acknowledges himſelf liable to all the frailties of nature. Tho' always upon his guard againſt faults, he is ever ready to acknowledge the commiſſion of them. He is, in ſhort, a man without blemiſh, who is always ſtudying to amend; and a perfect man, who is ever ſtriving to make himſelf more perfect.

THIS picture of an initiate, of which I have here given but a faint ſketch, tranſported Sethos's admiration. He ſaid to Amedes, Father, how came it to paſs that the prieſts ſpoke ſo indifferently of theſe laſt diſcourſes, which I juſt now heard; that was, no doubt, one of their niceſt trials, to ſee whether I had

had a taſte for virtue; whether the ſplendor of it would attract my notice; and whether I ſhould be ſenſible of its charms? Oh! it is now I begin to live; 'tis only the true initiate, the virtuous man, knows the ſublimity of his being; he alone enjoys his mind; thoſe who ſet their hearts upon other objects, are not worthy to be call'd men. Theſe laſt diſcourſes are ſo far from being of little moment, as the prieſts ſeem'd to inſinuate, that they will enable me to anſwer all the queſtions they may put to me. I ſhall talk from the fountain-head; and all I have to do for the future, will be to conform the reſt of my life to my anſwers. But, father, continu'd he, I muſt have been ſtrangely blind hitherto, not to perceive in you thoſe ſublime virtues, of which I have now ſo glorious an idea. It was, without doubt, that humility and indulgence wherein partly conſiſts the character of a true initiate, that have conceal'd you from my ſight. The king, my grandfather, and the queen, my mother, ſaw you thro' this veil, when they ſingled you out for their counſellor and their miniſter. Son, anſwer'd Amedes, it is ſufficient for me if it be true that I have not diſhonour'd the title I bear of an initiate; but it is for another man to give true luſtre to it: The greatneſs of your birth impoſes laws on you of a larger extent; but then it furniſhes you with greater powers for the practice of eminent virtues, and actions of of generoſity. I was ſenſible of my incapacity to educate a prince like you, and therefore I immediately borrow'd the aſſiſtance of all the ſchools of Memphis, to teach you the ſciences under maſters more able than myſelf; and I have endeavour'd to add to the vigilance with which a governour ought to attend a private education, that emulation which is rarely ſeen in a pupil, unleſs in a publick one. But the ſciences are nothing in compariſon to virtue. Who could better inſtruct you in that than thoſe men, who have attain'd a conſummate knowledge of all laws divine and human? Common fame gives ſome ſmall advantage in other particulars to certain prieſts of Egypt above thoſe of Memphis; but, at the ſame time, allows the preference to theſe in the knowledge of morality. What more proper time could they take to diſcourſe to you of virtue in the moſt ſublime manner, than while you are preparing for the initiation? This privilege, which has been coveted by the greateſt men, and which, in their eſteem, crowns a long ſeries of wonderful actions, is become a part of your education, and of conſequence, my ſon, is an engagement to you to begin where they left off.

THE day after theſe twelve days, the high-prieſt, follow'd by ſeveral others, came into Sethos's apartment the moment after he was

riſen,

risen, and said to him, Son, I come to propose the three questions to you, which you must give answer to in nine days. All our instructions said he, and even your reading will be laid aside for that time: We suspend even our common conversations, and you are not allow'd to speak to any of us in particular till the expiration of that term. It is from the gods alone you must henceforth intreat that knowledge you may stand in need of. For these nine days you shall lie in the sanctuary behind the statues of the three deities, that the goddess Isis may, if she please, instruct you even in your dreams. We shall every morning, when you awake, and before the gates of the temple are open'd to the people, offer a sacrifice to her, and invoke her to pour her wisdom into your soul. You may spend as much time in the temple as you shall think convenient; and in our gardens you may meditate upon your answers. In the mean time, to alleviate your solitude in some measure, you will be sent for twice every day to our table; but you must observe a profound silence, and keep up strictly to the austerity which was at first prescrib'd you for these nine days; during which, you must fast with bread and water. Give now attention to the three questions I have to propose to you: What is the principal virtue of a hero? Does heroism consist in exceeding the bounds

bounds of duty? Is it heroick to ſacrifice even one's honour to the intereſt of our country, or the general good of mankind? The high-prieſt, having twice more diſtinctly repeated theſe three queſtions, retir'd with the prieſts that were in his company.

SETHOS being now the ſecond time left alone, the firſt thing that he did, was to write down the three queſtions propos'd to him, that he might not forget them. The firſt reflection he made, after conſidering them in general, was, that the prieſts, who, from the firſt day of his coming thither, had inform'd him, that their inſtructions, and his examination would turn chiefly upon his condition; had diſcourſed very little to him upon the duties of a king in particular, and had made no manner of mention of them in their queſtions. He concluded from thence, that they at leaſt foreſaw he would never attain to the royal dignity, and that all he was to expect was, to be a hero: After having utter'd ſome ſighs for his misfortune, and the frailty of his father, he reſolv'd to ſubmit to the deſtiny the gods had prepar'd for him, and promis'd, with their aſſiſtance, to conform himſelf to it.

GOING out of his apartment towards the temple, he perceiv'd there was a profound ſilence

ſilence throughout the whole houſe. And, indeed, during theſe nine days, the prieſts, and all that inhabited this vaſt manſion, took care not to talk in his preſence; and in his abſence they only whiſper'd, and that but upon emergent occaſions: At other times the prieſt and prieſteſſes walk'd, and diſcours'd together at different hours in the garden. But during theſe nine days, Sethos never ſaw any body there but the prieſts, who by turns watch'd the Ox Apis that graz'd in the park, which was in the middle of it. The women from the city came to the prieſteſſes, or to the ſacerdotal palace by the ſtreet-way, but the prieſteſſes never open'd the gallery-doors to them. Theſe doors were even ſhut to the prieſteſſes themſelves during the nine days, and they had no manner of communication with the inward part of the houſe, tho' their huſbands were always allow'd to go to them. Both men and women, that had any buſineſs with the prieſts, were not at any time admitted farther than the outward halls: ſo that no alteration being made without, it was never known in the city when there was a candidate with the prieſts: and this, as well as the other ſecrets of the houſe, was kept as inviolably by their wives, and the officers of the ſecond order, as by themſelves.

SETHOS was not a little ſurpriz'd upon being led into the common refectory,

fectory, to find the priests table no better serv'd than his; and that confining themselves, on his account, to the same fast which they had enjoin'd him, they had at each of their two meals no greater allowance than himself, viz. nine ounces of bread and a little water. He thence concluded, that the priests regarded the justness of his answers as a matter of very great importance; and that requir'd his deepest reflection. However, as those who aspir'd to the initiation, some of whom were officers of war, had not all the gift of elocution, nor were all capable of giving an advantageous turn to their thoughts, a fault in expression was no hinderance to them, it being by no means a trial of wit or eloquence which they pretended to put them to: all the candidate had to do, was to manifest that he possess'd an upright beneficent heart, purg'd from that errour, which is but too common in those who knowing their power, think their grandeur consists in setting themselves above all rule, and being fear'd by other men. It is true, when such persons did come under their hands, who were prompted to aspire to the initiation by no other motives but temerity or ambition, or who seem'd incorrigible; they took pleasure in ridding the world of them, by sending them to exercise their valour and cunning in their subterraneous mansions. Many of those conquerors and politi-

politicians ſo famed in our hiſtories would have been bury'd alive here. However, ſuch examples were very rare. They muſt have been very ignorant, who, before they attempted the probation, did not know that the character of an initiate was a compound of all the virtues. And if they did not know it before, muſt have been very untractable not to reform their judgments and manners by all the inſtructions and reproofs beſtow'd upon them during the courſe of the purification of their minds. It was next to an impoſſibility for an initiate, after being confirm'd, to degenerate from his profeſſion. There is no emulation among men more powerful than that of keeping up the honour of a ſmall ſociety into which we are admitted by merit and virtue. This emulation was, perhaps, not ſo efficacious in foreign initiates; becauſe not having the example of their brethren before their eyes, they might forget their engagements: But as they were only made partakers of the ſecond or particular initiation, they were not entirely of the ſame order with the Egyptian initiates, and the honour of their ſociety was not dependent on them.

SETHOS had already ſpent five whole days in meditating upon his anſwers; when notice was brought to the high-prieſt, that there was at the gate of the temple a young Carthaginian, who seem'd by his air and attendants, to be a person of the highest distinction. He publickly declared, he had been doom'd by the senate of his city to repair to Memphis, to seek atonement for the death of his brother, whom he had had the misfortune to kill in a battle.

THE

THE

LIFE

OF

SETHOS.

BOOK IV.

ABOUT twenty years before, a Tyrian, by name Zoros, of the offspring of Cadmus, a man of valour and knowledge, had laid the foundation of the city of Carthage, or at leaſt had enlarg'd the bounds of Carthada. In his frequent voyages to eſtabliſh a trade on all the coaſts of the Mediterranean, he had found no place for a ſettlement ſo convenient as this little city, built upon that agreeable ſhore, which has ever ſince been call'd, The ſojourn of the nymphs. He at laſt reſolv'd to ſettle at Carthada, and to inlarge it. To this end he carry'd all his veſſels thither, laden with immenſe riches. He was receiv'd with joy by the inhabitants, who were not yet arriv'd to that pitch of opulency they ſoon after attain'd to by his aſſiduity. He enlarg'd and embelliſh'd it to ſuch a degree, that it was hardly known to be the ſame; and he preſerv'd its ancient name, only adding to it a Phœnician termination. The memory of Cadmus, from whom Zoros was deſcended, and whoſe virtues he purſu'd, made him valu'd, not only by the citizens of Carthage, but of all thoſe cities which were built by this hero 200 years before, in the neighbourhood of it; and with which the country call'd Zeugitania was fill'd. Thus Zoros, in a very ſhort time, form'd a conſiderable ſtate: but to render his growing authority more acceptable, he choſe to give his government the form of an ariſtocracy. He inſtituted a ſenate compos'd of ten citizens of Carthage, and of two of every other city, and for himſelf he only retain'd the title of prince of the ſenate. This, according to my memoirs, is the true origin of the city of Carthage, and conformable to the teſtimonies of Philiſtus, Appianus of Alexandria, and ſome others of our authors, put together; for the hiſtory of Dido is poſterior to this epoch

by

by ſome hundreds of years; and it is beſides certain, that this fugitive princeſs only built the citadel of Byrſa, as an addition to this city, which was long before founded.

THE high-prieſt would immediately have known the name of the young Carthaginian, whoſe fame was already ſufficiently ſpread, but he would declare it to none but to him in perſon, thinking thereby to inſinuate himſelf into his eſteem. He was not yet acquainted with the character of theſe inflexible men, who, in points of religion, were no reſpecters of perſons. The high-prieſt ſent to acquaint him, that he ſhould not receive him in the temple, but he muſt preſent himſelf at the gate of their college. That, in the mean time, he might have forborn divulging himſelf an action which demanded an atonement, and that theſe circumſtances ought to have been reveal'd to the prieſts alone. The Carthaginian, who was more aſham'd of this reprimand than of his odious exploit, in which he privately gloried, ſuffer'd himſelf to be led peaceably to the gate appointed. They made him come in alone, and told his attendants, they would hear no more of him till after three days. The high-prieſt, to whom he was introduc'd ſtanding in the midſt of his companions, without allowing him time to ſpeak, told him, That before he made enquiry whether he had ſlain his brother spontaneously, or by accident; whether it was an actual assassination, or a murder committed under the pretext of the publick good, or his own defence; they all look'd upon the fatal occasion which had brought him to this unfortunate action (so repugnant to nature) as a great mark of the anger of the gods pour'd down upon him: That he wou'd be put three days under strict confinement, and wou'd be allow'd but what was barely necessary for his subsistance. According to the laws of Egypt, added he, not only he who kills, but he who does not, to the utmost of his power, defend a person that is attack'd, and in danger of being assassinated, is guilty of death. We don't subject strangers to our laws, knowing, that with many, the punishment of homicide extends no farther than exile; and the favourable tribunal of atonement is not sanguinary even in Egypt. We endeavour to inspire a fear of the gods, and a terror of their judgments into those Egyptians who are brought before us only for accidents or involuntary misfortunes, and into those strangers who are often sent to us for their crimes; that as well one as the other may depart from hence more circumspect, and, if possible, more virtuous than the innocent themselves. However said he, to conclude, prepare to morrow to give a faithful account of your action in our full assembly. 'Till then, we will hear nothing concerning

concerning you. If your confession be then sincere, it will absolve you before the gods; but if, on the contrary, it is false or disguis'd, notwithstanding the exteriour expiation you will receive, you will carry away your eternal damnation.

THE next morning the Carthaginian was sent for out of his prison, and brought as a criminal, cloath'd in sackcloth, into a great oval hall. The high-priest was seated at the upper end, and all the other priests on each side of him on seats something lower than his, as at the tribunal of the labyrinth. Initiates were allow'd to assist at these courts: so Amedes and Orpheus were present at this: they were plac'd below all the priests, and young Sethos sate without the row, and below the initiates. As it was the trial of a foreigner, who could not know him, and as his exercises were so far advanc'd, they thought it might be of advantage to him to hear judgment pronounc'd in a cause, which appear'd to be of importance and singular. The Carthaginian standing, and bare-headed, thus address'd himself to the court in the Egyptian tongue, of which he was perfectly master.

VENERABLE chief of this sacred college, and you the priests of the great goddess Isis; you see here before you Saphon, the son of the renowned Zoros, founder of Carthage, the establisher and prince of his senate. Tho' my brother Giscon * and I were twins, the prerogative of elder brother has never been disputed me. However, my father, who begins to advance in years, having purpos'd to settle the succession, during his own life, call'd my right in question, and annex'd to the glory of filling his place on the throne, a condition, which he offer'd my brother equal with me. The condition was, that which ever of us should, within the course of three years, perform the most heroick action, should be declar'd his successor, by him and by the senate. I won't attribute this thought of my father's to an unjust prædilection in favour of my brother, tho' my friends had before warn'd me of it: I rather choose to believe, that, enjoying the benefit of many victories I had gain'd for him; and considering, that by the success of my arms I had added all Numidia to his dominions, he did not question but I should carry the prize before my brother; and that so, adding the right of merit to that of my birth, I might thereby obtain a greater influence over the people I was to govern after his death. I don't pretend by this discourse to insinuate that my

* Saphon and Giscon are mention'd in ancient authors, who have wrote of Carthage, as very nearly related; and some place them before the Trojan war. See Mariana's history of Spain, l. 1. & 2. and the remarks of father Charenton.

brother

brother wanted valour. However, he not only had never attempted to inlarge the new empire of Carthage, which he might have done on the other side; but he even never assisted me in my expeditions. Since we have been both of age to bear arms, his only exploits have been to repulse the Barbarians, who made frequent incursions into our southern provinces upon which they border'd, and who sometimes advanc'd to the very gates of Carthage. But to do justice to his vigilance and patience, 'tis certain he never had the opportunity of attacking and defeating more at once than parties of forty or fifty of these rovers: so that all these skirmishes join'd together, were in no measure to be compar'd to the glory and advantage of three or four victories I had obtain'd, and which began to make our empire one of the most powerful hitherto known. This was the state of affairs when my father made us both the proposal I have mention'd, in the assembled senate. I immediately concluded, that heroick actions were alone to be sought in war; and being persuaded that the principal virtue of a hero is valour, I prepar'd to fulfil the condition prescrib'd, by taking arms, and extending the conquests I had already begun.

TOWARDS the conclusion of the two first years I had advanc'd beyond Numidia, and conquer'd all Mauritania Sitifensis, so call'd from

from its metropolis Sitifi, which I had taken after a long ſiege. I propos'd to carry my arms to the foot of mount Atlas; and ſparing none but the ſacred country of the Heſperides, I did not deſpair of reaching the banks of the ocean in the courſe of the third year. But my deſigns were interrupted by an unexpected and ſurprizing account I receiv'd from Carthage, which oblig'd me to return thither. My brother diſappear'd the very day after the propoſal made by my father; and I concluded from that time, that he had given up all pretenſion: But I was inform'd at Sitifi, that he was gone over to thoſe rambling nations who before us'd to invade our territories, and whom he himſelf had ſo often drove from our frontiers. I was inform'd he ſpent the two firſt years of his abſence in going, with innumerable hazards and fatigues, either to their caves, which were many miles diſtant one from the other; or to their tents, which were frequently remov'd: That, by force of reiterated invitations and remonſtrances, he had at laſt prevail'd upon them to unite, and to form a civiliz'd nation, to build cities at proper diſtances for their common conveniency, and to lay the foundation of a metropolis for the center of their dominions. We ſoon got intelligence, that, on the other ſide of the mountains, which we look upon as our borders to the ſouthward, all diligence was imploy'd in raiſing the walls of the

the city of Capſa, ſituate on a river which empties itſelf into the ſea over-againſt the little Syrtes. Thus theſe people, who before were known by no other name than that of their unhappy profeſſion, rovers, affected now to to be call'd Capſans, and demanded reſpect from their neighbours, and even from us. We muſt allow, that being now taken up with their ſettlement, they had for ſome time forbore their irruptions into our territories: But you will eaſily conceive, O! ye wiſe prieſts of Memphis, what an uneaſineſs an empire thus riſing up in the neighbourhood of our own, muſt cauſe us. I therefore thought it for my honour, and a duty incumbent on me, as well as for the intereſt of Carthage, to oppoſe the riſe of this ſtate. I prepar'd therefore to fall upon them in their forts, which were not yet finiſh'd, before their militia or even their republick could be regulated. As I had already a large army, I was preſently in a readineſs to march. As ſoon as my brother had notice of it, he ſent heralds to meet me; who, however, call'd themſelves deputies from the Capſans, and not from him. They declar'd, that they had no intention of living in enmity with the Carthaginians; that their whole deſign was to form a republick like ours; with this difference, that the inferiority of their numbers depriv'd them of all thoughts of acting upon the offenſive: that they had begun to build

forts

forts and ſtrong holds, and ſhould finiſh them, only to defend themſelves againſt their neighbours, if they ſhould be ſo unjuſt to oppoſe their eſtabliſhment. I anſwer'd them, It was enough for me to look on them as enemies, and even as criminals, that their chief was a ſon of the founder of Carthage, who, inſtead of acting in conjunction with his brother for the glory of his nation, deſtroy'd the hopes he had of making it one day the head of all the inhabited Africa, by erecting a republick in rivalſhip to his own; and who, if he was ſuffer'd to go on, would for ever ſet bounds to the Carthaginian empire towards the ſouth. They reply'd, they had, indeed, follow'd the counſels of my brother, in forming themſelves into a ſociable and reaſonable people, with whom we might enter into an alliance, and who would be our ſhelter againſt the incurſions of the Garamantes and other barbarous nations leſs civiliz'd than they had been. And farther, that my brother had accepted of no command amongſt them; and that in caſe of a battle, it was with them alone I ſhould engage. As my motive to this expedition was ſtate-policy, which would not allow the delay of a negociation; and beſides, as my whole aim was the performance of heroick actions, I told them, in a word, I would give them my final anſwer in battle.

I THERE-

I THEREFORE follow'd the heralds in their footsteps; and tho' I led a whole army, they had enough to do to be more expeditious than I was. I intended to have pass'd the mountains, and have met them at the foot of the walls of Capsa: But as soon as the Capsans had receiv'd my answer, they prevented me, by crossing these mountains themselves, and thereby gain'd the advantage of fighting only on our territories. I was surpriz'd to discover, from the eminency of a little hill at some distance from them, an army that seem'd to be of about 40000 men, who had the mountains on their rear, thro' the passages of which they might easily be supply'd with fresh troops. However, as my army consisted of 100000 men, I thought my self in a condition to attack them. I halted a day and a night behind the hill which cover'd us, knowing, that as soon as I came in sight, I must engage. The enemy, on their side, as if they were as much inclin'd as I to end the quarrel by a battle, had left a large plain before them, whither I led my troops in battle-array: They even gave them time to post themselves, designing, without doubt, to engage them all at once. But then attacking us in front, and on both sides, they added to the order and resolution of disciplin'd soldiers, as they actually now were, the cunning they prac-

tis'd

tis'd in former times, of giving the onset, and then immediately retiring. The battle, which began before noon, had already lasted full five hours, and we began to lose, by far, more men than they: I therefore resolv'd to make directly up to my brother, whom I had long known by his Carthaginian armour, and the motions he gave himself in the army he commanded; though, for shame, as I presum'd, of being in arms against his own Father, and of staining himself with the blood of his own country-men, he never lifted up the visor of his helmet. Notwithstanding his activity, which carry'd him to every part of the battle where he thought his presence necessary, I soon came up to him. Traiterous son and brother (said I, accosting him) let the death of one of us put an end to this battle, too bloody for thy country. Without answering me, he with his sword put by the blow I had aim'd at the bottom of his helmet: But as he turn'd about to go away, I thrust mine to the hilt under his armour; and in the same instant he fell dead at his horse's feet. This blow chang'd the face of the battle: The Capsans retir'd in good order thro' the passages of their mountains, an dwe remain'd masters of the field of battle. However, as I perceiv'd they put themselves in a posture to dispute the passage, and that my army, which was diminish'd 30000 men, was weary'd and disheartned, I retir'd, and for this time abandon'd the design I had of razing the walls of Capsa; so my brother's fatal enterprize yet subsists, notwithstanding the defeat of the Capsans, and his death.

As soon as we return'd to Carthage, my father let me know, that the first time he saw me should be in the senate: He there, in my presence, declar'd to the whole body assembled, that the affliction he could not forbear labouring under for the death of my brother, notwithstanding his infidelity, to which he always gave the name of evident, had depriv'd him of that freedom of mind which was necessary to form a sound and upright judgment, with respect to me; and that therefore he referr'd it wholly to them. After a long deliberation, during which I retir'd, I was call'd in again; and the eldest senator, speaking in the name of the rest, said, That the senate, judging only by the exterior of things, and willing to prevent the danger of so ambiguous an example as that of my brother, was about to condemn his memory, tho' with regret, as having been slain in arms against his father and his country; That in relation to me, without any decision on the condition prescrib'd, and annulling the proposal which had been made us, since my brother being dead, and I alone, it was now become unnecessary, they

they confirm'd to me, even with the consent of my father, the succession to the principality of the senate, to which I had before a natural right by a moment of primogeniture; but that to avert from me the anger of the gods, who alone know the grounds of things, and as a reparation of the prejudice that might be conceiv'd against me of having, under an honourable pretext, rid my self of a dangerous competitor, I should repair to the priests of Memphis, the most renown'd of all Egypt for their knowledge in religion and morality, and humbly supplicate the atonement of my crime from them: This, O venerable chief, and ye most sacred priests, is a faithful relation of my case, and the cause which brings me before your tribunal; I intreat you will add to the expiation I desire for what is past, your wise instruction for my future conduct.

As soon as the Carthaginian had finish'd his discourse, the high-priest made him sit down on a stool which was plac'd behind him, and spoke as follows: Saphon, Son of Zoros, we have long since had a very great value for your father, the pacifick founder of Carthage, whose exploits have always tended to the good of mankind. All the judgments of your senate, which have come to our knowledge, have given us a great

idea

idea of their wisdom. We honour'd the virtue of your brother, before the last battle, which you have related to us, and of which we had before no particular account. With respect to you, we perceive, by your discourse, and we knew before by your fame, that you are a great warriour; but your principles are not conformable to ours. We have here a pupil, whom I will order to speak, and you shall learn from the mouth of a beginner, how much the instructions of our goddess are superior to those confus'd and tumultuous ideas of the greater part of mankind; and especially of those who give themselves up to the blind passion of war. The high-priest immediately call'd Sethos; who approach'd him with great marks of surprize, modesty and obedience. He plac'd him standing opposite to the Carthaginian, and order'd him to give such answer to the discourse he had heard as the goddess should inspire him. The high-priest look'd upon it as a happy rencounter, that there appear'd some heroick actions in the history of Saphon and Giscon; and he did not doubt but Sethos would in this discourse make use of what he had been five days in preparing, in answer to the three questions propos'd to him, viz. What is the principal virtue of a hero? Does heroism consist in exceeding the bounds of duty? Is it heroick for a man to sacrifice even his honour for the interest of his country, or the advantage of mankind? Before the young prince began, the high-prieſt told Saphon, That the birth of this young man alone would give him right to anſwer him; and beſides that, they were all there preſent to lead him into the way of truth and juſtice, if he might happen to depart from it. It was upon this circumſtance, to which Orpheus was witneſs, that he eſtabliſh'd it as a rule in Greece, that the expiation might be given by thoſe kings who were initiated to the myſteries of Eleuſina; as Bellerophon went to receive it from Proetus, king of Argos, not to mention many other examples. Young Sethos thus began his diſcourſe:

ISIS, great goddeſs of the Egyptians, vouchſafe to guide my tongue, and ſuffer me not to utter any thing that may be unworthy of the inſtructions your ſacred miniſters have given me in your name. In my opinion, Saphon, you did not rightly take the ſenſe of the propoſal made you, when you believ'd that the heroick action requir'd of you, conſiſted in aſſaulting your neighbours, and ſubduing them without diſtinction. I don't hint at the conqueſt you made of Sitifi after the condition preſcrib'd, becauſe as you have not ſaid for what reaſon you took arms againſt that people, your relation (to which alone I ought to confine myſelf) don't furniſh me wherewithal to judge whether your conqueſt was good or evil. I am, however, perſuaded, that if you aſſaulted it for no other reaſon, but to gain the glory of having done an heroick action, that very intention has made you fail of it; becauſe an heroick action cannot have the glory of him that does it for its object and aim, but muſt neceſſarily have in view the intereſt and advantage of others. You have given a long account of the motive which led you againſt the Capſans; and your relation of it alone, in my opinion, is ſufficient to ſhew the injuſtice of your cauſe, which ſets you at yet a greater diſtance from heroiſm; becauſe an heroick action proceeding from a principle of virtue, it is impoſſible that virtue ſhould ſubſiſt with injuſtice. In reality, you have yourſelf refuted the pretext of the danger of a republick being erected adjoyning to you, when you allow, that the Capſans, being buſied in their ſettlement, had forbore their inroads into your dominions. Theſe incurſions are dangers which thoſe ſtates that are too near the ſavages can hardly ever free themſelves from; becauſe theſe people never forming themſelves into great bodies, it is impoſſible utterly to root them out; and, ſlipping by without being perceiv'd, they find paſſages by the ſides of thoſe fortreſſes and walls, which ſtop whole armies. Thus your oppoſing, on account of a very diſtant danger, the riſe of a republick, which, by the narrow bounds of its territories, in comparison of the extent of your empire, could not cause you any apprehension; which, besides, offer'd you its friendship and alliance, and which itself defends you from other more dangerous barbarians, would have brought your country into a present and continual evil, to obtain the honour of a victory profitable to you alone: An example which has been but too often given by those warlike princes, who have sacrific'd not only foreign and innocent nations, but the estates and lives of their own subjects, to their particular fame. You was, I think, yet more in the wrong, by alledging to the Capsan heralds the hopes your nation had conceiv'd of overcoming all the habitable lands of Africa: For, besides that your country has no more right than you to make unjust conquests, the dominions of the Capsans themselves became habitable only by the care they had taken to cultivate their grounds, and to separate them by cities, since they were become a civiliz'd people. So that by attempting to destroy them, it was not your fault, if your country did not remain surrounded, as it had been before, either by dens of thieves or frightful desarts: and you have imitated, at least on this occasion, those conquerors, who, in all appearance, would reduce the whole world into one vast desart.

THE beginning of all these errors has been the false idea you have conceiv'd of the character of a hero, when you imagin'd his chief virtue was valour; whereas valour itself is rather a natural and advantageous disposition of the mind and body, than a virtue. We may make, as of several other the like qualities, a good or bad use of it. It is often found in wicked men; and has sometimes made those men bad, who without it would have been good. Valour can alone become laudable and honourable when it is employ'd and directed by a superior virtue. This virtue, in a subject or citizen, is the love of his prince and his country, guided by his obedience alone. In a prince, or the head of a republick, it is the love of his people, heighten'd by the justice he observes with regard even to his neighbours and his enemies. In the hero, to conclude, it is the love of mankind in general, or humanity guided by a zeal founded upon a lively hope of the protection of the gods. So it is this courageous humanity, this zealous love for mankind, which is the chief virtue of a hero. True courage, which, taken in general, is agreeable to every condition, and even to both sexes; but which, apply'd to war, is call'd valour, consists always in facing every danger in the pursuit of our duty. It is this only view of our duty which distinguishes true and virtuous valour from blind fury and unjuſt violence, and which renders heroiſm itſelf reaſonable. But I have been taught that there are two ſorts of duty: one of condition, and the other of inſpiration: The duty of condition regards thoſe, who being neceſſary to their country or families, or who even miſtruſting their capacity, wiſely confine themſelves to perform the common obligations of their condition, preferable in moſt men to all other. The duty of inſpiration is only proper to thoſe whom the gods ſeem to have ſingled out of the common order of men, to lead them to works more ſublime in themſelves, and of more advantage either to their country, or to mankind: and this laſt duty, generally pointed out by the ſingular junctures into which providence puts ſome men, becomes the duty of a hero. To perform it, requires a valour exalted above that of vulgar conquerors; and thus we ſee that the true hero or benefactor of mankind has always been eſteem'd the moſt courageous of men. A heart thus inſpir'd, a man indued with this genuine heroiſm, runs no hazard of ſtopping in the midſt of his courſe; nothing is dangerous to him, but going beyond the bounds of his duty; and his whole attention is to reſiſt every motion of an extravagant valour or magnanimity; that is, which would only tend to his own glory, without turning to the advantage of other men, to whom he has devoted his labours and his life, He knows that ſublime virtue is approv'd, not by works of ſupererogation, but by an entire and perfect accompliſhment of thoſe which his duty requires of him. This duty is as extenſive as the publick good; but then the publick good gives bounds to it, which he will never go beyond. In ſhort, the hero, far from hunting after vain-glory, expoſes himſelf, for the ſervice of his country, or mankind, to the capricious conſtructions and unjuſt judgments of thoſe very men he is ſerving. Uncapable of committing a baſe action, under any pretext of advantage whatſoever, he never ſacrifices that real honour which is inherent in him: but being ſtedfaſt in his undertakings, for the accompliſhing of them, he readily ſacrifices that ſeeming honour which depends upon the tranſitory opinion of envious or miſinform'd perſons. By theſe ſigns, Saphon, the true hero, has been diſtinguiſh'd; and by his example we ought to learn, that thoſe actions which make the leaſt ſhew, are not always the leaſt heroick.

ASSOON as Sethos had finiſh'd this diſcourſe, he turn'd about towards the high-prieſt, who gave him a ſign to return to his ſeat, and then addreſs'd himſelf to the Carthaginian in the following terms: Saphon, ſaid he, the ſame ſpirit which inſpires all the ſervants of our goddeſs, has made this young man ſpeak, as we ourſelves would have ſpoken. The image he has given you of a hero agrees with that of Giſcon, your brother, in the two firſt years of his expedition, And, indeed, in thoſe enemies, who coſt him ſo much labour while he defended your dominions from their inroads, he diſcover'd men who in that quality were worthy of his affection and tender regards; and, in ſerving his country, he imagin'd he might ſerve them too. According to your own teſtimony, he underwent all the labours and dangers which attended this duty of inſpiration: and to perform it, he, from the beginning, expos'd himſelf to diſadvantageous ſuſpicions, which you yourſelf have countenanc'd, and through which your father and your ſenate alone have diſcover'd the truth. But we make a diſtinction between theſe times, and thoſe in which, according to your relation, your brother march'd the Capſan troops into the dominions of Carthage. They had a right of advancing that length to oppoſe your attack, but he had no authority to lead them thither. This laſt circumſtance is the more blameable in him, and eſpecially in the battle with the Carthaginians, in which he commanded in perſon; as he thought it was contrary to his duty to accept of any dignity among the Capſans, and as, in all appearance, he had put them into a condition of defending themſelves. But let me tell you, you ought to reproach yourſelf for the wrong he has done. Unjuſt proceedings

proceedings often perplex virtue itſelf. Your brother's death has been an atonement to the gods for him; and we ſhall concur with you to appeaſe them in your favour.

HOWEVER, notwithſtanding the injuſtice of the motives which engag'd you in the Capſan war, and urg'd you to the murder of your brother; as both have been cover'd with the ſpecious pretext of ſerving your country, your ſenate has wiſely decreed you ſucceſſor to your father. The title of heir to a crown, or other paternal dignities, do not require thoſe refin'd virtues which are inſeparable from a hero: and it is even for the advantage and eaſe of the publick, that ſucceſſions be rather dependant on the order of birth, than on the difficult and often dangerous eſtimate of perſonal merit. Is ſeems even as if your brother yielded up that right of ſucceſſion to you, which he knew he had no pretence to, by leaving Carthage to purſue his heroick deſign of civilizing a barbarous nation. It is your duty, Saphon, to govern your people according to the maxims you have here had a glimpſe of, and rather as a juſt prince than a great commander. This laſt quality, which is glorious in a man of your age, who bears arms for the ſervice of his father, is by far leſs ſuitable to the head of a great republick, who has actually taken upon him the care of his people, and the maintenance of their

laws.

laws. We are not ſo unjuſt, as not to ſet a value upon your ſkill in the art of war; nor do we condemn all your victories. We know that the Nomades, before you conquer'd their country, were as unciviliz'd as the Capſans before your brother's expedition. We even know, that you was careful to preſerve the fertile meadows of Numidia; and that your father, to this day, treats that country as one of his moſt faithful provinces. To conquer nations, who are deſtitute of maſter and laws, in order to make them more happy and more polite than they were before, is allowable. It is even blameleſs to ſubdue people who have a chief, and are ſubjected to laws, when they are unjuſt and irreconcileable enemies to your country, as we have been inform'd the inhabitants of the Mauritania Sitifenſis, which you have very juſtly brought under your yoke, were, with regard to Carthage. All you have hitherto been wanting in, has been to know the true maxims of morality, and how to guide your valour, and the other noble qualities the gods have endued you with. For want of this knowledge and uprightneſs of intention, it has happen'd, that either your actions have been unjuſt, or even thoſe actions which have been good in themſelves, have not been acceptable in the eyes of the gods. We ſhall here put an end to the inſtructions you yourſelf have deſired. Reflect on them in ſilence the remainder of this day. To-

morrow

morrow you ſhall paſs thro' the corporal expiation; and the next day we ſhall offer the expiatory ſacrifice. The Carthaginian would have offer'd ſomething in his own defence; but the officers of the ſecond order, who had the care of his perſon, and who led him away, inform'd him, that he was not allow'd to reply; and that, beſides, it would be ſuperfluous before a tribunal of mediation and grace. As ſoon as he was retir'd, the high-prieſt aſk'd all his companions, if they did not think Sethos had in his diſcourſe fully anſwer'd the three queſtions which had been propos'd to him ſix days before. They all reply'd, he had ſufficiently reſolv'd them; and that, on occaſion of the hiſtory of the Carthaginian and his brother, he had made his anſwer as extenſive and as preciſe as could be requir'd of him. If ſo, ſaid the high-prieſt, we will finiſh the nine days faſt, and invoke the gods, that they will eternally imprint in the mind of this young prince, thoſe maxims which they themſelves have inſpir'd him with: And I believe we may likewiſe diſpenſe our houſe from that ſilence which they muſt otherwiſe have kept three days longer in favour of any other candidate who had not finiſh'd ſo ſoon as this. This ſilence would even be difficult to keep amidſt all the ceremonies of atonement for the Carthaginian. I believe we may admit Sethos to them, becauſe, by the anſwers he has given,

he

he has already merited the privilege of the manifestation. The priests were unanimously of the same opinion.

THE next morning at break of day, the priests of the expiation, attended by several officers of the second order, went to fetch the Carthaginian out of his prison; in which was a door that open'd to the subterranean canal, which the candidates must pass in their trials for the initiation. This door was near the water-fall, above the bars through which the water enter'd into that canal. This door they open'd on the inside for him to go out. Both sides of the water were made light by means of torches, and discover'd to his eyes a frightful preparation of machines, and of people appointed to manage them. On the bank on his side stood a vessel of brass, fill'd with a thickish liquor; and close by the water, a piece of red-hot iron, of the length of the tallest man, and hollow'd out in its breadth, which was about three feet, so that it resembled a long and large pipe cut in half the length-ways: It was supported by iron-feet over a fire of coals, and one end of it was a little sloaping towards the water: An officer of the second order held the end of a rope of about the thickness of a little finger; which crossing the breadth of the canal, was wound round the concave circumference of a very large wheel on the other side: Thro' the

center

center of this wheel went an axle, to which were faſten'd two ſtrong handles to turn it by, and ſeveral men ſtood ready by them to that end. Several prieſts, and ſome initiates, together with Sethos and Orpheus, were ſeated, on the right and on the left, by the ſides of the wheel. As intrepid as Saphon was, he could not forbear aſking the chief prieſt of the expiation, the only prieſt that was with him, what was to be the nature of his puniſhment, that he might prepare for it? The prieſt anſwer'd him, that he had ſome reaſon to call the purifications he was going thro', a puniſhment; but however, that if he could bear the ſimple agitations of his body, and above all, would not ſuffer himſelf to be overcome by a fear (which they ought not to ſuſpect in him) he would come out of them as ſound as he went in. They made him ſwallow ſome drops of a ſtrengthening liquor; after which, they tuck'd up his hair under a cap of incombuſtible linnen: they next ſtript him ſtark-naked, and laid him upon a ſheet on the ground, ſtretch'd out at length: There, he who held the cord ty'd his two wriſts croſs one another, and ſtretching out his arms to their full length, he bound his feet together with the ſame cord, leaving as much rope as was neceſſary to go from the wriſts to the feet, without hurting the natural ſituation of his body. All this was done with a wonderful quickneſs and ſleight of hand, and

without

without giving him the leaſt reaſon of complaint. In this condition ſix men lifted him up, and deſiring him to cloſe his mouth and eyes, plung'd him over head and ears into the braſs veſſel, which was fill'd with a diſſolution of garlick, ſaffron, oil of worms, and other ingredients; which, when mix'd, had the infallible virtue of reſiſting the force of fire *. Theſe officers took care, during the ſhort time they held the patient plung'd in the veſſel, to ſhift their hands continually, that every part of his body might be ting'd with the liquor. Immediately afterwards, they laid him on the bed of red-hot iron: and the property of the ointment was ſuch, that it made the body ſlide rapidly from it, and fall in an inſtant into the water; where were officers naked, ready to receive him, that he might not ſtrike againſt the banks which were ſhelving; and others plung'd in and follow'd him, that he might not touch the bottom. In the mean time, the wheel, to which the rope was faſten'd, turn'd round with a regular motion, to draw the patient over in ſuch a ſpace of time that he might not be ſuffocated by the water. He came out feet foremoſt; and being drawn to the wheel, with his head hanging downwards, he was faſten'd to it by leather ſtraps under his arm-

* Erant ex Ægyptiis qui faciem certis iunctam ſuccis in ahena ferventia citra noxam immergerent. Epiph. ad finem panarii ſeu librorum adv. hæreſes.

pits;

pits; and in this condition the wheel was turn'd three times quite round with him upon it. From this, Orpheus took his idea of the fable of Ixion. He was then loosen'd from the wheel; and being laid on a bed, was carry'd into an upper chamber, where the priests, who were physicians, gave him all sorts of restoratives that might be necessary for the relief of his body or mind. However, he was afterwards carry'd back again into his prison, where he was to lie the following night. By this description we see that the three parts of corporal atonement for criminals, answer'd exactly to the three trials of the purification of the body preparative to the initiation: but there was this difference, that these trials of candidates for the initiation were voluntary; whereas criminals, being always bound, were forc'd by the hands of others to undergo their punishments. There were, indeed, atonements of a more moderate nature for crimes less atrocious than murder.

THE third day, before sun-rise, the preparations for the expiatory sacrifice were begun. I shall not give the particulars of a ceremony, which lasted almost a whole day; I shall only observe, that it consisted of two principal parts, both of which were perform'd in the temple; but the former, with the gates shut. In this it was they undertook to appease Typhon, the mischievous genius or deity, which the Egyptians look'd upon as the instigator of all the crimes of men, and the author of all their evils. From thence Zoroaster, and the sages of Persia, took their evil genius Arimanus, who was always the opposer of Orimasus their universal benefactor; the Greeks, their Apopompean and Apotropean deities in opposition to Jupiter Olympus; and the Latins, their Averrunci, opposites to their assisting Jupiter, (*Jovi juvanti*). In Egypt their custom was, on this occasion, to lead a red bullock (of which colour they suppos'd Typhon to have been) into the hinder part of the sanctuary. The priest, chief of the expiations, laid his hand on the head of the victim, and pronounc'd these words, of which part are related by Herodotus *: "May the guilt of the criminal here present, "with all the unhappy consequences which it "ought justly to draw upon him, his family "and country, pass into this animal, which we "sacrifice to thee, O Typhon! as a representation of the death of him who is the object "of your hatred." In that instant the bullock was knock'd down by a blow between the horns; and the priest having cut his throat, sprinkled the criminal, who was yet cloathed in sackcloth, with his blood. But whereas in other sacrifices, the priests, and even those

* Lib. 2.

who

who made the offering, divided and carry'd away the victim in pieces for food; every part of the expiatory victim was cast out into the fields.

THEY next endeavour'd to appease the manes of the dead. Those who came thither to obtain the expiation, found round about the temple sellers of images of men and women, of ordinary workmanship, and always plac'd upon little pedestals. They were of gold, silver, or brass; and their height from three to twelve inches. They were made use of in this ceremony to represent indifferently the person, or sometimes even the deity offended. The sellers put those who demanded admittance to the expiation in mind to take one in with them, of matter and height proportion'd to their circumstances. Saphon, before he enter'd, had not been wanting to choose one of gold of the largest size; which he was to leave in the temple for a retribution according to custom. The priest having set it before him on a table, to represent Giscon, pronounc'd his encomiums in the name of the guilty, who was always suppos'd to confess the good qualities of the person he had murder'd. In this elogy, which was prepar'd the evening before, and written at length in their ritual, the priest read several particulars of the life of the deceas'd, which he knew by

 other

other means than by the confeſſion of the criminal, and at which he was often aſtoniſh'd. By practices of this kind, manag'd with a great deal of cunning, the prieſts had acquir'd the fame of having ſecret knowledge, and heavenly revelations.

To conclude; they purify'd the air round about the criminal, by means of a ſuffumigation compos'd of ſixteen drugs (a cubick number.) Plutarch has preſerv'd a liſt of them in his treatiſe of Iſis and Oſiris; and the receipt of it is yet found in our diſpenſaries, under the name of Trochiſk of Cyphi *. All this being perform'd, he was put into a bath; at his going out of which, he was cloath'd with the habit he had on when he came into the college. They then preſented as well to him as to the prieſts and initiates, among whom was Sethos, bread and wine; which they eat and drank on the ſpot in ſilence. After this he was conducted thro' the outward paſſages of the ſanctuary into the nave of the church; but he was as yet guarded by officers of the ſecond order. Then the children of the prieſts enter'd, either to wait at the altar, or to perform the chorus's of muſick. The gates of the temple were open'd, and the high-prieſt offer'd, in the front of the

* Marſh. p. 203.

ſanctuary,

ſanctuary, that ſacrifice to the propitious deities, which they call'd pacifick, and in which they offer'd a white lamb.

BEFORE the gates of the temple were open'd, Sethos, who was not yet to be ſeen, was gone up into his ſeat; and after all the ceremony was over, the Carthaginian, (who was to faſt this third day till after ſun-ſet, which was not yet approaching) was led away.

THE moment they all went out of the temple, thro' the end of the ſanctuary, to return to the college, news was brought the high-prieſt, that there was a candidate in the ſubterraneous temple, who without doubt would ſoon appear. The high-prieſt and his companions, who were yet together, plac'd themſelves in order behind the triple ſtatue. Quickly afterwards they heard the noiſe of the wheels inclos'd within the pedeſtal; and the prieſts ſaw a man come out, who was not arm'd with a helmet and cuiraſs, like Saphon, but who otherwiſe had as perfect a reſemblance of him, as could be between two twin-brothers. The high-prieſt congratulating him, as cuſtomary, on his addreſs and valour, ventur'd to call him Giſcon; which ſurpriz'd him extreamly. But having afterwards made him kneel down, and having pronounc'd over him that form of words, in which they call'd him, New Votary of the great goddeſs Iſis; the candidate aroſe, and ſaid, "Venerable prieſts of Memphis, I ſhall not conceal from you either my condition or fortune; and I plainly ſee, by the knowledge you have of my name, it would be to no purpoſe to do it: but I myſelf muſt confeſs, that if you judge of me by the diſadvantageous opinion the world has of me, I am unworthy to be the ſervant of your goddeſs. I am, indeed, Giſcon, that unfortunate Carthaginian, proſcrib'd by my fellow-citizens, and baniſh'd by the Capſans. The firſt make me criminal for commanding an army againſt my country; and the ſecond, for refuſing to bear arms againſt it. The Carthaginians believe my death certain, and look upon it as a puniſhment for a battle I had no concern in; and the Capſans, a vagabond people, of whom I have form'd a republick, already renown'd, have baniſh'd me, as a man who has refus'd to encounter with their greateſt enemies, the Carthaginians." Here the high-prieſt interrupted him, and ſaid, "Giſcon, we already know the greater part of your hiſtory. We have approv'd of the beginning of it, and have condemn'd the concluſion, in the manner we have been inform'd of it: But your innocence is now confirm'd to us by ſeeing you alive. That, however, is not ſufficient: Saphon, your

"brother,

" brother, who is actually in this houſe, and " on whom we have juſt finiſh'd the cere- " monies of atonement, which your ſenate " enjoin'd him to ſeek here for your ſuppos'd " death, muſt be a witneſs of it. By that " we make a conſiderable breach in our rule, " that no candidate is allow'd to diſcourſe " with any prophane perſon, till the courſe " of his exerciſes be finiſh'd. But as it is " the duty of a good man to clear himſelf " as ſoon as poſſible from crimes laid to his " charge, it is ours to facilitate the means of " it. Your brother, in carrying your juſti- " fication before you to Carthage, will carry " at the ſame time his own; and after having " been purify'd here before the gods for his " unjuſt and wicked intention, he will clear " himſelf, in the ſight of your father, your " ſenate, and your people, from the ever " odious name of murderer of his own bro- " ther." The high-prieſt firſt made Giſcon drink the cup of oblivion; and while he was drinking it, pronounc'd the uſual form of words: but he added, that while he was relating to his brother, in their preſence, what he did during the battle; how the perſon who was kill'd inſtead of him came by his armour; and finally, why, when baniſh'd by the Capſans, he came into Egypt; he ſhould be very careful not to make any mention of thoſe firſt trials of the initiation which he had gone thro'; of the opening of the pyramid thro' which he enter'd; or of that of the pedeſtal of the triple ſtatue of Oſiris, Iſis, and Horus, thro' which he now came thither. After which, the high-prieſt made a ſign to have Saphon ſent for.

GISCON had time enough, before his brother came, to tell the high-prieſt, that he had always had an ardent deſire of being made an initiate at Memphis, and to receive of him and his companions thoſe precepts and examples of virtue which made them eſteem'd thro' the whole world; but that ſince his misfortunes, he could hardly pretend to a title ſo honourable, or to burthen a body of men, whoſe reputation was ſo precious, with a man every where regarded as a criminal. However, continu'd he, reflecting at the ſame time, that the gods are the refuge of the unhappy, and that perſecuted innocence finds a ſure ſanctuary in them; What more favourable opportunity could I have of offering myſelf to them, than my exile itſelf? and what more preſſing reaſon to devote myſelf intirely to their ſervice, than the ſtate I was reduc'd to by injuſtice and ingratitude, of being no farther ſerviceable to mankind, unknown, and fearful of being known? I travers'd Ciniphi, Tripolitania, the country of the Naſamones, and the deſarts of Marmorica: In Libya I paſs'd by the temple of Jupiter Ammon, which I ſaluted at a diſtance,

tance, without daring to approach it. I knew at Carthage, and from the very time I firſt aſpir'd to the initiation, that the opening of the pyramid was the way to it, without, however, knowing that it led into this holy temple. But I had heard mention made of the dreadful inſcription at the bottom of the well; and of the perilous purifications of the body, which were previous to the preparations of the mind. I reſolv'd, when I left Capſa, to undergo the danger of the former, without any farther pretence to the latter; or at leaſt, to give a ſincere relation of my name and circumſtances to the holy prieſts, who were to receive me. At my arrival, yeſterday evening, in the borough, neareſt the pyramid, my hoſt, whom I only made acquainted with the deſire I had of viſiting it, made me a preſent of a lamp, which he told me was proper for my deſign. I departed at ſun-riſing; and being about two hours afterwards at the foot of the pyramid, I aſcended it with a reſolution of periſhing, if the diſgrace I labour'd under, with regard to man, was an effect of the wrath of the gods themſelves; and abandoning my juſtification to time, the diſcoverer of all things. But what ſhall I ſay? My indifference, with regard to death, ſtrengthen'd me againſt it, and has led me to you, O moſt holy prieſts of Iſis, ready to ſubmit to the lot you may judge me worthy of upon my own confession. The high-priest answer'd, Giscon, the thoughts of the gods are not conformable to those of men; and we ourselves shall better judge of your past conduct by the account you are going to give of it in the presence of your brother.

UPON that Saphon came in; but it is impossible to express the confusion which arose in his mind, at the first sight of his brother. He was not long in reflecting how he came into the hinder part of the sanctuary, from whence he himself was but just departed: but he now first conceiv'd, that another besides his brother might have worn Carthaginian armour in the battle. Asham'd of his error, which he perceiv'd was very palpable, he had a violent suspicion that the priests themselves had had Giscon with them several days, and made a secret of it to him, to make him undergo the horrible fatigues of the atonement, for a crime of which he had rashly and falsely accus'd himself. He remember'd, at the same time, the instructions he had so lately receiv'd from a master hardly come to man's estate, who had destroy'd the pretended heroism of his exploits, and had shewn him, that valour, his favourite virtue, had till then been in him only a blind and pernicious passion. He saw this brother living, who was pronounc'd a greater hero than himself, even at a time when he was thought dead as a crimi-

criminal. In a word, he found himſelf plung'd into an humiliation, againſt which he could find no remedy in his mind. Happily for him to recover his ſurprize, his brother Giſcon was to ſpeak firſt; and he thus began his diſcourſe:

BROTHER, theſe venerable prieſts enjoin me to appear before your eyes this very moment, to juſtify us both; myſelf for having commanded an army of Capſans againſt the Carthaginians; and you for having imbrued your hands in my blood. However ardently I purſued my deſign of forming the republick of the Capſans, and whatever diligence I us'd to put them into a ſtate of defence againſt the aſſaults of their neighbours; I had declar'd to them, that tho' I was ready to ſacrifice my life for them againſt all their other enemies, I would never take up arms againſt my country. I did not even ſcruple to tell them, that I was only theirs for a time, and that after having executed the deſign I had conceiv'd ſo much to their advantage, as well my perſon as my ſervices were devoted to my father and my country. I had given them this notice in time, to remove any ſuſpicion that might ariſe of my having united them only with a deſign to deliver their whole nation with greater eaſe into the hands of the Carthaginians. Notwithſtanding all this caution I had taken, as ſoon as they were

were advis'd of your march towards Capſa, they gave me to underſtand in their council of war, that they ſhould eſteem me as a coward or a traytor, if I did not take the command of their army againſt you. I anſwer'd, That I forgave theſe their injurious terms, the remains of their former ferocity, but that I was led by maxims ſuperior to theirs; that no human conſtraint ſhould ever make me depart from a reſolution which I had not taken till after having maturely conſulted the laws of juſtice and honour. I even added, that tho' I was oblig'd to them for the confidence they had plac'd in me, in which they were not deceiv'd, if they kept within the bounds they had preſcrib'd them, they acted contrary to common prudence in preſſing me to accept of the command of an army, which I ſhould lead but by force, if I were capable of yielding to their deſires. That thus, all I could adviſe them to, was to inform you by heralds of the equity of their pretenſions, and the injuſtice of your aſſaulting them: But I oblig'd them, for the maintenance of their own ſovereign authority, to enjoin thoſe heralds to ſpeak in their name, and not in mine; and above all, that they ſhould inform you in expreſs terms, that as I had not accepted of any office among them, it would not be with me you were to engage in battle. I know all this was faithfully related to you; and by this you might at leaſt have

have ſuſpected I was not that commander you kill'd. In the mean time the Capſans, full of indignation at your anſwer, immediately nam'd for their general the perſon I had recommended to them as the moſt proper amongſt them for their chief after my retreat, the firſt to whom I had communicated the deſign I had of uniting them, and who had been my chief inſtrument in that undertaking. They moreover ſtript me of my armour, and put it on him, to deceive you, and, againſt my will, to make me liable to the ſuſpicion and appearance of being concern'd in an action in which in reality I had no part. They immediately paſs'd the mountains which ſeparate them from the dominions of Carthage, and they affected to lay waſte on their ſide a greater ſpot of ground than was neceſſary to incloſe their army. The manner of the battle you are better acquainted with than I who was not in it: But the Capſans who, in defending their own country with all the reſolution of a new-form'd republick, had loſt but very few of their people, return'd to their city, where they kept me ſtrictly guarded. There they elected in my preſence, and without conſulting me, a new general; to whom, however, I ſhould have given my vote. After which, they enjoin'd me, by a decree in form, to depart their dominions, without offering me any thanks

thanks for the past, or indeed any other insult for the present.

IT would have been natural for me to return to Carthage; and by shewing myself there, to justify the only thing which could be imputed to me as a crime, during the two years of my absence. But I had been inform'd, as well by your answer to the heralds, as by other means, that you had, as well in your army as throughout the whole nation, cast a blemish upon the enterprize I had just succeeded in, of giving laws and manners to the Capsans. Reason made me first conceive, and experience has confirm'd it to me, that this was the only expedient which would free us from these rovers, who never invaded us but in separate troops, whom 'twas impossible for me to rencounter in their own territories, and from whom we had even nothing to fear, but by their being dispers'd. This thought had long revolv'd in my mind, and the choice our father had left us of our expeditions, when he engag'd to declare him his successor, who should perform the most heroick action, gave me an opportunity of putting it in execution. But having no design to dispute a right, which was yours by birth, I left to you those glorious advantages which you might render our empire by the fame of your arms, and went to seek at a distance an obscure

obscure service, very dangerous in its execution, and very doubtful in its success. I must confess, however, I did not expect you would have imputed to me as a crime an expedition actually accomplish'd to the benefit of our country, and of which it had already gather'd the fruits in the security of its highways, and the tranquillity in its plains. I thought it my duty to let the storm of persecution you had rais'd against me, pass over; and I would not oppose the proscription you had drawn upon me from our senate, tho' chiefly grounded upon the false supposition of my having been in the battle, and of my death; and I very well know my father was, in some measure, persuaded of my innocence; and that the senate had not condemn'd me but with regret. But I am come into Egypt, to lay myself at the feet of these holy priests, as the source of all justice; persuaded, that a decision from this sacred tribunal, will re-establish my blemish'd honour more securely, than an inconsiderate return could have done. I have even no farther desire of returning to Carthage, after what has happen'd; and it shan't be my fault, if I don't end my days in this holy temple.

THE high-priest, then beginning to speak, said; Saphon, before you answer your brother what you may think proper, and that you may have occasion to speak but once, I myself

myself will put a conclusion to his discourse, by telling you, That not only his conduct has been unblameable from the first to the last step of his expedition, but he has fully gain'd the advantage of you in having perform'd the most heroick action. He has, however, no right to the prize your father had set upon it. Whatever motive the wise Zoros may have had, the gods, more prudent and mighty than he, have brought matters to their true period, and have drawn even from the error of your senate, the just sentence they have pronounc'd, by securing to you the succession to your father. Giscon, as you have heard, gives his consent to it; and he could not oppose it, without losing before the gods and men, the glory of those great works he has hitherto perform'd. We don't, however, approve of the resolution he seems to have brought with him hither, of renouncing the service of his country. The gods, who have no need of us, look upon the services we do to men, who are the work of their hands, as the surest mark of our piety towards them; and a perpetual retirement is only commendable in those who never could, or can no longer be of service to other men. It is true, the instructions we may go in search of, or our meditations at different times, and especially under misfortunes, contribute greatly to our perfection, and render us more useful for the future. And thus your brother ought to be thankful

thankful to the gods for the miſchance which has led him hither, to receive the initiation, to which we are going to prepare him: But as ſoon as he is made partaker of it, we ourſelves ſhall ſend him to Carthage, that he may there continue to ſerve his country under your illuſtrious father, during the remainder of his old age; and under you, when you ſhall be inveſted with his dignity.

SAPHON, then lifting up his eyes and his hands to the triple ſtatue, ſaid; Iſis, great goddeſs of the Egyptians, I at laſt yield to your wiſdom. I for ever diſclaim my blind projects, and vain exploits; and am too happy that even my tranſgreſſion has been imaginary. I accept with an entire ſubmiſſion, and a profound gratitude, thoſe inſtructions which I have receiv'd from your holy miniſters, and from the youngeſt of your diſciples. They have all been confirm'd and juſtify'd by every circumſtance of this adventure, which is viſibly a work of divine providence. My dear brother, I am going to prepare the way for your return to Carthage, by the moſt authentick juſtification of your actions which I ſhall be capable of giving. The teſtimony of theſe holy prieſts will be without doubt more reſpected; but it ſhall neither be more faithful, nor ſo ready as mine. The high-prieſt made a ſign to Giſcon to go to his brother; and they embrac'd with

with all imaginable tenderneſs. Saphon was once more led into his apartment; and as the ſetting ſun began to quit the horizon, he there found a handſome but frugal repaſt, and a vaſe fill'd with excellent wine. It was left to his choice, either to go out that evening, or to take his repoſe there in the bed he ſaw prepar'd. But Saphon, after having accepted of the refreſhment ſet before him, and being inform'd that his ſervants attended without, expreſs'd his gratitude in a polite manner to the prieſts who bore him company, and who waited on him to the gate of their college.

WITH regard to Giſcon, as his exerciſes were not to commence till the next day, he was conducted into the ſame apartment Sethos had, till then, poſſeſs'd; but from whence he was that day to remove into thoſe deſtin'd for the initiates, who had always lodgings in the colleges of the prieſts; in which, if they thought fit, they were allow'd to ſpend their days. Antient hiſtory gives us examples of kings, who were initiates; and who having, either by reaſon of their age or infirmities, given up the cares of government to worthy ſucceſſors, had deſired no other retirement.

ALL the initiates were allow'd this firſt evening to ſee the candidate, for whom a great

great entertainment was prepar'd, but none eat with him. The priests, who had carry'd Sethos thither, engag'd him to relate to Giscon all that had pass'd with regard to his brother, and even the part he had had in the instructions which had been given him. This recital inspir'd the Carthaginian with an extraordinary respect for this young prince; who, for his part, had before conceiv'd a very high esteem for this stranger, whose eminent virtue might have done honour to Egypt itself. And thus they cemented those bonds of solid friendship, which will prove of such assistance to Giscon, to deliver him from misfortunes which a fatal passion will plunge him into in the sequel of this history.

BEFORE Sethos was led into the Carthaginian's apartment, they made him break his fast with a regulated quantity of wholsome and succulent food, and a little wine. But as this fast had been of long duration, and the austerity of it had been increasing for near three months, till it came to its extreme; the priests, who were physicians, were to preside at all his meals for the twelve following days, to bring him by degrees to his usual way of living. These twelve days were allotted for the manifestation, the third and last part of the initiation, which was rather a recompence for the exercises that had preceded, than any exercise in itself.

Human curiosity was here fully satisfy'd, by a discovery of the sacred mysteries, and other secrets of the Egyptian priesthood: and in imitation of the greatest travellers upon earth, the initiates, visiting the subterraneous dwellings of Egypt, travell'd, as it were, into another world.

THE first of these twelve days, at the dawn of day, the candidate was led to the triple statue; and being made to kneel before it, the high-priest consecrated him first to Isis; who by the wisdom she had inspir'd him with, had render'd him worthy of being admitted to a revelation of her mysteries: Secondly, to Osiris, the benefactor of mankind; to the service of whom he had, in imitation of his great example, devoted himself: And lastly, to Horus, the god of silence, and of the secret to which he was going to bind himself. They then immediately caus'd him to read the form of a terrifying oath. He swore never to divulge to any prophane person the least of what he was to see in these twelve days, or at any other time, in the subterranean temples of Egypt; submitting himself, if he violated this secret, to the vengeance of all the deities of heaven, earth, and hell; declaring himself, in this case, guilty of death, and subscribing before hand to the execution of this sentence, which they look'd upon as pronounc'd. It is certain, that

that the bare obſervation of their religious ſecrets gave the initiates, as well as the prieſts, a fund of wiſdom and diſcretion, for which they were reverenc'd, and which procur'd them, as well from princes as private perſons, an entire confidence of ſecrets in every kind. They however recommended, not only to initiates, but to young prieſts and officers of the ſecond order, not to affect that reſerv'd air, which ſerves only to excite in others a uſeleſs curioſity, and which, in ſome meaſure, diſcovers the ſecret they are ſolicitous to keep. Thus they accuſtom'd themſelves to a certain affability, which did not give room to the greater part of mankind to ſuſpect they knew more than they ſaid.

THEY then open'd to Sethos the ſubterraneous paſſages, which extended in a ſquare from the ſanctuary of the temple to the pyramid; that is, in length and breadth, about four thouſand paces, and which conſequently correſponded with the ſuperiour temples of ſome little towns dependant on Memphis. But, according to cuſtom, they gave him, as a guide, the laſt admitted Egyptian initiate, who happen'd to be in the houſe; becauſe, in fact, the prieſts, who were in a meaſure reſerv'd even to initiates, ſuffer'd them barely to ſee, but did not explain to them, till after a conſiderable time, the ceremonies or ſecret tranſactions they had ſeen. But the initiate, who conducted him, was allow'd to communicate his conjectures, which generally did not go far.

I MIGHT here properly enough make an invocation like that of poets, who undertake to give a description of hell. That I may be allow'd to reveal those things which I have learnt, and to bring to light what has been done in the bowels of the earth, and under the impenetrable veil of a profound silence. Sethôs was no sooner descended into these subterraneous mansions from the superiour temple, than he was extremely astonish'd to hear the cries of children. Orpheus, who was as much surpriz'd at it as he, since feign'd, That those children that dy'd at the breast, were plac'd at the entrance into hell. But these were the children of the priests, whose mothers were always sent to lie-in in the apartments which were there prepar'd for them. The reason of this practice was, to accustom the constitutions of these children, from the very moment of their birth, to these subterraneous habitations, in which they were to pass a great part of their life. And besides, they would not suffer any sort of noise or disturbance, nor even any paternal frailty to interrupt the priests in their meditations and studies; and they were taught to look upon their children from that instant, as appertaining to the sacerdotal college, and not to them.

them. Hence it was Lycurgus took his plan and motive for the publick education of the Spartans. The Egyptian priestesses suckled their children themselves, if the state of their health allow'd it; or else the wives of the officers of the second order serv'd them for nurses. These apartments the initiate only saw at the door, and for an instant. The priests, who were physicians, were alone permitted to go in, and they directed the oeconomy of them. The women and children were treated with a great deal of indulgence; for tho' the latter were destin'd to employs, some of which were very laborious, the Egyptians believ'd nature must be left to fortify itself, before they exacted any thing from it: but at the age of five years, these children went into the common halls, design'd for the most early instruction of youth, where they had masters who taught them to read and to write the vulgar or prophane letters *. They frequented these halls three years; from whence, however, they return'd every noon and evening to their mothers. Till then, the children of both sexes and orders had their education together, were kept within sight, and even watch'd in the night-time. But at eight years, they were separated according to the two orders; the first of which was, of those who by birth were allotted to the exer-

* Vid. Clem. Alex. Strom. lib. 5.

cises of the mind; and the other of those whose business was the work of their hands. The males were likewise separated from the females, and the sons of the priests one from the other, according to the different studies they were to follow, with a view to the different functions and professions of the sacerdotal families. These differences form'd however but four classes or schools: 1. Sacred or hieroglyphick literature, for those who were to succeed the priests employ'd in publick and private instructions on religion and morality. 2. Jurisprudence; from whence were taken those priests who were counsellors and judges in the cities. 3. Experimental physick, where the priests, who were to practise physick, had their education. And 4. Mathematicks, for those who were to profess any part of them. From that time they were likewise distinguish'd, both boys and girls, by their robes of four different colours, such as the priests wore under their tunicks of fine linnen in the publick exercises of their separate professions, or in the Isiack pomps and processions. These four colours were black for the first class; red for the second; violet for the third, and blue for the fourth. The education of these children was in general very rigid, because they were ty'd down to an extreme regularity, and were to be brought up to the highest perfection. But their masters, who themselves were supervis'd by attentive

tentive superiors, were never more severe one than the other; and the young disciples, knowing upon what principles their founders acted, did not think themselves unhappy.

BESIDES this, there was every day, about noon, a publick school, which they call'd, The School of Language. Even the daughters of the priests, who were kept in a subterranean apartment till the age of sixteen, under the government of the eldest and wisest of the priestesses, frequented these schools. There it was they were taught the rudiments and pronunciation, both simple and declamatory, of the Egyptian tongue. Advancing from year to year, they went thro' every species of eloquence and poetry; and they made the application of them either in the composition of history, or the expounding of the several duties of life, or the description of the human passions. The studies of these young persons were farther diversify'd by their sacred exercises to which they were accustom'd, and in which they were employ'd from that time; the boys alone in the superior temple, and both the boys and girls in the subterraneous; but preferable to every study: those who had a disposition to it, were kept close to musick, even tho' they neglected other exercises for which they had less inclination. It won't be amiss to observe in general, that in consideration of the great numbers of ceremonial or œconomical functions in which the priests were to be employ'd, they oblig'd none to persevere in the sciences but those who were proper for them; and that these were also afterwards more frequently than others dispens'd from their usual assiduities or exterior attendances.

THE period of every one of these schools was of ten years, and they had each ten professors, who succeeded one another, to receive every year those new scholars which were presented, whilst the others prosecuted and finish'd their course. The new initiate spent the first time a quarter of an hour in every one of these schools. They were always very full, because they were only kept in the twelve antient temples, and the priests of the towns dependant upon them, were oblig'd to send their children to the chief temple, that their education might be uniform. But we are not to believe that they were all sent back again to the towns from whence they came, as all the children born at Memphis had not therefore their establishment there. The high-priest and his counsel, wholly attentive to the reputation of the priesthood, plac'd them according to their talents, with a view to the different importance of the temples they were to officiate in, and they were chang'd as occasion requir'd. Memphis had the choice of the whole sacerdotal nome for

religion

religion and the ſciences; but by the ſubterraneous communication, a whole nome was in ſome manner but one ſingle houſe.

HOWEVER, after the age of nine years all the children began, at times, to frequent the upper houſe, to accuſtom themſelves to the exteriour air; on condition, however, that their mothers never ſuffer'd them to be ſeen in their apartments by any women from without, becauſe they were not yet bound by the oath of ſecrecy, and provided there was no candidate in the houſe; for in this caſe they only came thither to aſſiſt at the ſacrifices in the ſanctuary. This had more than once ſurpriz'd Sethos, who, during the time of his preparation, ſaw theſe children go and come, but could not gueſs whence they came, or whither they return'd. To conclude, at the age of eighteen the prieſts marry'd them to their daughters of ſixteen, as they judg'd moſt convenient; and after taking the oath of ſecrecy, to which their wives were likewiſe bound, they were added to the ſacerdotal college, and were lodg'd in the ſuperiour houſes; being however oblig'd to officiate in their turns in the ſubterranean: And then, though they were always oblig'd to follow the deſtiny of their family, and particularly, never to appear abroad but upon that footing; they were allow'd to ſtudy in private the other ſciences,

being

being persuaded that they were all dependant upon one another in some parts, and that there was no possessing any, without having some small tincture of several others. They never spoke, however, publickly, nor even to candidates; nor did they go to court or appear in the world till seven years afterwards; and till they had receiv'd all the instructions necessary to behave themselves in such manner as might be an honour to their body; provided even then, that their superiors judg'd them persons to be confided in.

THE officers of the second order, of whom we must now speak, form'd, with their wives, a numerous body of subaltern ministers, for the ceremonies of religion; domesticks for the priests or priestesses in the superior dwellings, or for their children in the subterraneous; and lastly, of workmen of every kind for their persons, houses and temples. As no stranger came in among them, the inward reparations and ornaments could be made by none but these officers, and the priests wore nothing about them that was the work of prophane hands. The priestesses were always distinguish'd from other women by a tunick of fine linnen, which they wore upon a robe of the colour which shew'd the class their husbands belong'd to. But as they wore above the tunick a mantle of silk of what colour they pleas'd,

embroider'd

embroider'd with gold, and dreſs'd their heads to their own mind, they were as magnificent as the Roman veſtals have ſince been, without ever borrowing any thing from without. Theſe workmen partaking of the ſame principles as their maſters, were generally much more ingenious than thoſe who work'd for the publick. But as they never wrought for any without-doors, their works ſerv'd as models, and excited emulation, without being the objects of envy and jealouſy. All the menachick arts, rang'd in order in theſe ſubterraneous habitations, form'd a long ſeries of curioſities; which Sethos being then oblig'd to take but a ſlight view of, pleas'd himſelf with reſolving to review again frequently. This ſubterranean city, which made two thirds of the whole ſquare, had ſeveral ſtreets, ſome larger, ſome leſs; and even ſquares, all equally illuminated with lamps. Since the firſt conſtruction of theſe dwellings, they had contriv'd to pierce holes in ſeveral places quite thro' to the ſurface of the earth; not, indeed, for the ſake of light, for it wou'd never have been ſufficient, but to receive a wholſome air into habitations fram'd by the prieſts, which the firſt founders never thought of. Theſe openings, which all anſwer'd to ſome of the ſquares underneath, terminated at top in the form of a well, in the court-yards or gardens of ſacerdotal houſes; ſome of which had never been built

built but for that purpose: and they found them, in course of time, very convenient to let down provisions, and to draw up the most unwieldy of their works. There were likewise, for the convenience of men, round about the inward walls, several rows of steps like unto those we have describ'd in the well of the pyramid: but towards the west, the depth was so great, that they could discern the stars at noon-day, and even some of the planets in their greatest northern latitude. And the priests soon took advantage of this appearance, to observe at different hours the motions of the stars and planets to the meridian, throgh the narrow cleft of the lids which they sometimes caus'd to be put over these wells.

As the new initiate employ'd several days in taking this view, he came out to take his meals and his repose, in some of the superior houses which lay most conveniently in his way. The guide had them all given him in writing; and those whom he met, directed them in every place what they had to do.

SETHOS came the fourth day to that place call'd, The Field of Tears *(Lugentes campi.)* It was an oblong, of the breadth of threeacres, and the length of nine, encompass'd by four walks, in which terminated several other of the subterranean passages, and was cover'd cover'd by a very high vault. Here the officers of the second order were punish'd for any crimes committed, according to sentence given by three priests; and by different chastisements in proportion to the heinousness of them. The most common crimes, which were for having certain number of times fail'd in the punctual observance of their different employs, were punish'd by hard and unprofitable labour for a certain number of days or hours. The men, for example, one or more together, roll'd a cylinder of stone, bigger or less, according to their number, up a sort of hill rais'd across the eastern end of the field; and the cylinder rolling down on the other side, they rais'd it to the top again in the same manner till it roll'd back again to the same place from whence it came, and there they begun again. The women drew water from deep wells, to pour it into a canal of flowing water drawn from the canal of the initiation; and which, after having travers'd the chief of the subterraneous walks, border'd the east end of the Field of Tears. Here is easy to discover the origin of the rock of Sisyphus, and of the vessels of the Danaïdes in Orpheus. These men and women were naked to their girdle; but it was their own fault if they receiv'd any corporal punishment: and Sethos was very well pleas'd to find the overseers employ'd in moderating the eagerness of those who were undergoing their penitence.

tence. But faults more heinous were attended with pains really afflicting. Tho' the priests and priestesses were liable to certain kinds of punishments, they were entirely hidden from the eyes of initiates, to preserve the honour of the priesthood; and from the secondary officers, to keep them within the bounds of that respect due to their superiors. This caution was never dispens'd with but in crimes of a scandalous nature, that had disturb'd the order of their house, or were publickly known. For such, they were condemn'd to one or more years of silence, which they were oblig'd to pass under-ground. Sethos saw several priests and priestesses, cloath'd in black, divested of the sacerdotal tunick, walking round the Field of Tears, and hiding their faces, or going into the prison which was on the side of it. There every one had his cell; but they had no conversation but with books, which were not refus'd them. To conclude; in case of violation of the secret, priests, initiates, and secondary officers were condemn'd to a punishment full of horror in its nature, tho' it might be short enough. It was to rip up their bosoms and tear out their hearts; which were given to be devour'd by birds of prey. It was even forbidden the prophane to ask questions of any one whomsoever concerning the secrets of the priesthood; and if by an extraordinary accident they did surprize any, they were under penalty of death, ty'd down to the same secrecy as the priests themselves. But whole ages hardly furnish'd such an example; and it was only upon the idea they gave Orpheus of the punishment of a revealer of their secrets, that he invented that of Prometheus and Tityus: but he took the gigantick length, which he gave to the body of Tityus in his fable, who, according to him, being stretch'd out at length on the ground, cover'd nine acres, from the real length of this field.

SETHOS advancing yet farther, came to an inchanted place call'd, The Elysian Fields. Here we must represent to ourselves a garden of about three quarters of a league in length from north to south, according to the situation of the pyramids, and of eight hundred paces broad from east to west. This breadth began the last third of the whole square, reckoning from the superior temple. Eight large parallel walks, which travers'd at equal distances the whole subterranean city, led to these Elysian fields, and began in some measure the garden, because they were adorn'd on both sides with great vases of flowers or fragrant shrubs. The priests, to embellish their Elysian fields, had employ'd whatever human invention, rais'd upon poetick ideas, could imagine. The light came from above to the whole extent of its superficies: but as it fell to the bottom from the height of one hundred and

and forty feet, it was something weaken'd, and the shadows of the trees, with which this garden was fill'd, weakening it yet more, at full day it seem'd but to enjoy the light of the moon. This situation has, perhaps, given some room for a description of the garden of the Hesperides, so as we read it in Scylax, the geographer. Those minds which have experimented great passions, know how far a light thus allay'd, is proper for gentle dreams. This it was that put Orpheus on giving the Elysian fields a peculiar sun and stars, tho'. they had no other light but from the sun and stars of our world. This immense opening was bounded at top, as the other, in an enclosure intirely wall'd round, which belong'd to the priests. The walls of these Elysian fields, which terminated on the south side in an oval, and were cut off in a strait line by a stately edifice on the north, seem'd to support the heavens on the entablature on the top of them. The oval end appear'd to be a prodigious water-work, which to the eye, deceiv'd by the height and distance of the object, seem'd to proceed out of the clouds; and which, after having form'd several large canals, was lost, like all the waters of these subterranean mansions, in the bowels of the earth: but besides all this, hidden pipes furnish'd water playing out in fountains in the midst of an infinite number of basons. This whole garden was divided into walks, groves,

groves, and labyrinths, adorn'd with excellent ſtatues and fine groupes of braſs, marble and porphyry. The beds of the parterre were long cheſts ſet into the ground, and fill'd with earth brought thither, in which grew not only the moſt beautiful flowers, but other ornamental plants, as myrtles, laurels, and orange-trees. In the middle of this whole ſpot of ground were mark'd out large ſpaces, which ſerv'd as areas or circus's for divers exerciſes of the body; where not only the ſecondary officers, in ſeveral of whoſe functions a great activity was requir'd; but the children of the prieſts, both boys and girls, agreeable to their ſex, were train'd up in them. Their firſt view in this, was to form and render the body active in general, as with other Egyptians. The fruits of this care was to draw a great number of people into their temples, by the exactitude and gracefulneſs with which they perform'd the numerous ceremonies of their religion. And in the common occurrences of life, tho' the prieſts and prieſteſſes were more reſerv'd, and had more modeſty in their behaviour than worldly people, there was obſerv'd a grace and an eaſineſs in their poſture and carriage, which the knowing often took for a model.

BUT they had a reaſon of much greater importance to them, to make their children expert in all thoſe exerciſes which have ſince compos'd the art of ſerious repreſentations among the Greeks and Romans. It was by means of theatrical ſcenes, that the prieſts of the principal temples of Egypt, and eſpecially thoſe of Heliopolis and Memphis, anſwer'd thoſe queſtions which were propos'd to them concerning future and hidden things*. They look'd upon this manner of anſwering as leſs hazardous for them than the deciſive oracles of Butos, or the aſtrological predictions of Thebes, and capable at the ſame time of cauſing more ſurprize in thoſe who conſulted them, and who fancy'd they ſaw the very thing in queſtion. The greater part of the enchantments, related in fabulous hiſtory, were only ſuch plays. Theſe repreſentations were perform'd at Memphis, in that building which form'd the northern extremity of the Elyſian fields; and which, to attract the greater veneration, had the frontiſpiece of a temple. The prieſts of the firſt claſs, or thoſe who apply'd themſelves to ſacred literature, preſided over theſe plays, and their children were train'd up to them; tho' among the other claſſes, they took both prieſts and prieſteſſes who ſeem'd to have the greateſt talent for theſe exerciſes, and

* The grounds of all this may be ſeen in the 11th chapter of Meurſius's Eleuſinia. M. l'Abbe Banier likewiſe gives an explication of the enchantments practis'd in the temples of the antients, which comes up to this. Orig. des fables, tom. 3. p. 168.

they

they employ'd both men and women of the ſecond order to ſerve at them. The prieſts, who were mathematicians, put in practice whatever experience had taught them in the mechanicks, for the probability of the material ſhew, and the motion of the machines introduc'd therein. The opticks were in every part obſerv'd with ſuch nicety, that the ſenſes were faithful while they gave falſe ideas; and the objects themſelves could not have appear'd otherwiſe than their images ſeem'd to do, in the perſpective of their theatre. We muſt likewiſe allow, that as they had no occaſion for an entire amphitheatre, they plac'd the perſon, or few perſons, they were to anſwer to at each time, in ſuch a point of view as was an infallible illuſion to their ſight.

BUT all this was nothing in compariſon to the meaſures which the knowledge they had of the diſpoſitions of the ſoul and body enabled them to take, to prepare their ſpectators for this illuſion. They made them ſometimes wait whole months; and during that time, they endeavour'd to get partly out of them, and partly by other means, thoſe circumſtances which were preliminary to the matter which gave them uneaſineſs; that they might compoſe their verſes, and prepare the decorations of their ſcenes accordingly. They then receiv'd thoſe who conſulted them into the private apartments they had in the temple: And besides the mysterious ceremonies they perform'd before them there with the gates shut, they fed them for several days together with nothing but light food and delicious liquors, in which they mix'd soporiferous potions. At last they took up a great stone towards the bottom of the temple; and there they saw, by the favour of a gloomy and sparing light, an easy slanting passage, by which they were to descend. They were plac'd in a sort of car, which was only open before. The priest, who was chief of the divination, plac'd himself by them; and if they were women, they were accompany'd by a priestess, who was allotted them from the beginning, as a companion and adviser. This car, compleatly mounted upon low wheels, which were hidden, and making no noise, was push'd gently from behind down the easy descent, as if it went of itself, into one of the walks we mention'd above, which, in some measure, began the Elysian fields. The car was first set in motion, and continued in it by officers of the second order, who came, without being seen, out of doors of this subterraneous passage, and who were reliev'd by others from space to space. And thus it went on in an equal motion to the Elysian fields, at the entrance of which they alighted.

THO' this place ſerves for a daily walk to all the ſubterraneous inhabitants, yet when any ſuch perſons were expected, every thing was ſo order'd that they ſaw none but whom, at a diſtance, they took for heroes or heroins, wiſe men and virtuous women. The prieſt and prieſteſs, who did not ſuffer them to be out of their ſight, nam'd the chief of thoſe whom they ſaid had been beneficial to human ſociety, either by their great ſervices, or by wiſe inſtructions, or at leaſt by good examples. They let them ſee at a greater diſtance vaſt crouds of thoſe, who, tho' their virtues had been bury'd in obſcurity, had not been the leſs punctual in the obſervance of them during their lives; nor were they leſs rewarded for them after their death. The light fell equally upon all their faces, they were not, however, to be diſtinguiſh'd. Nearer were thoſe who had ſubdued the greateſt of human paſſions, love and anger; and next to them, thoſe who had only given way to chaſte and lawful love; or who had only follow'd the motives of a juſt anger againſt the wicked, for the benefit of the good, and the advantage even of the wicked themſelves. All theſe poſſeſs'd the bottom of the Elyſian fields, which was the moſt agreeable part. On the ſide of them, in the wings, were thoſe who had done great actions, but had ſuffer'd them to be eclips'd by great and frequent frailties; or who, in the course of their glorious undertakings, had sometimes taken the counsels of their passions for the counsels of virtue. In another part, to conclude, were those whom love had never indeed prompted to commit a crime; but who, by means of this passion, had been render'd supine and backward in the practice of their duty, and for ever averted from the heroick course they had begun to pursue. The same restless spirit which had tortur'd them in their life, but above all, a regret for having in this manner travers'd their fate, follow'd them even in death. In vain the women they had lov'd, represented to them how satisfy'd they ought to be with the fame they had acquir'd: they had not that serenity in their countenances, which is the effect of accomplish'd virtue, and these women turn'd aside to weep. At these sights such persons thought themselves truly transported into the habitations of the other world, and believ'd none to be really alive but the priest and priestesses who accompany'd them.

THEY were next conducted to the theatre, which they were told was the temple of divination. At their entrance, a noble stair-case presented itself to their view; but thro' the steps they perceiv'd, as in a great cavern, flames, which arose from a canal of spirituous and sulphurous waters, which they had set on fire. This canal, tho' but narrow, by an effect of the opticks, seem'd to them a river of flames, of which Orpheus made his Phlegeton. Beyond the flames they saw men and women clad in skins, which fitted so close to their bodies, that they seem'd naked. Frightful figures of the Eumenides or Furies were continually scourging them: the vaults resounded with the reiterated blows, which however not giving any wounds, shew'd they met with bodies capable of sustaining eternal torments. These objects were shewn them as long as was thought proper, according to their character; and they even acquainted them with the causes of these different punishments, such as they generally might apply to themselves. They were at last brought to the front of the theatre, where the priest and priestess always seated themselves by them. There, besides the chorus's, which, with the help of proper musick, represented in as lively, and in a more affecting manner than nature itself, either people or armies, according to the subject, the actors and actresses, by means of imperceptible masks, and other secrets of the Pantomime art, counterfeited the visages and voices of those persons the consulters were concern'd for.

THO' the priests did not give answer to every thing they were consulted about with so much ceremony; and these theatrical representations were in reality not perform'd above twice or thrice in a year; there were, however, every day general preparations or representations of scenes invented on feign'd subjects. The children of the priests regularly attended them. The priests and priestesses who actually officiated below, and even those of the superior mansions, came thither by turns, either to act parts, or to give their advice. Initiates were likewise admitted, and heard: and as they made trials of the effects of their decorations and musick, these rehearsals or proofs of shews were finer than the most finish'd pieces in the world. The Egyptian priests and priestesses had their places assign'd them in the latter, as among the Greeks and Romans since. It was surprizing enough to hear with how much judgment they gave their opinions of them; because even those who had receiv'd answers from them in this manner, believ'd they had seen apparitions, and not representations. I am the shorter in the description of this sacred anecdote, because we shall see an example of it at large in the last book, of which Sethos himself will be the object; but the consultation will be at Heliopolis, where the priests, as we have before hinted, were more expert in divination than those of Memphis.

I SHAN'T, however, quit this subject without removing an objection, which may arise

in

in the minds of our readers, how the priests of Memphis, so enlighten'd, and so punctual in every article of morality, could thus deceive mankind. The key to this mystery is, that they themselves were seduc'd. It was a constant maxim amongst them, that divination was inherent to the priesthood. They prepossess'd their childen with this opinion from their infancy, as they themselves had in like manner receiv'd it from their fathers. Their sacrifices, fastings and scourgings, preparatory to their answers, not in the presence of those who consulted them, but amongst themselves, sufficiently evince this truth. In like manner, all the measures they took besides to get information of facts, their assiduities, as well in their closets as private conferences, to endeavour to foresee future events, by the circumstances of times, places, and persons, were in their minds but so many natural means which they thought themselves oblig'd to make use of, lest they should tempt the gods, and by their temerity draw upon the priesthood the loss of so precious a gift. With an eye to the same precaution it was, that they were more or less precise in their answers, according to the inspirations they believ'd they had receiv'd. They did not, however, attempt to conceal the secret of this practice from their initiates. On the contrary, after having acquainted them with their principle, they were glad to get light from them on

several

ſeveral queſtions they propos'd them, as from men who had more knowledge of the world than they themſelves. As for their preparatives to work thoſe who conſulted them up to an illuſion, or, as they call'd it, an extaſy; they had another view in them, which they look'd upon as very commendable, with reſpect as well to them, as to other perſons to whom they might relate their adventure. It was to inſpire in them a love and fear of the gods; not only by a previous view of the Elyſian fields, and of Tartarus, of which they let them have a glimpſe, but by the great leſſons, either given them in form, or cunningly inſinuated in their ſcenes. Indeed, in courſe of time, when the practice of divination paſs'd into Greece, or as it remain'd in Egypt, the intention of the diviners became exceedingly deprav'd: For, not to mention the palpable cheats of real impoſtors, only deſign'd to trick men of their money, and to corrupt the virtue of the women, the prieſts of ſome temples have had recourſe to magick operations and horrid ſorcery, which they thought a ſurer method to diſcover hidden cauſes than the invocation of the gods, or human and natural enquiries. But, in ſhort, the reſult of all theſe conſiderations taken together, is this, that thoſe of our Grecians who have attributed every kind of divination to deceit, have, in this point, had but a faint knowledge of mankind, and that the prepoſ-

prepossession and enthusiasm of those who pretended to this gift has had a greater part in the error of divination, and has kept it up longer than fraud alone would have been capable of. However, as both these causes give equally place to truth, which becomes more and more manifested, divination loses ground daily; and we may, without being masters of that art, foretell its approaching and entire extinction. On the side of the Elysian fields, advancing towards the pyramids, was the last part of these subterraneous mansions, or the Pantheon of the priests of Memphis: On occasion of which I shall observe, that whole Egypt was call'd, The Pantheon of the Universe. Tho' the whole extent of these subterranean habitations was in general call'd the temple, properly speaking, the pantheon alone deserv'd that name. The entrance to it was thro' several very deep arches, plac'd behind the trees on the west-side of the Elysian fields. The roof of this temple was not extremely high, exceeding only by ten feet the height of the arches, which were of twenty feet: but tho' the breadth was but of forty feet, the length was extraordinary, being equal to that of the Elysian fields, comprehending even the depth of the theatre. Less would not have been sufficient to contain all the deities of Egypt in separate chapels; nor was there a chapel allotted to every one: for the Egyptians ador'd, at least, the thirty thousand deities, of which Hesiod the poet tells us. The sanctuary of this temple was consecrated to Isis, the mother of nature, or nature herself. Her statue was there plac'd upon a pedestal, much the same as Apuleius, in his Metamorphosis, represents this goddess appearing to him in a dream. The foremost chapels on the right and on the left, contain'd each separate the image of one of the chief deities, which by the Romans, to whom Pythagoras brought them out of Egypt, were call'd *Cosentes* or *Selecti*, q. d. counsellors of Jupiter, or chosen for his counsel *.

NEXT to them came the demi-gods, call'd *Semons* or *Medioximi*, half men, or middling deities. The images of these, as many of them as were known by name, were plac'd several together in the succeeding chapels. The last chapels continu'd to the line of the frontispiece of the theatre, and were appropriated to that infinite number of unknown deities, who, according to them, had their habitations neither in heaven nor hell, but were dispers'd in the air, upon the earth, and in the waters. They were represented by general figures, or such of which one serv'd for a whole kind. These idols were plac'd in their several chapels, with their faces all turning towards the bottom of the

* See Kirk, tom. 1. p. 174, 175.

temple, as that of Isis was in the sanctuary: but the bottom of the temple, from the line of the frontispiece of the theatre to the wall at the end; thro' which there was no entrance, was reserv'd for the mischievous gods, otherwise call'd evil genius's. Typhon was represented standing, leaning with his back against the wall, and of the same height; his arms stretch'd out reach'd the walls on the right hand and on the left; near in the same manner as the statue of Serapis, the Pluto of the modern Egyptians, in his temple, which we now see at Alexandria *. But Typhon had the figure of a man only from his head down to his navel; he was represented with flames proceeding out of his eyes and mouth, and from the trunk of his body two enormous dragons, which supply'd the place of thighs and legs †. His fingers were vipers, agreeable to the description which Hesiod gives of Typheus, and Apollodorus of Typhon, which were the same. From the bottom of the temple to the line of the frontispiece of the theatre were twenty chapels on each side, in which were the images of the malign genius's, which, like the figure of Typhon, fac'd the good deities, to shew their opposition to them. The walls and roof of the temple, as well as of the arches on each side, were adorn'd with hieroglyphicks, which contain'd

* See Kirk, tom. 1. pag. 199.
† See his fig. in Kirk, ibid. pag. 211.

the

the hiſtory, as well as an account of the worſhip, of the gods in the pantheon. Here were perform'd every night, from ten till two, ſeveral ſorts of ſacrifices and ceremonies; at which were preſent all the inhabitants of thoſe lower manſions, even the priſoners of the Field of Tears, as well as thoſe who had fail'd in the trials of the initiation, the prieſts and prieſteſſes of the upper houſe, when they would, provided they did not neglect their common functions elſewhere, the greater part of the initiates, and the new initiate and his guide the three laſt days of the manifeſtation.

As theſe nocturnal ceremonies began before the end of the natural day, they firſt offer'd their devotions to thoſe divinities to whom the day was conſecrated. Moſt of them had their peculiar victims; and they even knew the ſeveral ſorts of wood which they were to uſe, either to burn the victim whole, or ſome parts of it *. The wood was ſet on fire, according to the different dignities of the gods; either by the ſun-beams, brought thither by means of a parabolical glaſs, as the ſacred fire of the veſtals, or by the ſparks from a flint ſtruck by a ſteel; or laſtly, by the flames of a lamp. The Greeks

* See for this whole account, Kirk, tom. 1. Syntag. 3. cap. 9. & 10.

and

and Romans adopted these niceties, and carry'd them so far as to observe the difference of fountains from whence they drew the water to extinguish the fire with which the victim was consum'd. As in Egypt they have no other water but that of the Nile, they made use of that only in their sacrifices; but they fetch'd it every day out of the great channel of that river for the use of the pantheon. This, perhaps, gave occasion to those authors whom Diodorus follow'd, to say, that three hundred and twenty priests of Memphis brought every day water out of the Nile the distance of several furlongs.

SOME of these deities had only sacrificing priests, and others none but priestesses. But at midnight the sacrificing priest for the day, follow'd by two lines of priests, came out of the last arch towards the bottom of the temple, on the side of the Elysian fields, and went into the sanctuary to the statue of Isis. They were accompany'd by a great chorus of musick form'd by other priests, priestesses, and even their children of both sexes, and of all ages from nine years upwards. When the sacrificing priest was come to the statue, the two lines of priests stopp'd, and made room for the offering which follow'd to pass betwixt them. And here the truth of the historical fact obliges me to say, that this offering was carry'd by priests daughters, to the number of eighteen, two and two, naked, and having each a basket of fruit, or other presents, according to the season. These girls began this office at thirteen, and continued it till their marriage. The sacrificing priest receiv'd and emptied all these baskets upon a great square altar, on the foot of which was this inscription; which being copy'd from the Egyptian upon a marble, is yet to be seen in a temple of Capua *. *Te, tibi, una, quæ es omnia, Dea Isis.* That is, We offer thee to thyself, thou only and universal deity, goddess Isis. The maidens who brought the offering, retired behind the sanctuary, and the priests went into it, to accomplish the ceremonies, which lasted near two hours, always accompany'd with the sound of voices and instruments. These ceremonies differ'd in the four seasons, as did the hymns, which were the subject of their musick; many of which were afterwards sung in the superior temple, and from thence came into the mouth of every Egyptian, for the beauty of their verses and tunes, which were sometimes heighten'd by novelty.

THESE were the mysteries of Isis; the secrecy of which made them so respected in the flourishing ages of Egypt; and which having been reveal'd during the confusion

* See Kirk, tom. 1. pag. 188.

of

of wars, and the oppreſſion of conquerors, have ſerv'd as an example or pretext for that licentiouſneſs which has ſince ſpread itſelf over the temples of Greece and Italy. By all the memoirs that have come to my hands it plainly appears, that the prieſts and aſſiſtants in antient Egypt never made an ill uſe of what paſs'd before their eyes in the Pantheon. Orpheus has expreſs'd the deſcription they were ty'd down to on this head by the awfulneſs of the place, under the image of Tantalus ſtanding in the midſt of water, but not being able to drink. Lycurgus, carrying his ideas yet farther, ſuppos'd that wiſdom which reign'd in Egypt throughout the whole ſacerdotal order, in which no inſtance has been known of any diſorder ariſing from a paſſion for women, was owing to their ſeeing them in this manner naked every day. And this it was made him eſtabliſh in his republick the luctations or wreſtlings at which the youth of both ſexes perform'd their exerciſes naked in the ſight of the whole world. He ſaid, the Lacedemonian women were deck'd in the circus by the publick modeſty, from what he had heard the prieſts in Egypt ſay, that theirs were deck'd in the Pantheon with religious holineſs. However, a long experience has convinc'd the wiſe of the truth of that ſentence of the old Latin poet Ennius, who ſays, that nakedneſs expos'd to the eyes of the citizens, is the original ſource of all the diſorders of a republick. *Flagitii principium eſt nudare inter cives corpora.* A very faint knowledge of the Greek and Roman hiſtory is ſufficient to give us an idea of that ſhameful exceſs to which the firſt communication of the myſteries of Iſis diſcover'd, carry'd thoſe nations. The Egyptians themſelves, fallen from their priſtine auſterity, had introduc'd into the temples, which they were allow'd to erect out of Egypt, and eſpecially at Rome, ſuch an extravagant licentiouſneſs, that the ſenate made ſeveral decrees to aboliſh thoſe temples they call'd Memphitick. Popular ſuperſtition, ſupported by a habitude rooted in debauchery, had render'd theſe decrees of no effect, till the conſul Paulus Emilius himſelf took an ax, and began the demolition of them. Theſe temples were re-eſtabliſh'd under the dictatorſhip of Sylla, and deſtroy'd again by the conſul C. Calpurnius Piſon *. The emperors, ſucceſſors of Auguſtus, rebuilt them, or pull'd them down, according as they prov'd enemies or fathers of their country; and the vigilance of that moſt holy and pious prince Marcus Aurelius Antoninus, who now governs the world with as much wiſdom as glory, has enough to do to prevent thoſe infamous practices from being reſtor'd every day in ſome part or other.

* See on this ſubject T. Liv. dec. tom. 1. 9.

SETHOS,

SETHOS, to omit nothing, enter'd, after the ſacrifice of the laſt day of the manifeſtation, thro' one of the weſtern porches of the Pantheon into that walk, which ran along the bottoms of the pyramids; and having found the iron grates which bounded it on the northern ſide, he had the ſatisfaction of touching it on the inſide, as he had done without, when he was with Amedes at the bottom of the well of the pyramid. By that, he in ſome manner bore teſtimony to himſelf, that he had happily accompliſh'd the painful and perilous courſe of the initiation. He lay, however, that night, according to cuſtom, in the ſubterranean manſions; while preparation was making againſt the next day for the magnificent proceſſion, which they call'd, The great Iſiack Pomp, or, The Triumph of the Initiate.

THE evening before, ſix officers of the ſecond order appear'd on horſeback before the king's palace, which, as we have already ſaid, was oppoſite to the temple at the other end of the ſquare: and there they proclaim'd by ſound of trumpet, that the next day a new initiate would appear. They afterwards made the ſame proclamation in every ſtreet of the city thro' which the proceſſion was to paſs. They did not mention the initiate's name, but they declar'd him to be an

Egyptian. For with regard to foreign initiates, the proclamation was only made at the gate of the temple; becauſe the proceſſion, which was not near ſo pompous, went only round it. This was always agreeable news to the kings, who believ'd they thereby gain'd a faithful ſervant upon all occaſions. But it was yet a greater joy to the people, who look'd upon the Egyptian initiates as wiſe mediators between the king and them, and as powerful protectors about his perſon. As many years generally paſs'd without their attaining ſo great an advantage, the rarity of it enhanced the value, and inſpired every one with an earneſt deſire to ſee this ceremony. Upon this particular occaſion the diſpoſitions of the court were alter'd. They had then no ſuſpicion there that the new initiate was Sethos. Every one thought him out of Memphis, and ſome even believ'd him out of Egypt: and beſides, conſidering the corruption of manners, and meanneſs of ſentiments in which the greater part of the courtiers were plung'd, they look'd back to the age of fables for thoſe heroick times when kings or ſons of kings were candidates for the initiation. Seſoſtris, who was initiated at Thebes, was the laſt king of Egypt, who had the ambition to aim at this dignity. And thus the queen, in imitation of thoſe mothers who think they have taken great care of their children, when they forbid them all exerciſes

that

that require resolution and courage, did not fail, when she heard the news, to observe to the ladies about her, that if she knew one of her sons should desire to be initiated, she would soon prevent it: and the judicious company was very much dispos'd to applaud her. As for the king, as he did not meddle with the affairs of state, and only employ'd his servants in his amusements; he was very little affected with the merit of the initiation, and propos'd to himself no other satisfaction in it, but the pleasure of seeing this pomp pass under the windows of the palace.

THE whole night was employ'd in adorning the inside of the temple with whatever the priests had most magnificent in their treasury; and the citizens of Memphis prepar'd the streets, and embellish'd the outsides of their houses with their most precious moveables. A little after sun-rising, the temple was open'd to the people, and in the middle of the sanctuary they saw the tabernacle of Isis, which was brought up from the subterranean temple. It was a large coffer, cover'd with a veil of white silk, embroider'd with hieroglyphicks in gold, over which was a black gauze, to signify the secret of the mysteries of the goddess. Before the procession mov'd, they offer'd a sacrifice to her; during which, the daughters of the priests, who never appear'd abroad but on the festivals of Isis, danc'd, by turns, grave dances to the sound of instruments alone. Immediately afterwards the march began towards the city. The six officers, who had proclaim'd the ceremony, went first, sounding their trumpets from time to time; and two lines of guards of the same order march'd on each side of the procession, the whole length of it. Of the four classes of priests, the mathematicians, the physicians, and the lawyers went first, preceded by their children in the same order, and in the same habits as themselves. All the priests wore a black robe under a tunick of fine linnen; but over the tunick, the three first classes of the procession wore robes of blue, violet or red; of which one part cover'd their heads. Between the two lines march'd, one by one, priests, whom they call'd Pastophores: instead of robes, they had cloaks of the colour of their class; and they carry'd the books of Mercury, from whence they borrow'd their sciences *.

AFTER this first part of the procession, came a priest of the first class in a black cloak, who carry'd in both hands the famous Isiack table, resting upon his breast; it was of copper, but border'd and travers'd with plates of silver, upon which were engraven

* Clem. Alex. Strom. lib. 6.

the

the emblems of the mysteries of Isis, represented by the figures of men and women, standing or sitting, and of which some had the heads of beasts *. He was follow'd by the daughters of the priests, clad in tunicks of fine linnen, over robes of the colour of their fathers class, and having over their tunicks a sort of scarfs, each of a different colour, embroider'd with gold, with golden tufts, and fasten'd on their left shoulders with a precious stone. They were dress'd in their hair with tufts of herons feathers, and adorn'd with ear-rings, necklaces of pearls, and bracelets of an inestimable value. They form'd four lines, and went arm by arm, two and two. The priestesses, who were governesses, went in the middle, cloath'd all in black, excepting their tunicks; and on the sides of these extraordinary beauties, which were but seldom seen, the guards were doubled. By the bare description of Apuleius, we find that even other women, who were initiated to Isis, since the devastation of Egypt, have taken the place of these damsels in such sorts of processions, at which even the other priestesses did not assist before. After these damsels, came a very great choir of musick, compos'd of priests and their children, who proclaim'd the approach of the tabernacle of Isis. It

* See Kirk. about this table; OEd. Ægypt. tom. 4. pag. 80. & seq: and the Ant. of F. Montfaucon, vol. 2, part 2. page 331.

was carry'd on the shoulders of eight priests: but immediately preceding it, went maidens of the second order, clad in habits of white woollen, very fine, and adorn'd with flowers, who having citerns and tabors in their hands, danc'd before the tabernacle a sort of light dances; the imitation of which the Greeks have carry'd too far in their Orgies. Others of these maidens, who went on each side, burnt perfumes; the smoke of which surrounding the tabernacle, it seem'd to be always in a cloud. The high-priest walk'd alone after the tabernacle. He was cloath'd in white under his tunick; and over it with a purple robe lin'd with ermin; the train of which was carry'd by two children of the second order. He had a sort of mitre on, peculiar to him alone, and he only had the augural staff, which all other priests bore in his absence. He was follow'd by the priests of the first class, or interpreters of the sacred literature, whose books were likewise carry'd by Pastophores. Two among them carry'd a pole on their shoulders, upon which was plac'd the augural or divinitory urn; it was cover'd by an astrolable, a quadrant and a compass. For tho' astrology was more in use at Thebes than in the other temples, astronomical instruments were every where the symbols of divination. All the priests of this class were cloath'd, under and above their white tunicks, in black. The antientest went

went nearest the tabernacle. So, contrary to the order of the three first classes, they were follow'd by their children, the two lines of which were clos'd by the four prefects of education. Here, properly speaking, the Isiack pomp ended. It was seen upon other occasions, but had never been so numerous, and so magnificent as on this.

THE last part of the procession, or the triumph of the initiate, had a military appearance, even with regard to those who were not warriors; because it was suppos'd, that they defended their country in their way; and besides, the initiates were indifferently of every profession for the service of the king and of the publick. At the head of the second interval, appear'd, under the sound of fifes and kettle-drums, three standards flying. The first bore the symbol of the kingdom of Memphis, which was the Ox Apis; the second that of Egypt, which was a sphynx; and third that of the whole world, which was a serpent, biting his tail, in the form of a circle This was to signify the order according to which the initiate devoted himself to the service of mankind. The initiates appear'd next; they were but few in number in every nome: and those who had any employs, either in war, or in the provinces, did not quit them to be at this ceremony. However, if there were any initiates of another

ther nome, they had their places here according to the order of their reception, for all the initiates of Egypt made but one body. They march'd one by one in their usual habits, that is, in a vest of fine linnen which reach'd but to their knees, and which they never went without; and over their vest was the robe of their dignity or function: on the side of them, and out of the rank, went the foreign Initiates, if there were any in Egypt: and thus it was that Orpheus assisted at the triumph of Sethos. According to this order it often happen'd that generals and even princes, who were younger in the initiation, gave place to mere citizens.

At last appear'd the new initiate, having at his right-hand the youngest of the priests, and at his left the eldest of the initiates. For this first day he was cloathed only in a white tunick, with a train trailing after him of the length of his body: Over it he had a shoulder-belt, white border'd with black, at which hung a sword; the hilt of which was only of steel: instead of a girdle, he had a fire-colour'd scarf, embroider'd with gold: He had a chaplet of myrtle on his head, and in his hand he held a large branch of palm, as the symbol of peace: His head was cover'd with a white veil, which fell over his face and breast, thro' which he could see enough to walk by; but which hinder'd every body from

from knowing him. Behind him follow'd a triumphal chariot, drawn by four horses in front. Four virtues held a triumphal crown over the empty seat; and images of the vices enslav'd, border'd all the circumference of the footboard. This chariot was, excepting some symbols, like to that in which generals made their entries into the chief cities of Egypt, at their return from any signal victory. But the initiate never went into his; to shew that he did not aspire even to those exterior honours which his great actions might merit. In this ceremony the initiate had at all times been receiv'd with great acclamations of the people. But the extravagance and injustice of Daluca's administration, made the hopes of some relief of yet greater concern to all the inhabitants of Memphis. Flowers and sweet essences were scatter'd in abundance on the initiate from the windows and streets. No musick was ever so affecting as the concert of benedictions they bestow'd upon him. It was for this reason, though the joy had been less at other times, that the initiate always went veil'd; that he might apply no part of these transports of publick affection to himself, and that he might, on the contrary, suppose they were only due to the high esteem had for a body, whose examples he was hereby taught to follow, and whose glory he was encourag'd to maintain.

SETHOS, after having in this manner made a circuit of a great part of the city, came to the ſquare, in which was the king's palace. The king, the queen, and a croud of courtiers waited their coming, in a long balcony, adorn'd with rich tapeſtry. Oſoroth, who by nature was good, ſeem'd to take part in theſe rejoicings, as the acclamations proclaim'd their approach. As far as he could ſee the laſt diviſion of this pomp, and above all, when he diſcover'd the head of the initiate, which was at leaſt equal to the talleſt, he felt a ſoft commotion, which immediately rais'd in the queen, who was an enemy to all good, a very lively jealouſy: But her confuſion was ſenſibly increas'd, when the initiate aſcended a high ſcaffold, erected according to cuſtom, before the balcony of the palace. Here he kneel'd down on a cuſhion, and made a profound reverence to the king. Then riſing, he drew his ſword, as offering it for his ſervice. At this action, which the young prince perform'd with a wonderful grandeur and noble air, Oſoroth, almoſt with tears in his eyes, ſtoop'd, and ſtretch'd out his arms as to embrace this initiate. He then turn'd to the right and to the left, to inſpire every one with that tender admiration with which he himſelf was pierc'd. The people, encourag'd by this example, vented thouſands of joyful accla-

mations

mations addreſs'd to the king. They wiſh'd him to be their maſter, and to continue ſo during a long courſe of life. At the ſame time they fix'd their eyes upon the queen in a manner, which tho' no otherwiſe inſulting, than in their ſecret intentions, ſhe however perfectly comprehended. This lady, who, in compliance to the king, was oblig'd to conceal that real rage, which gnawed her very ſoul, under a forc'd ſmile, was for a long time the object, not only of the people, but even of the courtiers, who deteſted her, tho' they were become her ſlaves. But her diſorder was yet infinitely greater, when the initiate was gone down from the ſcaffold, and return'd to the temple, holding in one hand his naked ſword, and in the other his branch of palm croſſing one another. For the king took this occaſion to aſk the queen after his ſon, who, he ſaid, had the ſame ſhape and gaite as the initiate. He added, that he wiſh'd it had been Sethos, and that he ſhould think it a happineſs in his old age to have a ſon who might deſerve ſo great an honour. The queen, who was confirm'd in her belief of Sethos being abſent, becauſe ſhe did not ſee Amedes among the initiates, inform'd the king of the journey for which Sethos and Amedes had deſir'd leave three months before. The king took it ill ſhe had not acquainted him with it. He even ſaid, if ſhe

she had inform'd him of it, he should not have been so long absent, but have been back again time enough to have seen a triumph which would have stirr'd up his emulation. But the hour of Osoroth's conversion was not yet come, and he had more violent shocks than that to suffer before he could be awak'd out of his lethargy; or rather, the present object, which always affected this prince, soon gave way to other impressions.

IN the mean time the initiate being enter'd into the temple, ascended a very high throne. The uppermost step was large enough to hold three or four people together. Two officers of the second order follow'd him thither, and drew two large curtains before them. While certain hymns were singing below, which explain'd, in the nature of a prophecy, those benefits which might be expected from an initiate of illustrious birth, Sethos put on his common habit over his white vest; and in about half an hour, the curtains being drawn away, discover'd him to the people, with which the temple was crouded. The acclamations were doubled at the sight of him, and the news was instantly carry'd to the king. The queen, who was present, was cast into an excess of despair, which she was oblig'd then to dissemble,
but

but which will ſoon produce very fatal effects. In the mean time they had further information, that Sethos was to ſtay the remainder of the day and the enſuing night in the college of the prieſts; where there were to be great rejoicings on account of his reception.

THE

THE

LIFE

OF

SETHOS.

BOOK V.

THE next morning Sethos and Amedes went to the palace to the king's levee. Oſoroth, in the preſence of ſeveral of the grandees who were in his apartments, receiv'd his ſon with open arms. He thank'd Amedes for having procur'd him the advantage of the initiation; and he told the young prince, that the war which the kings of Thebes and This had but then jointly declar'd againſt the kingdom of Memphis, would

would ſoon give him an opportunity of employing his ſword, which he had devoted to his ſervice at the ceremony of the foregoing day. After a converſation which ran wholly upon general topicks, the king ſeeming inclin'd to be alone, Sethos retir'd. He was follow'd by the courtiers, who thought things would ſoon take another turn at court, and that Sethos would have a great ſhare in the diſtribution of military employs.

The queen in the mean time had form'd a new plan of politicks, which ſhe propos'd to follow. Her chief aim, to which every thing was to be ſubſervient, was the deſtruction of Sethos; and the diſpoſition towards a war, which, 'till then, ſhe had been diſquieted at, was thought of ſervice for the execution of her deſign. Among other things, ſhe reſolv'd to let the return of the king's inclination to his ſon take its free courſe, and particularly not to interrupt the general tendency of the court, and of every order of the kingdom to court the favour of Sethos. This trial laſted about a fortnight, during which time, however, ſhe carefully kept on her ſide the ſecrets of the ſtate, and the key of the treaſures deſtin'd for the expence of the war. None of the officers of the army were yet named. At the expiration of this term, ſhe pitch'd upon a moment ſhe thought the moſt favourable to

 ſucceed

ſucceed in a private conference ſhe had deſir'd with the king.

My lord, ſaid ſhe, you have had time to make trial of the conſequences which may attend the too ſignal marks of confidence in a king to his ſon, the heir to his crown, to whom a whole kingdom adheres, as their future and undoubted maſter. You already ſee the court of prince Sethos more frequented than your own; and the people, flatter'd only with the hopes of his reign, ſhew a more fervent affection for him, than you perhaps found in them for your own perſon when you firſt aſcended the throne. It is in vain we pretend to diſpute this privilege to youth, if we once ſuffer them to take advantage of it. But I dare affirm, that the art of government preſcribes very different maxims. Witneſs, my lord, your royal father, who poſſeſs'd this art to a degree beyond any of his predeceſſors. You know in what manner the great Seſonchis behav'd with regard to you; I won't ſay to the age of ſixteen, which is that of the prince your ſon, but to the age of fifty, at which your reign began. During ſo long a guardianſhip he never imparted any of his deſigns to you; and twice or thrice when he, at your ſollicitation, ſuffer'd you to give proofs of your valour in war, it was barely in the character of a voluntier; and he always named

named his generals to his own mind, even for thofe expeditions in which you ferv'd in perfon. In the mean time you never afpir'd, without his knowledge, to titles eminent and proper to win and feduce the people, fuch as is that of an initiate. I don't, however, impute to the young prince a defign which is far above the reach of his age, and which fhews us in him an example of an initiate of fixteen years, not to be parallell'd in our hiftories. The only author of this project is Amedes, a man of a dangerous virtue, who leaves no ftone unturn'd to be reinftated in the miniftry, in order to weaken that fovereign authority in you, which I exercife in your name. I know it is through his intrigues that the king of This, who had not before joyn'd the king of Thebes, has taken up arms againft you. The latter is only induc'd to war by an ancient jealoufy of the kings of Thebes againft the kings of Memphis, and he makes no other demands but that of fome places which he pretends belong to his frontiers. But the king of This, as brother to the late queen Nephte, and uncle to prince Sethos, prefumes to concern himfelf with the affairs of your ftate. Under the colour of the chimerical defigns he imputes to me, he has the affurance, at the inftigation of Amedes, to demand of you, that a greater regard than hitherto be had to the young prince at Memphis, during your life-time. It is my duty, my lord, to inform you of these conspiracies, which are forming, as well within as out of your dominions, against your sovereign power. It is your fault if they be not stifled in their birth; but I can't go about it effectually without your approbation.

THE king, who seem'd himself to have acquir'd a greatness of soul and a more elevated mind upon the initiation of his son, answer'd Daluca: That he approv'd her care for whatever concern'd the authority of his government: But at the bottom, added he, in the disposition the late king, my father, left the minds of his subjects, I find I have power sufficient, and all that is wanting is a due management of it for the good of my kingdom, and the security of my people. Besides, added he, the universal and constant testimony of all men, and even of all my predecessors, won't suffer me to entertain any mistrust of the initiates. Sesonchis himself, whose example you alledge, and who understood mankind better than any prince in the world, made use of Amedes, during the whole course of his reign, in the most secret and difficult occurrences, and seem'd always perfectly satisfy'd with his conduct. Amedes always declining the office of prime minister has been the only reason why I burthen'd the late queen and you

you with the weight of this office. In effect Osoroth, judging of others by himself, and only reflecting upon the cares and fatigues of the administration, did not so much as think what might be, at least for persons of a certain rank, an object of desire and ambition. You may remember, continued he, that at your entrance upon the administration I advis'd you to Amedes as an assistant, and I should advise you to it with more earnestness at this time, when the cares of an approaching war seem to me more perplexing to a person of your sex; but that I would not have Amedes be absent from my son in the first campaign he is going to make. I don't propose, however, to give my son, for his first trial, the command of my troops. On the contrary, Amedes shall make him pass thro' every degree of military service, and the prince shall begin by obeying those, over whom he will soon command. I therefore expect you give me a list of the chief officers who are to serve in this war, and especially the name of him you design for general: for it is time we go to meet the enemy. Daluca answer'd; That tho' she herself had continued to provide for the frontiers, she, as well as the whole court, had believ'd, for a fortnight past, that the king, in conjunction with Sethos, would make choice of proper commanders. But, as it was not so, she would the next morning bring him a liſt of the general officers for his approbation, and that then they ſhould depart without delay.

THE queen had at that time the liſt about her, with a deſign of ſhewing it to the king at the concluſion of this conference. But this prince had by his anſwers put her ſo far beſides her meaſures, and ſeem'd ſo little ſenſible of the fears ſhe thought to ſurprize him with, and ſo eaſy with regard to thoſe ſhe intended to render ſuſpected, that ſhe had not the courage at that time to offer him a liſt of men according to the humour of her new-modell'd court, and conſequently without virtue or merit. The old officers, who were yet living, were not indeed remov'd, but all the vacancies were fill'd up with young men, who were the moſt devoted to thoſe ladies who had taken them off from their military exerciſes, or at leaſt who had made them return, as ſoon as it was in their power, from thoſe expeditions of little moment, which had offer'd ſince Daluca's adminiſtration. The general ſhe had nominated was a man of thirty years of age, more fitting to diſtinguiſh himſelf in war by his pride and preſumption, than by his prudence and valour. Full of ambition, which wanted virtue for its ſupport, he ſought more the envy than the eſteem of other men, and being a ſlave to Daluca, ſet as great a value upon her ſpirit of intrigue, as her quality of a queen. The difficulty was to make him acceptable to the king in the new circumſtance of the change which ſeem'd to appear in him, and above all of the concern he had to take to place his ſon in an army made up of good troops and experienc'd commanders. However, ſhe was under an abſolute neceſſity of having a general of this character to impart her deſigns to: She employ'd the night following to fortify herſelf with reſolution and aſſurance to employ her utmoſt influence to get this general confirm'd. She knew very well, that by this choice ſhe put the affairs of the kingdom in ſome danger: but ſhe argu'd within herſelf, that being rid of Sethos, and remaining mother to the ſecond ſucceſſor to the throne, every thing would turn in her favour.

THE next morning ſhe accoſted the king with her table-book in her hand: My lord, ſaid ſhe, I have taken care to preſerve thoſe officers who have gain'd the greateſt reputation in the ſervice of the late king your father, in their ſeveral ſtations. You may, perhaps, think the general I have nam'd ſomething young; but, not to mention his other qualities, what I eſteem the moſt in him, and what the late king ſought the moſt in all his generals, is his aſſiduous and conſtant dependance upon the orders of the court. You, my lord, without ſtirring out of your cloſet, ought to be, like the great Seſonchis, the real and only commander of your armies. Your officers of war have no other intereſt but to give proofs of their valour, and to obtain teſtimonies of their zeal and ſervice: but you alone know how far your army is to be hazarded, and your enemy to be purſued. I therefore think it my duty to propoſe a general to you who will be led by your views, and who has no other motives than thoſe you ſhall give him. If this caution be at all times neceſſary, it is by ſo much the more ſo in a war to which you ſend a ſon, whoſe preſervation is, without doubt, your chief care. In my opinion, thoſe men are not to be entruſted with youth, who by being accuſtom'd to danger, are not apprehenſive of it, who take no counſel but of their valour, and wait for no order but opportunity. The king, being become ſomewhat haughty with regard to Daluca, interrupted her, by ſaying, that with ſuch a preamble ſhe might recommend to him the meaneſt ſoldier in the army. That in the mean time he knew that experience, valour, and ſometimes even the temerity of a general was the real ſecurity of an army. But to conclude, added he, let us ſee the choice you have made. The king, as ſoon as he had caſt his eyes upon the

the name of this perſon, who was called Thoris, ſaid to the queen; Madam, I am very apprehenſive that the zeal of my ancient officers will very much abate, when they find themſelves oblig'd to ſerve under a general yet more inferior to the greater part of them in birth and merit, than in age. But it is at your riſque he is going to the field. I give up this firſt campaign, which, in my judgment, will hardly be deciſive, to your miniſtry. The ſucceſs will ſhew you whether your eaſe and happineſs depend upon your own counſels and adminiſtration; or whether you ought not to put as well your own intereſt, as that of the ſtate, into other hands. As for my ſon, he ſhall have no other commander but Amedes, who himſelf ſhall have none; and they ſhall join ſuch bodies of troops as they ſhall chuſe, on ſuch occaſions, and for the time they ſhall judge expedient.

OSOROTH had hitherto experienc'd only ſuch wars as were without danger, and tended only to enlarge or leſſen the frontiers a few leagues, and which, never ſhaking the fate of a kingdom, ſeem only carry'd on to keep the officers and ſoldiers in action. So he thought he might very well entruſt the queen with the management of this, and that he had ſufficiently provided for the ſafety of his ſon, by exempting him from the

the commands of a general he had no good opinion of. He thereby fell into the error of thoſe who don't prevent diſtant evils, imagining that they know the juſt extent of them, and can ſet bounds to them at will. The queen therefore, finding ſhe had the power, at leaſt once more, to purſue her own meaſures, made this her indiſcreet choice publick. All well-wiſhers to the ſtate were uneaſy at it; but it was an alleviation to their ſorrow, when they foreſaw, that, at the expence of ſome batallions or forts, bad ſucceſs, more powerful than men, or even princes, would neceſſarily bring on Daluca's fall.

THE new general, notwithſtanding the troops march'd with all poſſible diligence, had time to make the ſtreets and houſes of Memphis ring with his pride and joy. His litter, borne by ſlaves in accoutrements of war, carry'd an air of triumph; he ſtil'd himſelf a Hero; and he told every one in expreſs terms, that the dignity conferr'd on him did not ſo much affect him, as the obliging manner in which it was done. The queen, indeed, that he might be the more ſenſible of the value of his employ, had not at firſt given him the uneaſineſs ſhe herſelf had gone thro', when ſhe propos'd him to the king. But the evening before his departure ſhe took him in private, and told him

him what repugnance the king had ſhewn on his account. He talk'd of you, ſaid ſhe, as if he had been inſpir'd by Amedes, Sethos, and the whole body of the initiates. Their principles are ſo differing from ours, that we ought not to wonder if they are our enemies, as we are theirs. My influence, however, has obtain'd your nomination, but you are not to ſuppoſe it ſo advantageous as it ſeem'd to be when I firſt laid the deſign. That was in the abſence of Sethos, when there was ſome appearance, that he, ſeeing me queen with an unbounded authority, and fearing that his younger brothers were preferr'd to him in his father's favour, had choſen to retreat out of Egypt, or was gone in ſearch of adventures in foreign countries. Then you would have had the command of armies for your life, and my eldeſt ſon, who is but ſeven years of age, educated in my ſight, and with my views, would have confirm'd you in that command during the whole courſe of his reign. The caſe is now very different. I don't mean becauſe the king has exempted Sethos and Amedes from your command, and left them the choice of what troops they ſhall think fit to join with, and of the enterprizes they ſhall judge expedient to engage in. This exemption is at leaſt ſo far to your advantage, that you are not anſwerable for the hazards they will expoſe themſelves

ſelves to. But what I plainly perceive to your diſadvantage, is, that immediately after the trial of this firſt campaign, the king will give the command of his troops to prince Sethos. If this ſhould happen, you will neceſſarily, by reaſon of your age, be degraded to the meaneſt poſts in the army, from which I have with pleaſure rais'd you. Don't ſo much as hope that I will employ my credit for your ſupport. As ſoon as Sethos is at the head of the army, I ſhall diſengage myſelf from a miniſtry divided in itſelf. The loſs won't be great to me: I ſhall remain queen, and the mother of two of the king's children; but I lament the lot of thoſe whoſe fortune is dependant on mine, and whom, however, I ſhall then ſtrictly reſolve to abandon.

THORIS, after having been a while ſilent, ſaid, Madam, what you do me the honour to tell me, opens my eyes. Your goodneſs in concerning yourſelf for my intereſt, teaches me, that it is my duty to be thoughtful of yours, which is inſeparable from that of the ſtate. Your adminiſtration has reſtor'd it to all the glory it ſhone with under the great Seſonchis; and it ſhall be a law to me to undertake whatever can ſecure to you that authority you are ſo juſt in the adminiſtration of. In vain our two greateſt enemies are exempt from the general command of of the army. If a profound reflection can furnish any expedient; if a continual attention can enable me to lay hold of some of those opportunities, the seeming hazard of which will remove all suspicion, I hope to make myself worthy of your choice. The good or bad disposal of things, a victory or the loss of a battle, the obedience or disobedience of your particular commands, may be of equal service to you. Say no more, reply'd the queen, remember only, that, in bold enterprizes, delay is generally more dangerous than a ready execution; and go with me to take leave of the king this instant. The king, at the first sight of this officer, only turning his head towards him, inform'd him, that he had exempted his son and Amedes from the command he was going to exercise over his troops. He added, that it was the queen who employ'd him, and that he wish'd he might answer the choice she had made of him. After which, continuing his discourse to the ancient officers who were about him, he told them, that after this campaign they would have the pleasure of serving under his son only. Upon this cold reception, the queen retiring into her closet, order'd Thoris to follow her, as if to give him his last instructions. There, laying aside all disguise in their discourse, they form'd the black design, which the approaching campaign was to furnish

the

the means to, and at the ſame time to conceal.

THE general rendezvous for the troops was in the neighbourhood of Coptos, a conqueſt of the late king's, which the enemy then threaten'd with a ſiege. This city was actually in the ancient diviſion of the kings of Thebes. It was even become, by their care and labours, one of the greateſt tradeing cities of Egypt. For they had caus'd a great road to be made, with inns at proper diſtances, from Coptos, croſs the ſands of the Egyptian Arabia, to that maritime city of the Arabian gulph, to which Ptolemy Philadelphus, after having embelliſh'd it, gave the name of his mother Berenice. From Memphis to Thebes, a diſtance of above one hundred leagues, there were an hundred ſtages or ſtables, of which Diodorus makes mention, each for two hundred horſes, to diſpatch the king's orders, and likewiſe for the convenience of travellers. But the temples, palaces, ſepulchres of all ſorts, coloſſal ſtatues and obeliſks, which appear'd to view, upon leaving the Panopolitan Nome to enter the Coptite, were of themſelves ſufficient evidences, that the latter, of which Coptos was the capital, had time out of mind been a province of the Dynaſty of Thebes. As magnificent as all the kings of Egypt had been in the publick monu-

ments

ments they had erected in different parts of their kingdoms; none of all the other kings, not excepting even those of Memphis, had near come up to the kings of Thebes in this regard. The great number of quarries, of stones, marble, and porphyry, of which the Upper Egypt is full towards the south, had furnish'd them with materials, and their immense riches had enabled them to make use of them. The nearer Thebes, the more numerous were these surprizing objects; which form'd on every side of this famous capital, since call'd Diospolis, avenues so stately, tho' seen at a great distance, that many have confounded them with the city itself. Thence it was that some have reckon'd Thebes four hundred and twenty furlongs, or seventeen leagues and an half long*, while others reckon but fourscore furlongs, or three leagues and one third †, which was the real length of the city, properly so call'd. From this same confusion other authors have said, that that part of Thebes, which was built on the east of the river, was extended very far on that side into the Egyptian Arabia, continued on the west of the river by the division of the Memnonium, and stretch'd towards the south to Syena under the tropick, which is near at forty leagues distance. This it was, in short,

* Cato, apud Stephanum. † Strabo l. 17.

that

that made Homer call Thebes, the city with a hundred gates; a determin'd number which only signifies a great many, as Diodorus remarks. Another error into which the real bigness of this city has made some Greek authors fall, and which has more regard to our present subject, a war between Thebes and Memphis, is the number of fighting men Thebes could send into the field. They have been made to amount to a million *. But this number denotes either the inhabitants of Thebes, comprehending even the women; or the body of all the soldiers of the whole kingdom, their sons included. We find in some memoirs which were known to Pliny †, that the king could range three hundred thousand men in the subterraneous passages of Thebes, which belong'd to him, not to mention those appertaining to the priests, and march them out of the city without the knowledge of the citizens. That was, without doubt, the state of the militia of Thebes alone. Mephres, who reign'd there at the time we are now speaking of, propos'd to invest Coptos with two hundred thousand men, and to have another body of one hundred thousand men, under his own command, to cover the siege. But out of an air of magnificence, which the kings of Thebes, as ancient con-

* Strabo l. 17. † L. 36. tom. 2. p. 375. Ed. Hard.

quetors of nations, had always affected, Mephres had in his army foreign troops of western Arabians, and Troglodyte Ethiopians, which he himself had brought under his yoke; but to whom he had left their customs and accoutrements of war.

THE queen of Memphis, on her part, having furnish'd the city with ammunition and provision, and plac'd a garrison of thirty thousand men in it, which was as many as the circumstances of the place requir'd, march'd likewise a defensive army of one hundred thousand men, commanded by Thoris. Amedes rejoic'd that there was a siege to be sustain'd in this first expedition of Sethos; because, having resolv'd to shut himself up with him in the city, the governor of which was a man of valour, and his friend, he thereby plac'd the prince out of the reach of his secret enemies. Before they left Memphis he advis'd him to put the casket, which the late queen, his mother, had given him at her death, into the hands of the priests; because the fate of man, especially when going to war, being uncertain, he would at least be sure, if he return'd, and whenever he return'd, of finding this resource, or the priests would employ the treasures of it in such a manner as he should direct them, in whatever part of the world he might be. This being done, Sethos departed with his governor three or four days after Thoris. But as Amedes would not extend the privilege of the young prince beyond the bounds the king had ſet, he carefully avoided whatever might have the appearance of a command. So Sethos was accompany'd only by Amedes, and the eight young lords his companions, who had deſir'd leave to ſerve with him as voluntiers. They had each their ſlave. Sethos had one whoſe name was Aſares, an Arabian by birth, as almoſt all thoſe of his condition are, who, in the ſequel of this hiſtory, has a very ſingular part to act. He was of the ſame age as the prince, and being of a very ſprightly genius, had taken advantage of the exerciſes both of the body and mind, which were enjoin'd his maſter in the courſe of his education. Having ſeen the benefits of virtue, he had reſolv'd to take upon him at leaſt the appearance of it, and even to purſue it, if it could lead him to that pitch of fortune which was his true aim. The queen had for ſome time before made attempts to corrupt him : but, ſeeming not to underſtand her, he had imbib'd a maxim, that if he muſt be a traitor, it ought to be for his own intereſt, and not for that of others. Our voluntiers enter'd into Coptos above a month before the enemy was in a condition to form any attack.

SETHOS was receiv'd by the inhabitants with an extreme joy, and he ſoon perceiv'd they were better pleas'd to be under the government of Memphis than that of Thebes, under which they were very fearful of returning. This fear had no regard to the kings, but to the prieſts, whom the kings of Thebes generally allow'd too great an authority over the people, which they abus'd by exerciſing a very troubleſome inſpection in the inmoſt receſſes of families, and, under the pretext of honouring or appeaſing the gods, burthening them with cuſtoms not only ſtrict but ſevere, which made their own religion inſupportable. Amedes took this opportunity of ſaying to Sethos: My lord, by your title of initiate you are hereafter above my inſtruction. But the uneaſineſs you obſerve in the inhabitants of Coptos, the ſubject of which you know, emboldens me to offer you yet an advice of importance, which was not proper for me to give you at another age, nor natural for you to receive from the mouth of the prieſts. All the morality, and all the virtue of a king conſiſts in a juſt combination of piety towards the gods, and goodneſs to his ſubjects; ſo that his piety towards the gods is blind, when it is hurtful to human ſociety; as his goodneſs to his people is pernicious, when it countenances in them an oblivion of the gods and their worſhip. According to this principle, it will not ſuffice that you are a religious man, you muſt likewiſe be a ſtateſman. By uniting theſe two qualities it is, that giving a reaſonable authority to thoſe who are to keep up good manners and the exerciſe of religion in your kingdom, you will prevent their deſtroying liberty, quiet, and particularly the publick diverſions. Theſe diverſions, kept within the bounds of decency, prevent real diſorders in the people they engage, and being turn'd as much as poſſible to a moral advantage, they even keep up politeneſs, and all the civil virtues in the minds of the populace. A virtuous and wiſe prince winks ſometimes at things in the publick which he won't allow in himſelf. But moreover, it is good to know, that as the juſtice of the gods is not the juſtice of men; that is, that as the gods, tho' infinitely juſt, do certain things which men could not do without injuſtice, ſo the virtue of a ſtateſman, which ought to be greater than that of private perſons, muſt not always be limited by that of private perſons. Devotion, I ſay, even the leaſt enlighten'd, is in this advantageous, that it keeps up a ſpirit of good manners in the people: but it muſt be govern'd, and never ſuffer'd to have the rule itſelf. It is allowable, and even praiſe-worthy to act with regard to ourſelves upon principles of devotion, but with other men we ought never to act but by reason. Thus a prince ought, above all things, to avoid making his courtiers believe, that devotion will make them acceptable to him; because, instead of bringing them to this inward sentiment, which is not to be inspir'd, he leads them into hypocrisy, and thereby renders them more impious and wicked than they were before. A prince ought to go further, and prevent whatever may disturb the publick tranquillity under the pretence of devotion. Men full of a blind and scrupulous zeal, on whom no passion has more dominion than that of guiding others, ought themselves to be carefully watch'd by their prince; that after having troubled the minds of those of his weaker subjects who give ear to them, they don't attempt to disturb common order among those who are not inclin'd to hear them. Don't confound this sort of men with hypocrites, but look upon them as much more dangerous: for hypocrites do no more harm under the cloak of religion, than will turn to their advantage; whereas scrupulous persons are capable, by their obstinacy, of doing harm to themselves and others. But retain above all, my lord, what I presume yet to add to this advice. As much king as you will be, you will never be preferr'd before this sort of men in the minds of the people, but as far as you are regular in your own conduct, and just in all your proceedings. Without this caution, these avengers of their own cause, which they take always for that of the gods, will attribute every unlucky accident, which may happen during the course of your reign, to your want of piety and justice. On the contrary, if you are irreproachable with respect to yourself, and just towards your subjects, you will make the odium of that injustice, which always accompanies the reformations and impositions of the men I am speaking of, fall on their own head. I allow that this evil is less to be fear'd at Memphis, where, excepting in those cases in which religion is concern'd, the priests never meddle with the affairs of private persons, but when they apply to them. There are none in all Egypt who better unite their piety towards the gods with their goodness towards men: and you know how much they recommend humanity and beneficence to those who have a superiority over others. The initiates of Thebes, tho' full of honour and courage, have always been more rigid in victories, and less forbearing in their vengeance than those of Memphis. In a word, the priests of Thebes establish religion by severity, and those of Memphis by indulgence. By this the latter have made themselves famous and respected throughout the whole world; while the others, by their

characters,

characters, can be agreeable but to very few, and do likewise much less good in their generation. Tho' religion is not dependant upon kings, and they ought not so much as to concern themselves with it, they have a great share in the exterior rites of it; and the tranquillity of their subjects is always their care. The kings of Thebes, who have not pursued these maxims, have suffer'd a power to devolve upon the priests, which has often been of great prejudice to the state, and which even to this day is vexatious to themselves. Not to mention the general alienation in the minds of men, occasion'd by the severity of their priests, an example of which you see here in Coptos; their history relates, that the ancient Amosis, an initiate of Thebes, the same who had the glory of abolishing human victims throughout all Egypt, gave so much liberty to the superstitious zeal of the Theban priests, that they drove out of the capital only, fourscore thousand persons, who could no longer bear up under the insupportable burden of ceremonies, which they impos'd upon them. Even to this day, now they are much milder, they take upon them to go at will into the most private apartments of the palace: and whereas in other dynasties, the priests make use of this privilege but as favourites, at Thebes they do it as inspectors; and the king has only the chamber of his nuptial bed, and that where the council of ſtate aſſembles, free from them.

HOWEVER, to quit this moralizing, which may begin to be tedious to you, I have already been thinking, my lord, to let you take advantage of this prerogative of the Theban prieſts for another uſe. Kings and princes can't always travel with ſafety in foreign countries: but as an Egyptian initiate, all the prieſts of Egypt are oblig'd, at your firſt demand, to ſhew you all the curioſities of their ſacerdotal Nome. They alone have the keys of this great number of publick monuments, which are tombs. They can go almoſt every where, from one to the other, by ſubterraneous communications, tho' at ſeveral leagues diſtance. With the prieſts of Thebes you may go as far as Syena and the Leſſer Cataract. You may viſit as much as you pleaſe of the kingdom, and enter even into the king's palace, without either he, or any of his officers, knowing that you are in his dominions. The people of Coptos themſelves will only believe you to be in the temple of Iſis, which is beyond the moraſs that defends one of its gates, and by which you will begin your private excurſion. It is true, you won't paſs thro' the ſtreets or publick ſquares, nor will you ſee hardly any thing of the cities and

and the buildings which are in and about them, but what you may diſcover from the tops of the temples, or the windows of the ſacerdotal colleges. It is likewiſe true, that in this journey you will gain no knowledge for the ſervice of the ſtate; for beſides the rigid ſilence the prieſts will obſerve with you on this head, agreeable to the laws of juſtice and honour, they will bind you by an oath never to make uſe, as an enemy, of what you will ſee as an initiate. However, as whole years would hardly be ſufficient to obſerve all theſe wonderful works, and as in appearance the ſiege of Coptos will be form'd within a month; I believe, my lord, it will be proper for you to confine yourſelf to a ſlight view of the Memnonium of Thebes, the city of Syena, and the neighbouring Cataract, which is the moſt remarkable; contenting yourſelf this time with what you may take a curſory view of in your paſſage, and with the anſwers the prieſts will give to your queſtions. I make your journey of mere curioſity by ſo much the ſhorter, as I extremely deſire you may view the obſervatory of Thebes at your leiſure, and have an opportunity of diſcourſing upon the ſubject of aſtronomy with the prieſts there, who, beyond diſpute, exceed the whole world in that ſcience. To this end I have already recommended you to two of the moſt noted prieſts, with whom

I have

I have had a friendly correſpondence ſince I laſt reſided in Thebes; they will continually attend you. But I believe in your abſence, which they have fix'd to three weeks, it will be proper for me to ſupply your room in Coptos, that I may anſwer the king, your father, when he may deſire to hear concerning you. During this time I will obſerve with aſſiduity, as well the interior and exterior of the place, as the preparations for the ſiege, that, at your return, I may with greater eaſe make you thoroughly acquainted with the actions we can enter upon when the attacks are form'd.

SETHOS anſwer'd Amedes, that tho' he could gladly have had him as a companion, and even as a counſellor, on this journey, yet he approv'd of his wiſdom in the meaſures he had taken. That he was therefore ready to depart that very hour, to be ſurer of returning before the ſiege began. Amedes led the prince immediately to the ſacerdotal college of Coptos. There he confided him to the care of the two prieſts, who convey'd him to the temple of Iſis in one of their own boats, which, as all other conveniencies of the prieſts for travelling either by water or land in Egypt, was free, even in time of war, not only from all attacks, but from every viſitation.

As short time as Sethos employ'd in taking a slight view of the curiosities, either exterior or subterraneous, of the Theban Nome; a fear of being tedious to the reader will make me yet more concise in the description of them. Sethos being arriv'd at Thebes saw the four chief temples of the city *, the ancientest of which was a miracle for its bulk and beauty. It was thirteen furlongs, or more than half a league in circumference, seventy feet high, and the wall twenty-four feet in thickness. All the ornaments of the temple, as well for the richness of the materials, as exquisite workmanship, was equal to the magnificence of the building, of which some part is yet standing. But the gold, silver, ivory, and precious stones were pillag'd when Cambyses set fire to all the temples of Egypt. Then it was that the Persians, transporting all these treasures into Asia, and carrying likewise Egyptian workmen with them, built the famous palaces of Persepolis, Susa, and some other of their cities. Of forty-seven tombs of their kings, which embellish'd Thebes or the neighbourhood of it, Diodorus only describes that of Ismandes or Osimanduus, which was call'd the Memnonium; this Ismandes or Osimanduus being

* Diod. 1.

no other than Mendes or Memnon, one of the ſucceſſors of Seſoſtris. This ſepulchre was ſix thouſand two hundred and fifty feet in circumference. The inſide of it was divided into ſeveral apartments, all differing one from the other. An account of them is agreeably given in this author; and Sethos view'd them all with admiration.

AFTER having viſited the Memnonium, the two prieſts, as they had agreed with Amedes, carry'd the young prince immediately to Syena, a place not ſo remarkable in itſelf, as for the way leading to it. This way was the more charming as it was not regularly border'd on the ſides, like a ſtreet, with palaces in a ſtrait line: But the proſpect of a fine champian country was every moment broken off by ſtately edifices, plac'd at unequal diſtances one from the other. But to ſay the truth, this continuation of Thebes divided itſelf on the right and on the left of the river into ſeveral towns which had their particular names; as Hermonthis, Tuphium, Latopolis, Elythia, Apollinopolis the Great, the Ombes, and laſtly Syena. To give Sethos an idea of theſe places, the two prieſts, deſigning to return with him by private paſſages, continued always in the high-road; but he was with them in one of their cover'd chariots, with thin curtains round it, which they could

draw

draw back at pleaſure, and thro' which they could ſee without being ſeen. They made him obſerve at a diſtance a ſquare temple, which had four avenues, each compos'd of two rows of treble columns, or columns plac'd three and three upon a triangular pedeſtal. On the cornices of theſe columns were alternatively a ſphinx and a tomb. Each double row was of five hundred pedeſtals or fifteen hundred columns, which in all made ſix thouſand columns, each of a ſingle piece, and ſeventy feet high. Diodorus makes no mention of this temple, but modern travellers yet ſee the remains of it *.

As ſoon as Sethos arriv'd at Syena they ſhew'd him the deep well, over which the ſun paſs'd perpendicularly the day of the ſummer ſolſtice, ſo that at noon the whole form of it was ſeen entire at the bottom of the water. This phenomenon, as well as that of the Obeliſks of this city, which at that moment gave no ſhadow, prove that it is ſituated exactly under the tropick of Cancer.

THE next morning they propos'd to Sethos to viſit the leſſer Cataract, which is not above four or five leagues diſtance from Syena; for the larger is near to Napata in Ethiopia:

* Paul Lucas has given a print of them. Voyage to the Levant, tom. 3.

The

The ſmaller is a chain of rocks, which on that ſide towards Syena appear of a prodigious breadth, and of the height of two hundred feet perpendicular from the ſurface of the river in its natural courſe. But at more than ten furlongs farther towards the ſouth begins the unevenneſs of theſe rocks, the cavities of which are ſo deep, that the water which paſſes over theſe frightful places, fall and daſh againſt the rocks with ſuch violence, that the noiſe of it fills the mind with terror as far as they are heard. However, the Nile in its increaſe abundantly fills theſe cavities, and covers them in a perfect level. It was then towards the end of the firſt month of its decreaſe; before which, the journey to Syena, as well as the ſiege of Coptos, would have been equally impracticable. But the Nile, which runs gently in the plains, has then at the Cataract the ſwiftneſs of an arrow from a bow. Sethos had the pleaſure of ſeeing the barks of travellers, which driving at this ſeaſon with the ſtream, make a fall of about two hundred feet without any danger *; an inconceivable trial in the firſt who ventur'd upon it. Here are likewiſe ſeen the remains of an aſtoniſhing work. The natural caſcade, which falls with the impetuoſity we have juſt obſerv'd, leaves a ſpace betwixt it and the perpendicular wall. The kings of Thebes

* Strab. l. 17. p. 818.

had caus'd a large platform † to be made, where they walk'd dry under the water; the motion of which forms it into a vaulted arch; and moreover, had caus'd to be hollow'd out of the natural rock, even with the platform, a vaſt grotto, enlighten'd by ſeveral rows of windows. Sethos allow'd, that this part of his journey very juſtly crown'd all the beauties of it. The two prieſts therefore conducted him back again to Syena. The Nile, along the banks of which they travell'd, and which they frequently paſs'd over on bridges, wholly employ'd Sethos's imagination, and gave him an opportunity of aſking his guides their opinion of the riſe of this river, and the cauſes of its inundation.

THE eldeſt of the two immediately anſwer'd, That the Egyptians being inclin'd to look upon the Nile as a gift immediately from the gods, or as a god itſelf, which had a temple at Nilopolis; they thought it beſt to leave the people in an ignorance ſo conducive to their piety. Indeed, continu'd he, the greater part of mankind is kept up in a greater veneration for the gods, by the peculiar operations they attribute to them, than by the effects which reſult from the general order of their providence. Therefore, not diſcovering to them the fact which is known

† Paul Lucas, tom. 3.

to us, we leave an open field for ſome writers, who, not having ſeen things themſelves, relate ſuch conjectures, with regard to the Nile, the falſity of which time daily diſcovers. Some have ſaid, that this river takes its riſe in the mountains of Atlas, towards the weſtern coaſts of Africa; and that traverſing all that part of the world, it came into Egypt by the northern confines of Ethiopia. Others, advancing ſomething nearer to the truth, tho' yet very far from it, bring the Nile directly from the ſouthern parts of Egypt, but, without reaſon, ſeparating Africa by the ocean at the Equator; then place the riſe of this river in thoſe lands which they ſuppoſe beyond it, and which they call the Anticthones, or the other world: So that, according to their notion, the Nile traverſes the ſea, without mixing its waters with that of the ocean. They call the mountains, where they imagine it to ſpring, the mountains of the moon, and place them ten degrees beyond the Equator *. It is more than a century ſince the ſacerdotal college of Thebes has ſacrific'd immenſe ſums to dive into the truth of this matter. Our prieſts, accompany'd by our officers of the ſecond order, have neither fear'd the danger nor the fatigues of travels by ſea and land, which they have undertaken, either

* See the chart call'd, *Antiquiſſima orbis delineatio*, appoſite to p. 84 of the 1ſt vol. of father Briet's book, intitled, *Parallela Geographiæ veteris & novæ.*

alone,

alone, or with sundry merchants, who coasted it to different ports of Africa: and it has appear'd, that the discovery of the rise of the Nile, which was the first motive of their inquiries, has not been the only fruit of them. They found out, that the western coast of Africa is not divided by the ocean under the Equator, nor bends toward the east, as is yet believ'd by most of the geographers, who stretch out this coast to the most eastern extremities of Asia, and inclose the Indian ocean in this space as a Mediterranean sea *. Africa, on the contrary, extends in a point declining towrads the west, to the thirty-fifth degree of southern latitude. The priest, who discours'd him, even shew'd him, on a small chart which he had about him, the situation of the eastern coasts of Africa to its point, and the turning of the western coasts, as well as the names of the principal inhabitants who dwelt as well on the one as the other, to the Fortunate islands. We know no other way at this time to these islands but by the Streights of Hercules's Pillars; and return the same way, for want of cultivating the knowledge the Egyptians

* This system has been reviv'd in the latter centuries; and Marin Sanuto, a Venetian, about 1330, publish'd a chart of it, which is in Bongar's collection, call'd, *Gesta Dei per Francos*. But see in the above-mention'd work of father Briet, the chart, intitled, *Agathodæmonis orbis descriptio*, opposite to p. 87. of vol. 1.

had of the whole compaſs of Africa. As for the ſprings of the Nile, continued the prieſt, we have found them in a barbarous kingdom of Ethiopia, for which we have yet no name, but the inhabitants call it Goiama. They are twelve degrees on this ſide the Equator, which brings them to twenty-two degrees, or five hundred and fifty leagues on this ſide the mountains of the moon. And we obſerve in general, that the geographical corrections almoſt always tend to diminiſh the diſtances of places reckon'd by the moſt antient geographers. Moreover, theſe ſprings ſeem to ariſe in a mountain cover'd with trees, which is flat at top. There we find two ſmall openings of ciſterns plac'd pretty near one to the other, like two eyes. But we can't ſound them, becauſe we are immediately hinder'd by roots of trees. The water has no iſſue but at the foot *. This river iſſuing from the mountain oppoſite to the north, ſoon forms a lake, call'd by the inhabitants Dambea, which is above ſixty leagues in circumference. At laſt, after many windings to the eaſt and to the weſt,

* This agrees with the deſcription father Kircher, OEd. Ægypt. tom. 1. pag. 57. makes of the ſprings of the Nile, on the relation of father Peter Pais, a Portugueſe jeſuit, who was the firſt diſcoverer of them; and with the map he gives of the courſe of this river into Egypt. M. de Liſle differs a little from it in his map of Africa of 1722. He has even plac'd the two eyes, mention'd in this deſcription, to the right of Minus.

it

it comes into Egypt, and traverses it almost in a strait line from the south to the north. We conceal this rise and natural course of the Nile from the populace, for the reasons I have already given. And with regard to travellers and mariners, it is just that they take themselves, for their interest and advantage, the pains we have taken for the mere benefit of information.

SETHOS, who from his soul disapprov'd of such a reserve, flatter'd himself, sooner or later, by some means or other, to verify what concern'd the coasts of Africa, and to render this discovery useful to mankind, without falling into the inconvenience of divulging a sacerdotal secret. This opportunity was to offer sooner than he imagin'd. In the mean time he thank'd the priest for this account of so many extraordinary things; and told him, that not to be too troublesome to him, he would entreat his companion to explain to him the causes of the inundations of the Nile.

THIS other priest answer'd him, that the explication would be short. The cause of the inundations of this river, said he, is the same as that which produces the river itself. Rains, which give the first birth to the Nile, are afterwards the cause of its periodical inundations. As the sun by its presence or absence, as well as by the directness or obliquity of its aspect, is the principal agent in the different dispositions of the earth, and of the air which encompasses it; its operations are more constant between the two tropicks, which include its annual course, than in the spaces beyond them to the poles, over which it has less power. For that reason the winds, which are caus'd by the rarefaction of the heated air, are more regular in the torrid zone than any where else. The heat of the days, and the coolness of the nights return always the same in the different months of the year. With regard to the rains, which are form'd of the exhalations and vapours dispers'd in the air; it is the sun itself which raises them abundantly in its perpendicular situation, and at the same time dissolves them into torrents of water. Thence follows, that differing from what happens in the temperate and in the frigid zones, which have summer when the sun approaches them, and winter when it departs from them; the winter, or the rainy season, in each of the two parts of the torrid zones, at least in Africa, is the time of the most direct passage of the sun over them. Now, as the sources of the Nile are in the northern part of this zone, the first streams of this river increase when the sun is in the northern signs, where it causes our summer. The same happens to all the rivers which have their spring in the torrid

torrid zone. But they are not all fill'd with a ſlime ſo beneficial as that of the Nile to fatten the ground. This diſcourſe brought our travellers inſenſibly to Syena.

THERE they enter'd the ſubterraneous paſſages, and they made Sethos continue in them as much as poſſible till they came to Thebes, that a view of the ſacred curioſities might ſucceed the ſight of the prophane. I ſhan't ſpeak here of the former, which were not very different from what Sethos had ſeen in the ſubterranean edifices of Memphis. The body of ceremonies were much the ſame. But in the Theban Nome they were animated by a ſpirit of rigour, which, in the opinion of Sethos, took off very much not only of their beauty, but their value; and whereas in the ſacerdotal Nome of Memphis, virtue was an exerciſe befitting men of honour, in that of Thebes it ſeem'd to be a labour for ſlaves. In the mean time, Sethos keeping theſe reflections to himſelf, came at laſt above ground again in the capital. The prieſts ſhew'd him all the beauties of their college, and reſerv'd their obſervatory for the laſt.

THE apartment which bore this name, was plac'd on the temple of the Theban Jupiter, and compos'd of two long galleries one over the other. The higheſt was terminated towards the north by two pretty low towers; and towards the south by a high cupola open on all sides, which was properly the place for observations. The lowest of the two galleries contain'd all the astronomical books. They were divided into two classes; one containing books of the elements, methods and systems; the noted authors of which were represented in a row of pictures, by which young students never pass'd without making a profound reverence. Thence the most eastern Indians took the exterior adoration they render'd to their first learned men. The second class contain'd a collection of immediate observations, made since astronomy was cultivated at Thebes. The columns of the syringes had preserv'd those anterior to the deluge, which were transcrib'd into these books; and in which they had remark'd and corrected the imperfections necessarily attending the first attempts towards the sciences.

SETHOS entring into this first gallery of books, saw three or four hundred priests of all ages, from eighteen years upwards, who were reading or writing in silence, on desks plac'd along the shelves. Our Grecians mention much the same circumstance of the observatory of Acanthis *. In the observatory

* See the preface of the Almag. of father Riccioli.

of Thebes there were, however, about twenty elders, to whom the youngeſt apply'd themſelves, and open'd their difficulties, whiſpering. They were not always courteouſly receiv'd; and theſe great maſters judg'd, that a too great liberty of aſking queſtions not only encourag'd idleneſs in young beginners, but accuſtom'd them, under the pretext of affirming nothing, to ſay a great many childiſh things. The prince's guides had already led him towards theſe prieſts, who were directors of the ſtudies; becauſe he had expreſs'd a deſire of ſeeing nearer at hand ſuch illuſtrious men, whoſe name alone had long before excited a veneration in him. They were advanc'd part of the way to meet him; and they took pleaſure in anſwering the queſtions he made concerning the different applications of the pupils he ſaw ſo attentive at their ſtudy. Some, ſaid they, continue the general tables of calculation begun fifteen hundred years ago, with regard as well to numbers, as to rectilineal or ſpherical triangles, to facilitate and ſhorten the computations the problems of aſtronomy engag'd them in. This long preparation ſhews that the Egyptians as well as the Greeks, had not the method which the latter attempted to find out, in order to ſave the enormous trouble of numerical multiplications and diviſions *. Others, farther ad-

* In this condition they were in before the invention of logarithms, and when they made uſe of Hervart's tables.

vanc'd, continued the priests, make calculations of the eclipses by tables already form'd, or calculate tables of the different planets by observations given. Some are oblig'd to give ephemerides for different places of the earth. The most experienc'd undertake ephemerides for the suppos'd inhabitants of some of the planets; and who, without doubt, think themselves at rest in the center of the universe, as we do. Others, to conclude, examine the courses of all the planets seen from the sun. These find the motion of the planets, which from the earth seem to us so odd, and so difficult to be brought to any certain hypothesis, to be, excepting some difference in swiftness, uniform and regular. The sun, which according to all manner of appearance, is not inhabited, is the only place from whence the planets would appear to move as they do, and where astronomy would be easy. But being upon the earth in a wrong situation for observation, we may say, that whereas in the other parts of physick nature seeks only to be conceal'd, in astronomy it seeks to deceive us.

SETHOS, charm'd with what he saw and heard, said to them; O ye venerable men, worthy of eternal memory and acknowledgments! these difficulties you have overcome, place you in the highest rank of all the learned men of the world, Astronomy, in the opinion of every wiſe man who ſets a true value upon things, is the higheſt attempt of human underſtanding, and of all inventions that which by its ſublimity and certainty does the moſt honour to mankind; becauſe it ſurpaſſes, in ſome manner, humanity itſelf. It is to you we are in general indebted for this glory; and it is you who have taught us what attention and ſtudy can render us capable of. As our Egyptian heroes have given to moſt civiliz'd nations thoſe laws in which their happineſs conſiſts, you furniſh them with means to enjoy, for the greateſt benefits of life, that heaven you have diſcover'd to them; you will leave it, as it were, an inheritance to poſterity *. The heavens, by your care, far better known than the earth itſelf, will ſerve alone to give an exact knowledge of the ſituation of every country, and the extent of every ſea, and will alone guide different nations to a deſir'd intercourſe one with the other. The eldeſt of the prieſts anſwer'd him, That they all receiv'd this compliment with pleaſure; not with reſpect to their perſons, but as regarding the whole ſcience, of which they perceiv'd by his diſcourſe he perfectly knew the application and uſe. He added, in a polite manner, that after having diſcours'd with him, they were going to ſhew him in

* *Cælo in hæreditatem cunctis relicto.* Plin. l. 2. c. 26.

the upper gallery their aſtronomical inſtruments; not as it was uſual with them to many initiates, for cuſtom's ſake, but to have his opinion and advice. Sethos, though he very ſincerely declin'd this reſpect, follow'd them, however, with great joy.

As they enter'd into this gallery at the ſouth end, Sethos immediately ſaw the cupola over his head; the light of which added greatly to the beauty of the gallery, tho' it had likewiſe windows on both ſides. This cupola, which was exactly round, was twenty feet in diameter. They always left hanging there the tube, which ſerv'd them to gather thoſe rays alone which proceed from the ſtar, and to guide the eye to follow it continually *. But when they would get up into the cupola to make obſervations, they made a floor in it, by means of joyſts and boards, which they thruſt out in a moment from the thickneſs of the roof of the gallery. Here Cheres ſaw all the repreſentations the Thebans had of the motions of the ſtars, either in relievo, as globes and ſpheres; or in planes, as the planiſpheres, analemmas, aſtrolabes, and every other ſpecies of aſtronomical projections. They did not omit ſhewing

* Tho' the antients had not the uſe of thoſe glaſſes, which are the moſt eſſential part of teleſcopes or perſpectives, they nevertheleſs made uſe of tubes, for the reaſons mention'd in the text.

him

him the ring parallel to the plane of the Equator, which the Egyptians, and even the Greeks make uſe of to know the exact moment of the Equinox, by the ſhadow which one ſide of this ring makes upon the other in the inſtant, when it happens between ſun-riſing and ſetting. Hipparcus and Ptolemy were both aſtoniſh'd to ſee ſometimes the moment of the vernal Equinox appear in the morning, and appear again at noon. The prieſts mention'd this phenomenon to Sethos, as they explain'd to him the uſe of this ring; and told him, that in this particular caſe, the true moment of the Equinox is at noon, and that of the morning only apparent; but that they had nothing yet deciſive of the cauſe of this appearance *.

GOING towards the end of the gallery, Sethos perceiv'd ſome prieſts who were calculating nativities and horoſcopes. In that, as we have elſewhere obſerv'd, conſiſted their divination. They added to it an enquiry, yet more ſtrict than that of the other prieſts of Egypt, into the ſecrecy of kings and private perſons. The young prince did not think it proper to aſk them any queſtions

* It is an effect of the aſtronomical refraction, which the antients perceiv'd; but which they neither meaſur'd nor made uſe of in their calculations of horizontal ſolar eclipſes, in which it chiefly takes place. See this article in the Almag. of father Riccioli, tom. 1. pag. 133.

on

on this head; not only becauſe they would have hid from him the grounds of their art; but becauſe he had heard of Amedes, and perceiv'd by the natural integrity of his mind, that they were not worthy his notice. So the prieſts led him at laſt to the inſide of the two towers, which were at the north end of the gallery.

THESE towers were round, like the cupola, and of the ſame diameter: but being level with the gallery, the half ſphere, which ſerv'd for a roof to them, did not begin till the height of twelve feet; becauſe they would not have theſe roofs cut the horizon of the cupola, which was higher than all the buildings in or about Thebes. In the weſtern tower was repreſented the hemiſphere of the firmament, which contains the ſix northern ſigns; and in the eaſtern, that which contains the ſix ſouthern. The circles of the ſphere were deſcrib'd in them as in our celeſtial globes; and all the fix'd ſtars were mark'd according to their bigneſs and reciprocal diſtances. The prieſts told Sethos, that an exact obſervation of the poſition of the fix'd ſtars, was their rule for an exact determination of the apparent courſe of the planets; becauſe they appear to our eyes to depart from or approach to certain fix'd ſtars. It is by that, continu'd they, that we have at laſt

hit

hit upon the theory even of the comets, ſo far as to foretel their return *. They added, that their forefathers having been as far as under the Equator, they had ſeen and obſerv'd the whole firmament; and that they did not believe the eye of man could perceive a ſingle ſtar which was not deſcrib'd in their two hemiſpheres. It is true, that whereas Ptolemy knew but of one thouſand twenty-two in the whole firmament, the prieſts of Thebes had plac'd in each of their hemiſpheres near a thouſand.

SETHOS having contemplated theſe ſtars, which were of gold on an azure ground, for ſome time, ſaid: O learned prieſts, allow me to expoſe to you a ſurprize, into which I fall as often as I obſerve the ſtars on planiſpheres or globes; and by ſo much the more, when I ſee them on theſe two magnificent vaults, into which you have brought them all; which is, that notwithſtanding the narrow limits of all theſe repreſentations compar'd to the immenſe extent of the heavens, the ſtars ſeem to me more ſeparated, and at greater diſtances

* Diod. lib. 1. ſect. 2. attributes this knowledge to the Egyptians. The Chaldeans, poſterior to them, and who allow'd them to be their maſters, had it likewiſe, according to Apollonius of Myndus, quoted by Sen. Nat. quæſt. lib. 7. cap. 3. Apollonius himſelf hop'd this art would ſoon or late be recover'd. See the hiſtory of the academy of ſciences, 1699. pag. 72. on the ſubject of a memorial of M. Caſſini.

 from

from one another, and above all, in an infinite less number, when so represented, than they appear in the firmament itself, where they seem to be crowded together in every the least space of so vast an expansion. At first view we think we see millions in that celestial hemisphere, in which the most quick-sighted eyes, such as yours, have never found one thousand. Thus, in this respect too, we say truly, as you have learnedly observ'd, that, in regard to astronomy, nature seems industrious to deceive us: but we must confess, that our sight does not give us the measure, greatness, and distances of things. There is, as we may say, a jarring between that and our imagination. Both one and the other have an opposite influence in our first views; and in many cases, sciences only can rectify them. In reality, while our imagination prodigiously increases the number of the stars, our sight diminishes yet more the extent of the firmament. I might, perhaps, undertake to prove, that the sky appears to us only as the half of a sphere, whose diameter does not exceed two hundred and forty feet. The priests, tho' accustom'd to all the paradoxes of astronomy, were astonish'd at the novelty of this proposition beyond expression; and they were more than ordinary attentive to what Sethos said. I believe, continu'd he, if one were to ask an indifferent person of what bigness the sun appears to him to be; he would

would account it about a foot in diameter; and indeed it ſeems to be a little more than a foot at the horizon, and ſomething leſs at noon. I will therefore ſuppoſe a foot as a mean meaſure, the exactneſs of which is here not neceſſary. Now aſtronomers have found, that the diameter of the diſk of the ſun is about half a degree of the firmament. Thus the ſun paſſing the day of the Equinox thro' half the circumference of the Equator, which is a great circle, goes one hundred and eighty degrees, or three hundred and ſixty half degrees, which is three hundred and ſixty apparent feet. The diameter of a circle being pretty near the third of its circumference, or two thirds of its half circumference, two hundred and forty feet muſt be the diameter of a circle, whoſe half circumference is three hundred and ſixty feet. Thence, continu'd Sethos, I venture to draw this conſequence; That if I was upon a plain horizon, ſuch as in the middle of an even deſart, or upon the ſea; and that, placing myſelf in the center of a half circumference drawn above me, whoſe diameter was two hundred and forty feet, or its ſemi-diameter one hundred and twenty feet, a diſk of ſilver, which ſhould take up half a degree of this circle, was to paſs this half circumference: I ſay, that not being otherwiſe inform'd of any thing by any other object, I muſt neceſſarily fall into two errors: The firſt, would be be to believe this disk as big as the sun; and the second, to suppose it plac'd, as well as the whole line it would trace, in the firmament, as I suppose the sun to be, tho' it be in reality a great distance from it. To conclude, said Sethos, carrying my idea yet farther, I am persuaded, that the semi-diameter of one hundred and twenty feet, given us by the observation I presume to lay before you, is very near the point of distance, at which common eyes begin to lose the power of judging of the real distances and bigness of things, unless the imagination be assisted by the comparison of the intermediate and neighbouring objects, whose distances or bulk are otherwise pretty near determin'd.

THE priests having heard this discourse, forbore all examination of the physical suppositions of the problem, and told Sethos: That they were much less affected with the brightness of his wit, and the depth of his knowledge, than the modesty with which he had deliver'd things the most singular in the world. Long may you live, O great prince, said they, long may you live, and be the glory of Egypt, by the perfection of all the talents, and of all the virtues, which are visible in you. It was a great satisfaction to Sethos to be approv'd in his attempt of doing some honour to the education of Memphis, in presence of the priests of Thebes. He thank'd them with the

the greateſt marks of gratitude for that openneſs of heart which they had been pleas'd to ſhew him, and for the generoſity with which they had allowed him, at leaſt, an acceſs to their moſt profound ſecrets. He added, that he ſhould deem himſelf happy if he could long continue to be their diſciple; but that his duty calling him back to Coptos, he deſir'd, as their laſt favour, that they would ſuffer him to be conducted thither that ſame day. The two prieſts, who had not forſaken him a moment, carry'd him back by the way he came, and Amedes, who knew the time of his return, was waiting at the ſacerdotal college to receive him.

THE young prince, upon ent'ring Coptos again, laid aſide all thoughts of whatever he had ſeen during his journey, to apply himſelf wholly to the affairs of war. The morning after his arrival, Amedes, viſiting with him the fortifications of the city, made him obſerve the difference of the works with regard to their different ſituation. The next day he ſhew'd him the works the enemies had begun ſince the fall of the waters of the river. As yet they were only the lines of their camp, defended by ditches palliſado'd, and in ſome places by walls. He told him, that theſe works would have been much farther advanc'd, and that there would have been a great many more nearer the city, but for the continual oppoſitions they had met with from the army of Memphis, and the frequent ſallies of the garriſon of Coptos, who often deſtroy'd in the night what the enemies had done in the day. But that at laſt the army of Thebes being ſuperior to that of Memphis, at leaſt in open field, the enemy was advanc'd to the point he ſaw; and that they would infallibly bring their machines in a few days to the very foot of the walls. He added, that Thoris, waiting 'till ſome favourable opportunity offer'd, did with reaſon confine himſelf to defend the avenues to Coptos on the ſide of Memphis, that the place might always be ſupply'd with neceſſary ammunition and proviſion during the ſiege; and that for this reaſon he had pitch'd his camp on that ſide. As ſoon as Amedes had done ſpeaking, Sethos ask'd him, if he had been of the number of thoſe who had ſally'd out to hinder the beſiegers works? Amedes having anſwer'd, that the governor had engag'd him to lead on ſome of theſe attacks, the young prince immediately reply'd, he deſign'd himſelf to be in the firſt ſally the governor ſhould order. But Amedes acquainted him, that he had promis'd the king his father, not to ſuffer him to go out of the place. My lord, added he, I have reaſons for it which are not ſo evident that I could open them to the king, and which you will

will likewiſe diſpenſe with my communicating to you. But the promiſe I have made him is binding on this head, and forbids me ſallying out myſelf as long as you are in Coptos. However, to let you ſee that my aim is not to be an obſtacle to your valour, nor even to ſcreen you from the common perils of war; you ſhall enter into action as often as you pleaſe on the walls, where you won't fail of ſeeing very vigorous engagements. Towers of wood or ladders will raiſe the enemy within reach of our javelins, and even of our ſwords, and battering rams will make breaches in our walls, which we muſt defend man for man. I ſhall here take occaſion, in anſwer to the reproach caſt upon the Egyptians by ſome Greek authors, that they did not excell in the art of war, to ſay, that it was they, who in the perſons of Oſiris, Seſoſtris, and Memnon, produc'd the firſt conquerors in the world. That afterwards they courageouſly drove away from the heart of their dominions, both the Arabians who had ſeiz'd them by ſurprize, under the ſhepherd kings, long before Sethos's time, and the Ethiopians under king Sabacon, two or three hundred years before the invaſion of Cambyſes. But moreover, ſetting aſide their bravery; it is certain, that their ingenuity and power had furniſh'd them, long before the Greeks, not only with all ſorts of arms and inſtruments of war, the invention of which Herodotus * attributes to them, but with those offensive and defensive machines which the latter afterwards put in use at sieges.

SETHOS examin'd with attention all those which were prepar'd within the city. As those provinces which are never so little distant from one another have yet different customs, he compar'd the machines of Coptos with those he had seen the models of at Memphis; and arguing upon this subject with the engineers, he endeavour'd to discover the singular advantages of one over the other.

RETURNING from the temple of Isis, by the way of the morass, the young prince had already observ'd, that the foot of the wall on that side was wash'd by the water. But taking a view of this part from the inside of the ramparts, he observ'd that the enemy, who was master of the adjacent parts, had since cover'd the water with a great number of flat boats. The governor knew it; but he did not conceive they could make any great advantage of them: and having a watchful eye over the rest, he look'd upon the morass itself as a defence which nature had furnish'd him. It was, however, on that side the first attack on the town was made; because the

* Herodot. lib. 3. & Clem. Alex. Pædag. lib. 2.

enemy built very much upon the ſucceſs of a machine they had newly invented, to ſcale the city from the moraſs. They began, by covering the whole ſurface of the water with boats; and faſtening then one by the other, they form'd a floor as firm as if they had lain on dry ground. This work awaken'd the governor's attention, and he began to think more ſeriouſly of defending this part of the walls. Sethos, who was ſtanding by his ſide, told him, that he call'd to mind an expedient, the firſt idea of which he had found in the hiſtories of Egypt; that he would go and confer thereon with the engineers, and that in an hour he would offer him this invention ready for execution: that in the mean time, he had the confidence to promiſe him a ſucceſs from it as happy as it had been in former times. The governor, a prudent officer, anſwer'd him; That independant of the good or bad ſucceſs of this project, the whole kingdom was happy in having a prince who knew how to think, and above all, who was willing to ſubmit his thoughts to the examination of experienc'd perſons. That he waited with impatience for his propoſal, which he was before-hand very much diſpos'd to follow.

THE ſame day, the enemies having cover'd their boats with planks, brought all the pieces of the great machine they had prepar'd; and they had taken their meaſures ſo well, that it requir'd a very little time to put it together. Sethos, whose design the governor had approv'd of, was very diligent in observing, thro' private chinks in the wall, what he could discern of this machine, and of the effect it could have. The engineers had orders to come frequently to him, to know whether, upon what he might from time to time perceive of their works, it might be necessary to make any alteration in the iron hooks he had already order'd in the general view of his design. He saw nothing that made it worth while to make any change in the form he had at first given. His intention was, to let the besiegers put their machine in a condition to work without interruption, that his counter-battery might make the greater havock amongst them. However, to give them no suspicion of his private design, he ply'd them with arrows shot at random from the top of the wall. They had taken the precaution to screen themselves from them; for the greater part of their barks, especially those in which their work oblig'd them to be most, were cover'd with boards slanting on the side towards the town.

NIGHT being at last come, they perceiv'd that the enemy had chosen that time to put their machine in practice. It was a large lodge or shed open before, and capacious enough to hold fifty soldiers. It was to rest upon

upon the brink of the parapet of the ramparts; the height of which, the besiegers engineers perfectly knew. The body of this lodge was to be supported in this manner by long, strait stakes, of which only the hindermost were upright or perpendicular to the barks. All the rest serv'd as peers or jaumbs, being fix'd obliquely into these, in the same manner as is practis'd with galleries of wood which have a great bearing out. In this form it was something like the Sambuca of the Latins, so call'd for the resemblance it had to a harp, and which Marcellus made use of at the siege of Syracusa on the sea-side, according to the relation and description of Polybius and Plutarch. But the machine we are here describing, was more considerable in every respect; and the manner of erecting it very different. The workmen, turning their backs to the town, rais'd it as the semi-diameter of a circle upon supporters, plac'd and fasten'd in the boats, by drawing it with cords running in pullies, which were fasten'd to a sort of masts almost as high as the walls.

THE besiegers had not put any men into the row of boats which were nearest the wall, not to expose them to the great stones, and other heavy bodies, which the besieged might throw down upon them: but on each side of the machine were plac'd a great number of archers, to infeſt the beſieged on the ramparts with their arrows.

SETHOS, on his part, had cauſ'd to be faſten'd to the parapet a great number of ſtrong pullies, tackled with ſtrong ropes, at the end of which were faſten'd iron hooks of all forms. The enemy did not ſee theſe pullies, not only becauſe they had taken care to remove all light round them, and had kept only for themſelves as much as was abſolutely neceſſary for their work; but becauſe theſe pullies were plac'd between the heads of the ſoldiers, which Sethos, by a ſtratagem which ſucceeded, had ſome time before plac'd ſtanding upon the parapet. While the enemy, making a jeſt of this diſpoſition, , which to them ſeem'd fantaſtick, ſaluted them with their arrows; the eight lords, companions of Sethos, diſpers'd among thoſe of the front, but with their armour faſten'd behind to leſſer ropes, and holding in each hand one of the iron hooks faſten'd to the ends of the larger ropes, fell down, or rather were dexterouſly let down, as if they fell of themſelves, one after another, as dead men, into the neareſt boats. The enemy not thinking theſe ſuppos'd dead men worth their notice, and not having perceiv'd the ropes, hidden from their eyes by favour of the night, were only buſy, ſome in clearing the brink of the parapet with their arrows; and others, in

raiſing

raiſing their machine by force of labour. In the mean time, theſe young noblemen having, with great activity and addreſs, faſten'd their iron hooks to the hinder part of thoſe flat boats, which contain'd the workmen who were raiſing the machine, return'd to the foot of the wall, where they made, all together, a great cry; which was the ſignal for hoiſting them up immediately, and for hawling at once all the ropes to which the iron hooks were faſten'd. The diſorder which the firſt motion of the pullies caus'd, is inexpreſſible: It threw down all thoſe who held the machine ſuſpended in the air, and almoſt rais'd to its full height. The fall of it cruſh'd to pieces above two hundred men, engineers and labourers, who directed, or were aſſiſtant at the raiſing of it. All the ſoldiers in the ſhatter'd machine were kill'd or wounded. The pullies raiſing the ends of the boats neareſt the walls, made all the planks give way, and threw thoſe, who a moment before were inſulting the beſieged with their arrows, into the water. The greater part of the boats to which the hooks were faſten'd, being rais'd intirely out of the water, whirl'd about in the air by the force of their own weight hanging to the ropes, diſcharg'd themſelves of thoſe men who had taken hold of them for fear of drowning, and cruſh'd them to death afterwards in the other boats which had receiv'd them in their fall. Much in the

the ſame manner it was that Archimedes turn'd the effect of the Sambuca's, which Marcellus had caus'd to be apply'd to the Acradina of Syracuſa againſt the Romans themſelves; and thus Sethos, having no farther experience in war than what he had attain'd to from hiſtory and reading, made himſelf fear'd and reſpected, in his very firſt exploit, by Mephres, one of the moſt valiant kings the dynaſty of Thebes ever had. Something of the ſame nature has been ſince related of Scipio the younger, and of Lucullus, who only by reading of Xenophon had made themſelves great captains before they commanded the armies of the republick.

WHILE every body, and in particular the governor, were heaping praiſes upon Sethos; he himſelf was gall'd to the ſoul that he had not yet had an opportunity of giving any mark of his valour. He told the governor, ſhewing them his eight companions, that it was they, and not he, who had given the firſt proofs of their courage, as well in the ſallies they had been engag'd in during his abſence, as in the perillous undertaking of faſtening the hooks to the boats. But that he comforted himſelf with the hopes of partaking with them the danger of an exploit that he had projected againſt the enemy's towers, without going out of the gates of the city, ſince it was forbidden him. The governor

vernor answer'd, That it was not for him to exhort him to any thing: but that after the success of his first attempt he had not the power to dissuade him from any thing whatsoever. But nevertheless he rely'd very much upon the wisdom of Amedes, for the preservation of a prince who was already an object of wonder, not only to the king's subjects, but to his enemies.

MEPHRES, whose army was very numerous, had taken the very time in which this machine was preparing, and to be put in practice, to advance his towers. The continual skirmishes between his army and that of Memphis had not hinder'd him from levelling several passages thro' which these monstrous piles of wood, quite erected, were to advance towards the walls upon rolls. At sun-rising they saw two of them, of equal size, before that part of the wall which had the largest face towards the plain, and where the Thebans had already fill'd up the ditch. They were square buildings, of four fathoms each side, and higher by two feet than the parapets of the ramparts; before which they were plac'd at fifteen or twenty feet distance. Toward the top they had a floor, to which there was an ascent by a stair-case contriv'd on the inside of the timber. This floor was lower than the brink of the tower by the height of a tall man, to secure the besiegers from

from darts lanc'd in a direct line. But on that side which was towards the wall, there was upon the floor a broad bench, upon which the enemy were to mount, to annoy the the besieged, who might line the ramparts with their arrows. Besides that, every tower had a sort of draw-bridge of three feet broad, with iron rails on the sides about three feet high. These draw-bridges the enemy were to let down on the parapet, and by that means to endeavour to throw themselves into the city. Sethos, seeing these draw-bridges which as yet were erected in the air, and having observ'd the iron rails, smiling, said to his officers who were about him; These people surely are very awkward; we may, perhaps, let them see something more bold.

IN the mean time the ramparts were provided with soldiers commanded by the governor himself, who prepar'd to repulse the besiegers. Besides the arrows which they shot continually at the enemy in the plain, he order'd, that as soon as they observ'd them upon the floors of the towers, they should shoot arrows into the air that might fall down again on their heads. Sethos, on the contrary, wish'd, with regard to his design, that the floors might be full of soldiers, because he look'd upon them as so many men who should not escape. But observing that these arrows did not do them much harm, nor hinder them

them from exposing themselves to the danger, he did not contradict this order of the governor's, nor did he inform him of his project, to give him the pleasure of a surprize. He had, indeed, in the morning, desir'd that two long planks might be plac'd within the ramparts, over-against the two towers; one end of which resting upon the ground, and being rais'd by degrees, and supported from space to space with stones, the other end towards the parapet was of the same height as the towers. The governor let him make these preparations, thinking he design'd to place soldiers upon these planks, who being something higher might the better resist the enemy's descent into the ramparts. But Sethos, who had concerted his design with his eight companions, caus'd them to be arm'd, as himself, with light armour, and each a sword of a foot and a half long, broad at the hilt, and very sharp-pointed. The moment he thought most proper for his design, placing himself, with three of his companions, at fifteen paces distance from the foot of one of the planks; and the other five at the same distance opposite to the foot of the other, they all cry'd out at once to make way. Immediately taking a sudden jump all together with a surprizing vigour, they were seen, in a moment, running on the planks, rais'd in the air, and falling, with sword in hand, into the two towers. The governor, as well as all

all the officers and soldiers on the rampart, stood motionless at this sight: but the people in the towers, much more surpriz'd, thought them really fall'n down from heaven by a prodigy which foreboded their certain ruin. Indeed, having no other weapon but their bows, which they were going to make use of, by mounting all together upon the broad bench, they were all stabb'd before they had time to come to themselves. As the stair-case and bottom of the tower were fill'd with Theban soldiers, commanded to back those who were above; our young heroes threw all the dead bodies down the horizontal opening of the stairs; and they, being in armour, by their weight, either kill'd or overthrew all who were on the stair-case. Not satisfy'd with that, they took the levers, or other instruments of iron design'd to let down the draw-bridges, and with a wonderful quickness and dexterity loosen'd the planks from the joysts, which were more than sufficient for them to walk on; and throwing them down, they destroy'd those who were below in great numbers: They likewise ruin'd a great part of the stair-case, by leaving only such pieces of wood as were necessary for them, not to walk, but to jump or clamber from one place to another. At last, not designing to stay long there, they let down the draw-bridges, and return'd, running to the ramparts. But to deprive the enemies of the same

ſame opportunity, if they ſhould attempt to come up in their turns, Sethos caus'd the two bridges to be dextrouſly cut off cloſe to the parapet, and they fell at the foot of the wall.

THIS exploit had a far greater ſucceſs than Sethos himſelf had imagin'd. The firſt ſoldiers, who got out of the two towers alive thro' the doors below, cry'd out in a fearful tone, That certain Genii, enemies to the Thebans, were come down from heaven on the tops of their towers, had deſtroy'd their companions there, and were making frightful ravage. This notion, ſupported by the groans of thoſe within, and the noiſe of the boards falling, made thoſe who were poſted adjacent to the towers, fly to a great diſtance; and they did not ſcruple ſaying, that ſigns from heaven were ſuperior even to the orders of their king. Mephres, who ſaw theſe young men in the air, and could hardly comprehend this unheard-of example of intrepidity, the author of which he ſuſpected to be Sethos, plainly perceiv'd he ſhould not be believ'd if he alledg'd it. So, not to expoſe his authority, he choſe rather to give way to the ſuperſtition of his army. He gave orders the very ſame day to ſet fire at a diſtance to the two towers, ſince they were diſpleaſing to the gods. He even added, that as their great machines had not ſucceeded, they would, in the

the continuance of the siege, only make use of the battering rams, the most simple of all machines; which they could not do without, to beat down the gates, or batter the walls of a city they so lawfully attack'd.

THE governor and Amedes, on their part, wrote to the king of Memphis, to give him an account of what had pass'd from the beginning of the siege, and of the glory which the young prince, and the eight lords his companions, had acquir'd. Thoris in the mean time receiv'd from the queen reproaches, either private or express'd, in a doubtful sense, that his projects advanc'd so slowly, and that the affairs of war remain'd always in the same situation. He did not want this spur to his rage. The contempt he had always lain under, but into which he imagin'd he was fall'n by a comparison to Sethos, whose name alone fill'd the mouths of every one, cast him into a confusion, which began to be visible in his orders. In short, under the pretext of taking advantage of the disorder, from which the Theban army was not yet recover'd; he let the governor know, that he was resolv'd the following night to attack the enemy with the greater part of his troops, and therefore desir'd he would favour his design by a sally of the best troops of his garrison, at midnight, and on that side opposite to him. He sent him, at the same

time

time the word by which they might know one another in the dark. The governor consented to all, and let him know he wanted no other signal but that of the hour appointed. Thoris knew that Sethos never made one at the sallies: but imagining upon such an occasion he would be near the gate on the inside, he hatch'd the black design of giving the enemy an opportunity of entring into the city. To put it in practice without being discover'd, he took upon him to go in person to view the way they were to pass to encounter the enemy. When he went into the tents of the chief officers, he talk'd aloud to them of his design; he nam'd the gate the garison was to march out of, and gave them the word in such manner, that those who were round about the tent might hear it. Some of the eldest captains took upon them to acquaint him, that he would have done better to have spoken lower, because of the spies that king Mephres might have in the camp; and the rather, as it was for particular officers to give the word to the troops in the moment they were to march. As it was the intention of Thoris to have the project of his enterprize come to the enemy's ears, he soften'd his tone no longer than till he was out of the hearing of those who, from space to space, presum'd to give him the same advice. The general order, in short, was to march against the army of the besiegers the hour he had advis'd the governor. He foresaw that their march would soon be stopp'd by the army of Mephres, who was sufficiently inform'd of all. So he propos'd, after having engag'd them some time, to sound a retreat, under the plausible pretext of his design being discover'd, and so give the enemy an opportunity of cutting off the sally of the garison, and, perhaps, of entering the city. All this happen'd to the great misfortune of Memphis, as he foresaw; and to his own, which he did not expect.

MEPHRES had divided his troops into two bodies; the largest he commanded himself, and the other he sent under the command of one of his lieutenants against the garison. Thoris, at the head of his army, was immediately struck with fear at seeing the king of Thebes, who till then had never appear'd in person in any of the nightly expeditions, and with whom he had no thoughts of engaging. He remain'd at a stand, when the king fell upon him with his whole avantguard; and commanding two or three of his officers, who were nearest his person, to seize him without wounding him, he caus'd him to be led hand-cuff'd to the quarters where the prisoners he had taken from the beginning of the siege were kept: after which, rushing on the foremost ranks, he made a terrible slaughter. But the next commanding officer after Thoris, a prince of the blood-royal of Memphis,

Memphis, a man in years, and of great reſo-lution, taking the command upon him in the abſence of the general, gave immediate orders to the officers who were behind him to retreat with the army in good order and ſilence into their intrenchments; while with one ſingle cohort, which he kept, he would oppoſe the whole ſhock of the Theban army. The ſoldiers of this cohort, to the number of three hundred, drew together imperceptibly with their backs to the wall of a long temple they had behind them. There they withſtood all the fury of the enemy; and were almoſt all cut off, when the commander, directing his diſcourſe to Mephres, ſaid: My lord, you are conqueror of our firſt ranks, and of three hundred men which we were here; but the body of the army of Memphis is in ſafety. Be contented at this time with the remainder of theſe brave men, who ſurrender themſelves priſoners to you. The king inſtantly put an end to the battle: he order'd the ſoldiers to be convey'd away, and care to be taken of them, eſpecially of the wounded. Afterwards, giving his hand to the commander, he made him mount a horſe by his ſide, and told him, that he ſhould have no other chain but his word, nor no other priſon but a tent near to his own. Thus the king return'd into the center of his camp, to inform himſelf of what paſs'd on the other ſide of the city.

MEPHRES, to take advantage of the treaſon of Thoris, had given orders to his lieutenants to ſuffer the troops of the gariſon to advance very near to the camp, where they ſhould be receiv'd by a body of the army in battle-array; and that in this interval of time a certain number of batallions ſhould file off to the right and to the left, under favour of the darkneſs, and range themſelves near the gate the gariſon was march'd out at. He gave two words inſtead of one; that by which they were to know one another in the engagement, and that which, being common to them and the gariſon of Coptos, was to favour the entrance of the beſiegers into the place. The troops which were detach'd to the gate, had orders not to appear till the beſieged being beaten, as in all appearance they would be, fled, or at leaſt retir'd towards the city: but that then, mixing with them, and ſeeming to belong to them, they ſhould throw themſelves, in as great a number as poſſible, into Coptos.

THE attack of the gariſon, who were ſurpriz'd to find the enemy in ſo good a poſture of defence, was, however, very vigorous; becauſe the officers the governor had pitch'd upon were excellent ſoldiers, and ſeven of the companions of Sethos, who were with them as volunteers, encourag'd the troops

by

by their example. Tho' the Theban army not only receiv'd them in front, but attack'd them insensibly on the flanks too; the soldiers of Coptos held out this unequal battle with so much courage, that the besiegers, who were posted near the gate, thought there would be no fugitive at all, and that this pretext for throwing themselves into the town would fail them. In the mean time the Thebans, beginning to speak aloud, that the army of Memphis was defeated, and the general taken, about fifty of the most cowardly of the garison, who were nearest the gate, forsook their ranks, and took to their heels towards the city. The governor, who believ'd all his troops were defeated and following them, caus'd the gates to be open'd to receive them. The Theban soldiers, who had waited with impatience for this opportunity, join'd with them in great numbers: but the fear and disorder of the former soon made them known from the latter, whose outward appearance was more stay'd, and who affected too much to call out the word, that they might be suffer'd to pass. The governor, who was in arms within and near the gate, with the flower of his officers and soldiers, among whom were Sethos and Amedes, cry'd out at once: We are betray'd; let the gates be shut. This order had no effect, the besiegers having so crowded up the passage, that it was impossible to stir them,

 The

The governor had nothing elſe to do but to ſend for ſuccours from that part of the gariſon which remain'd in the city; and in the mean time to employ the men he had there to oppoſe this torrent. They ſuffer'd the ſmall number of the enemy that were enter'd, to be diſpers'd thro' the city, as not being able to do much harm of themſelves: but the governor, with the choiceſt of his ſoldiers, whom he had already got together, Sethos, one of the young lords, who alone remain'd with him, Amedes, and even the ſlave we have already mention'd, and who never left his lord, when he would ſuffer him to follow him, reſiſted the beſiegers, who were got to the widening of the gate, with ſo much vigour, that notwithſtanding all the efforts of thoſe who puſh'd them on behind, not any more enter'd.

AMEDES perceiving that Sethos, in the heat of action, was every moment out of his ſight, gave him a particular charge not to go without the gates. The young prince had indeed no intention of doing it: but a moment afterward, perceiving the enemy gave way, and being under the gate, back'd by all the ſoldiers who were behind him, he could not perſuade himſelf to loſe ſuch an advantage; but purſuing it, was got without the gate, with the young lord and his ſlave, before he perceiv'd it. They were all three ſoon

ſoon forc'd to retreat along the ditch on the left hand, to ſome diſtance from the gate, by the attack of freſh troops. Amedes himſelf, in oppoſition to his own orders, being engag'd under the ſame gate, and not being able to draw back without giving the enemy an opportunity of advancing upon him, and entring the city again, was likewiſe got out, and was forc'd towards the right hand by the troops of the king of This, by whom he was grievouſly wounded and taken priſoner. The governor knew there were perſons of ſuch diſtinction without the gates: but having charge of the place, he laid hold of the firſt favourable moment to ſhut the gate; and leaving only a wicket open, plac'd ſuch men there as he could depend on; not only to ſee whom they let in, but to procure advice every moment of the troops that were without, and, above all, of Sethos and Amedes. In the mean time the young prince, with his companion and ſlave, making uſe of their utmoſt cunning and activity, and favour'd by the darkneſs of the night, were ſoon at ſuch a diſtance as to be out of danger of being kill'd or taken priſoners. Then the reſult of their little council was, That the ſhorteſt and ſafeſt method for them was, courageouſly to overcome all obſtacles, and join the troops of the gariſon; who yet defended themſelves on the ſpot where they were firſt attack'd, and which they would eaſily find again by the noiſe. They order'd it ſo, by keeping all three together, that they got thither, after having kill'd by the way ſome of thoſe who attempted to ſtop their courſe. Having ſoon made themſelves known among the ranks, they, in ſome meaſure, renew'd their hopes. But Sethos ſoon after receiv'd a wound by a ſword under the bottom of his armour, which laid him flat on the ground for dead. His companion, who ſaw it, threw himſelf immediately upon him, to endeavour, with the help of his ſlave, to draw his body out of the fight. They had juſt ſucceeded in it, when the young lord got ſuch another blow himſelf, which laid him at a diſtance from Sethos ſenſeleſs and almoſt without life. The ſlave thinking his lord dead beyond recovery, with reluctance drew his ring from his finger, to ſhew that he had accompany'd him faithfully to his death. Being likewiſe reſolv'd to continue fighting near him, he had but juſt time in the tumult, to put this ring into his mouth. But he had hardly enter'd again into action, when, being on the flank of the batallion, from whence he had juſt remov'd his lord's body, the Arabian ſoldiers ſeiz'd him behind, and made him enter into the number of their priſoners. He us'd himſelf to hold his ring hid always under his tongue, having a confus'd idea that it might be a means to procure his enlargement.

THE king, tir'd with expecting in his tent the succefs of fo long and fo obftinate an encounter, came himfelf to the field of battle; and with an intent to fpare his troops for the continuance of a fiege, which he apprehended would not be foon at an end, he gave orders to found a retreat almoft as foon as he came thither. And thus the befieged, terribly leffen'd in number, and even not yet knowing their whole lofs, return'd, however, this time into the city with honour.

BUT what an affliction was it, not only to the governor, but the whole garifon, and all the inhabitants of Coptos, when they found Sethos wanting, as well as Amedes, the young lord, and the flave, from whom they might at leaft have learnt his fate! At break of day the governor fent to the king of Thebes to demand a truce for burying their dead. Having eafily obtain'd it from the king, who wanted the fame himfelf, he fent to take an exact view of the field of battle, hoping to find out thofe he was moft concern'd for, by their helmets or other armour, and in particular Sethos and Amedes, by their initiates vefts which they wore under their cuirafs. But the vagabonds who range about for plunder, as it generally happens, had already ftripp'd the dead, and the trampling of men

and

and horfes had disfigur'd the greater part of them. The governor was foon inform'd, that there were no marks to be found of the bodies either of Sethos, Amedes or the flave; but that they were bringing in the young lord, whom they found yet breathing on the fide of the field of battle, ftripp'd like the reft. While they were dreffing his wound, which did not prove to be mortal, he foreftall'd the governor's curiofity, and told him, with groans, that he had feen the young prince kill'd, and that he had affifted the flave in dragging his body out of the crowd; but that having been wounded himfelf in the very inftant, he knew nothing what was become of the body of Sethos, nor of the flave, who was then alive and well. The news of the young prince's death was foon known every where. On the one fide it came to the king of Thebes; and on the other to Amedes. The latter, being difcover'd to be an initiate by the officers of the king of This, who took care of his wound, which was more painful than dangerous, was laid in a litter, and fent as a prifoner of note to Abydus, diftant hardly a day's journey. The king of This having feen him, gave him a very favourable reception. Amedes, on his part, tho' after the death of the prince he had no thoughts either of returning to Memphis, or of remaining in the kingdom of This, foon mediated a peace between the two kings, father and uncle of Sethos, by diſengaging the latter from the league he had made with the king of Thebes.

THE day after the fatal miſtake, of which Thoris had been the cauſe, Mephres having receiv'd the news of the death of Sethos, ſent his compliments of condoleance to the governor, as repreſenting the king of Memphis. He added, that he was juſt going to take vengeance for it; and that he might come himſelf in all ſafety, or ſend whom he might think fit, to be eye-witneſs of it. The governor made anſwer, that he would give the king his maſter an account of this generous civility of the king of Thebes: But that not conceiving what ſort of vengeance he was about to take for the death of the prince, he begg'd he would excuſe his giving any anſwer on this head. At the return of the herald, Mephres aſſembled his whole army, and plac'd all the priſoners of Memphis in the midſt of the ranks. Theſe motions were obſerv'd from the top of the ramparts of Coptos, but they could not yet comprehend what they would end in. At laſt they perceiv'd Thoris bare-headed, and led between two men who held him bound. Then Mephres, beginning to ſpeak, ſaid: Soldiers of Thebes, and ye ſoldiers of Memphis; behold this deſpicable general, who, having no diſtinction either of birth or merit, has had the inſolence

to

to accept of the command of the troops of Memphis againſt an army which it was well known I was to command in perſon. However incens'd I am at the little regard which has been had upon this occaſion to a cuſtom ever obſerv'd by all the kings of Egypt when engag'd in war, I have ample ſatisfaction in the advantage we have had; and I believe Oſoroth will ſoon be more diſpleas'd at this unworthy choice, than I could be. If he govern'd of himſelf, I know what meaſures I ought to have taken with him to prevent this affront. But as I don't vouchſafe to enter into a diſcuſſion of the deference due to the blood-royal of Egypt with any but thoſe of the ſame blood; I have ſuffer'd this affront, reſolving to do my ſelf juſtice for it. I had even rather have given marks of diſdain than vengeance, with regard to a general ſo contemptible as this, had he only ſhewn his want of prudence and knowledge. But be it known to both nations, that this traytor has been the only cauſe of the misfortune which has this night befall'n the enemy's army and gariſon, and above all, the incomparable prince Sethos, the loſs of whom all Egypt ought to regret. This perfidious wretch it was, who, going yeſterday in the evening from tent to tent to diſpenſe his orders for the attack, thought he could not ſpeak loud enough of his deſign, and of the word he had ſent the governor of the city. In vain the moſt pru-

dent

dent officers of his army advis'd him, one after another, as he came to them, to ſpeak with more caution. He, without ceaſing, reſum'd the tone of his voice, with the apparent deſign of being heard by thoſe ſpies, of whom an abhorrence of Daluca's adminiſtration furniſhes me numbers. If he were my ſubject, and I would make him ſuffer the death he deſerves, he ſhould be examin'd in a council of war: But the chaſtiſement I confine myſelf to, even with regard to my priſoner, don't require my taking ſo many meaſures. It is expedient to ſecure here at leaſt ſome puniſhment for a villain, whoſe conduct might, perhaps, not be diſapprov'd of by the miniſtry to which the kingdom of Memphis is now a prey. The king, having ſpoken in this manner, caus'd Thoris to be ſtripp'd to the girdle, notwithſtanding the mournful proteſtations he made that the queen forc'd him to accept of the command; and that by giving his orders, without going out of the camp, he did not apprehend being overheard by the enemy. His hands being bound behind him, two men, one on each ſide of him, put his neck between two forks, and in that condition led him round the whole large ſpace, which was ſurrounded by the troops of Thebes and the priſoners of Memphis, while two other men ſcourg'd him with long rods. This has ſince been a puniſhment inflicted by the Romans upon thoſe who became

came the enemies of their country, previous to the ſtroke of the axe, and of which the bare recital given to the emperor Nero, made him determine to make away with himſelf, for fear of being overtaken in his flight.

AFTER the execution, the king ſaid: Officers and ſoldiers of Memphis, it is as much for your ſatisfaction as my own, that I have now given this example. You ſhall be judges of it yourſelf, by the good treatment you ſhall meet with till you are exchang'd. As for this wretch, I will ſend him bound hand and foot to Daluca without any ranſom. I ſet no value upon him, and ſhould be ſorry he ſhould be compar'd to the meaneſt of my ſoldiers who are priſoners The king, in reality, ſent him immediately to the firſt city of the kingdom of Memphis, where he knew the governor was a creature of Daluca. Thoris, upon his arrival, begg'd he might be conceal'd from the eyes of every one till he prov'd his innocence. This the governor readily comply'd with, and immediately diſpatch'd a meſſenger to the queen to know what he ſhould do with him. The queen, perceiving herſelf chaſtiz'd in the perſon of her general, ſent, with all diligence, orders to this governor, to make a ſhew of all imaginable kindneſs to Thoris under cloſe confinement, and to promiſe him from her a ſpeedy juſtification : but that he ſhould publiſh

lish every where to the world, that the queen would bring him to a trial. That, however, at the end of three days, he should cause him to be strangled in his bed by men whom he could depend on; and that afterwards he should spread abroad that he dy'd of grief. All this was perform'd to a tittle.

THE governor of Coptos had resolv'd not to write to the king till the evening of the day following the double battle which happen'd under the walls of the city, that he might employ the time of his delay in making all possible enquiry, and to gather all the news he could concerning Sethos. He had caus'd all the bodies upon which any marks of distinction were found, to be separated from the rest; for that not only Sethos, but three of the young lords his companions, were not return'd from the battle. Before they were put into the catacombs of Coptos, he caus'd more distinguish'd and honourable exequies to be perform'd for these than for the other, being persuaded that Sethos, tho' unknown, was among them. He at last wrote a letter to the king, bath'd in tears, in which he gave a particular account of all that had pass'd in that unhappy night, and to the moment he took pen in hand. The king, when he came to the article of his son's death, fell in a swoon. The queen, who had receiv'd this news by her emissaries, fifteen hours before him, having

having been from that time always near his person, did all ſhe could to recover him. As ſoon as he came to himſelf, he turn'd towards her, and in a tone, mix'd with grief and anger, ſaid: Oh! madam, theſe are the fruits of your pernicious adminiſtration; from this moment I deprive you of it. Go, and ſhut yourſelf up in one of your moſt diſtant palaces, and let me never ſee you more. The queen gave way to this ſtorm, and retir'd: but before ſhe departed, and took her two ſons with her, to a houſe of pleaſure ſhe had at ten leagues diſtance from the capital, ſhe eſtabliſh'd a private intelligence with thoſe, who looking upon her as mother to the preſent heir to the crown, and knowing the force of her policy, plainly perceiv'd ſhe would always be in ſome conſideration, and hop'd to ſee her again in greater power after her return than before her exile. The king, in the mean time, inſtituted that very day a council of men of pretty good intentions. This council will maintain the kingdom, during ſome of the next enſuing years, in a middle ſituation between proſperity and weakneſs; but which, approaching ſomething nearer to the latter than the former, will bring it to the very brink of its ruin, engag'd in a foreign war; which will be the principal ſubject of the laſt book of this hiſtory.

ASSOON as this council was establish'd, Osoroth, who had yet some hopes of hearing from his son again, imagining he must be stray'd away in the confusion of a night-battle, wrote to the king of Thebes. He intreated him to extend the generosity he had shewn, in being concern'd at the death of his son, so far as to cause enquiry to be made after him among the prisoners which might have been made by the several nations who serv'd under him. He inform'd him, that his son had a ring on his finger, the stone of which was an emerald; whereupon was represented a Horus, of whom one hand seem'd stretch'd out to another that held it, which was that of the late queen Nephte, under the figure of Isis, and had been separated from the rest of the stone, and made a ring for her; tho' he did not know what was become of that ring. That Horus held one finger of his right hand on his mouth; but that one part of his garment seem'd to be held by another hand, which was his own under the figure of Osiris, that he himself wore as a ring on his own finger. That, in short, if by a proclamation of these signs, prince Sethos might be brought to light; he offer'd for his ransom not only the whole Nome of Coptos, which he immediately resign'd to him, for the sake of peace, which he was resolv'd to purchase, but moreover the half of the remainder of his kingdom; an immenſe price for the perſon of his ſon alone. As ſoon as the king of Thebes receiv'd this letter, he order'd the contents of it to be publiſh'd in every place where priſoners of war could have been carry'd, promiſing beſides in his own name an extraordinary reward to thoſe who ſhould reſtore this prince, if, perhaps, he might not be dead.

THIS proclamation was publiſh'd, as in other places, at Compaſis, a city of the Weſtern or Egyptian Arabia, ſeven or eight leagues diſtance from Coptos, where the Arabians, who had taken Azares, had carry'd him. They knew nothing of his being a ſlave. On the contrary, having taken him fighting with an incredible courage, and being charm'd with his preſence of mind on the road from the field of battle to Compaſis, they look'd upon him as a perſon of diſtinction, and reſolv'd to conceal him from the enquiries the king of Thebes might make after priſoners of note. This opinion, which he had at firſt rais'd in them, he kept up in the two or three choſen men who guarded him. So, when the proclamation came to them, he thought he had room enough to ſay: My lords of Arabia, tho' I am an Egyptian, I have always had a natural propenſity to your nation. You have already an evidence of it in the eaſe with which I ſpeak your tongue. It is not yet time for me to tell you who I am. I have not the ring here describ'd; but, if you are wise and secret, I'll give an account of it in another place. Carry me only on the other side of the Red-sea to the great Arabians, from whom you are descended. I am dissatisfy'd with the administration of Memphis, as you are with that of Thebes; we may be of mutual advantage one to the other. These Arabians being astonish'd at this discourse, conceiv'd a new respect for their prisoner. They instantly led him by private ways to the haven of Berenice, where they embark'd him privately, as himself had desir'd; and having landed him at the port of Badios in Arabia Felix, some days afterwards he was conducted honourably to Meriaba, where the kings of that country held their residence.

THE fate of Sethos, who was not dead, as was suppos'd, had not been less singular. Some Ethiopian soldiers had made him prisoner towards the conclusion of the battle; they had perceiv'd a breath of life, which an hour's time had recover'd in him. Tho' they did not know him for the prince of Memphis, his noble stature, and the fineness of the steel of his armour, made them believe they should get a great ransom for this prisoner. Sethos therefore, not yet come to himself, was carry'd by these Barbarians to a city, call'd in our antient itineraries, Phœnicon *, twenty miles from Coptos on the way to the Red-sea. The Phœnician merchants had a settlement there of such importance, that it gave name to the place. The Ethiopian soldiers had pitch'd upon this place to carry the wounded men to, because the commerce of precious stones, with which they furnish'd the Phœnicians, made them very much esteem'd by them. There the Ethiopian soldiers stripp'd Sethos of his armour and garments, and threw away his initiate's vest, which was unknown to them, and all over bloody. They afterwards committed him to the care of some Phœnician physicians, of whom they made use themselves for their sick. These physicians, being of a nation more civiliz'd than the Ethiopians, took a peculiar care of this prisoner, whose wound had happily not prejudic'd his nobler parts. They were concern'd for him more on the account of his understanding, which soon was manifest, than for the orders they had receiv'd on his account. Sethos carefully concealing his name and birth from them, till he was able to judge what course to take, pretended to be a common soldier of the army of Memphis, call'd, Cheres: So that the Ethiopians, who came from time to time to enquire after him, began to cool on his ac-

* See the Geography of Cellarius, de Africa.

count. The Phœnicians taking advantage of this distaste, propos'd their selling him to them. The bargain was soon made; and Sethos, without yet saying any thing, from a prisoner of war, became a slave. His new masters waited only till he was in some measure recover'd, to carry him to the white Port on the Red-sea, where they were to imbark for a long voyage.

He was yet at Phœnicon, where, without making himself known, he had heard the false report which was spread of his death; the sorrow it had caus'd in the city of Coptos; the concern the king of Thebes had on that account, and the vengeance he had taken for it; when the publication of his father's letter was brought into the very chamber where he lay. The mention made in it of his ring, made him cast his eyes upon his hand the first time since his wound; and seeing that wanting, he stifled the first inclination he had to discover himself: But when, in the continuance of the letter, he understood that Osoroth offer'd the half of his kingdom for his ransom, the unreasonablness of that inspired him with the resolution of concealing himself yet more, and rather to bury himself alive, than be the cause of dismembring, in so frightful a manner, the second and most glorious monarchy of Egypt. As soon as the letter was read quite thro', he could not forbear ſaying aloud; That ſuch a priſoner, if he was yet living, would ruin his father's kingdom before he came to the ſucceſſion; and that it would be a happineſs for Oſoroth, if his ſon remain'd dead, as it was believ'd. This young prince ſtrengthen'd himſelf in theſe generous ſentiments, in the hopes of returning ſooner or later to Memphis in a more favourable and glorious manner; by a reflection on the dangers which the ill-will of the queen, whereof he had juſt had ſo terrible a proof, would expoſe him to every day, if he return'd to his own country; and, perhaps, yet more, by a private ſatisfaction ariſing from an idea of a long voyage he was going to undertake with theſe navigators, who were generally good friends to the Egyptians, from whom they took their riſe, and who ſhew'd a particular regard for him. To ſay yet more, he depended upon his initiation for a ſupply of all the virtues of which he might have occaſion under a diſguiſe, and an exile perillous, tho' prudent. To prevent therefore any importunate enquiries, he preſs'd his new maſters to convey him immediately to the haven where they were to imbark. They did it the very ſame day, by means of a litter, carry'd by men, to prevent the motion he muſt have ſuffer'd in any other carriage.

THUS

THUS the king of Thebes wrote to the king of Memphis, that all his enquiries, of which he gave him the particulars, were in vain. That he accepted of the Nome of Coptos, the only cauſe of the war, as having of old belong'd to the kings his predeceſſors: But that if even he had been ſo happy to find his ſon again, whom the governor of Coptos believ'd he had bury'd, he ſhould not have rated the ranſom of a prince, whoſe memory he himſelf honour'd, at a higher price than that of a reaſonable peace.

THE

LIFE

OF

SETHOS.

BOOK VI.

SETHOS, whom we ſhall call Cheres throughout the whole courſe of his voyage, in conformity to the name he had given himſelf, found at his arrival at the white Port a fleet of fifteen veſſels, mann'd with ten thouſand Phœnicians. The kings of Egypt, according to ſundry teſtimonies of antiquity, made uſe of this people to carry on a trade with foreign nations, and to navigate their

their own ſhips in diſtant ſeas. After having in vain attempted to cut the iſthmus, which ſeparates the Mediterranean from the Red-ſea *, they had confin'd themſelves to ſome canals, capable only of receiving veſſels of a middling burden. So they were oblig'd to let the Phœnicians have ſome ports of the Red-ſea, from whence they had a communication with the Indies. They had even about ſix years before made a very conſiderable ſettlement in the famous iſland of Taprobane, (now Ceylon) ſituate at the end of that great peninſula which ſeparates the Indus from the Ganges. Beſides the affairs of commerce, which carry'd them thither every year, they were going this time to carry ſuccour to their colony, whom the kings of the iſland threatned with an approaching expulſion. So this fleet, tho' conſiſting of merchant-men, was equipp'd for war. Cheres, as yet ſtretch'd out on his litter, was carry'd by them who bought him on board, of their general; to whom they preſented him as an Egyptian taken priſoner at the battle of Coptos by certain Ethiopian ſoldiers, who had ſold him to them for a ſum of money. He call'd himſelf a common ſoldier, who had indeed been reclaim'd by nobody: But, added

* Seſoſtris deſiſted from this undertaking; and Nechus, who afterwards attempted it, loſt one hundred and twenty-thouſand men about it. Vid. Marſh. pag. 376, & 531.

they,

they, for the underſtanding and parts, which were viſible in him, they hop'd, after his recovery, which advanc'd apace, their general would be glad to have him in his ſervice. He receiv'd this priſoner very favourably, and told him, that the Egyptians, tho' of the meaneſt rank, were always treated handſomely by them. That he might recover at his eaſe; and that he ſhould have no other employment impos'd on him than what he ſhould chooſe himſelf. They ſet ſail the very next day. The wind, which was, during the whole voyage, equally favourable, was no impediment to the patient's recovery. After two days he began to get up for ſome hours, to acquire a knowledge in navigation, by applying what he ſaw put in practice, without ſaying any thing, to the principles which he knew better than thoſe who made uſe of them. He heard, with pleaſure, the ſailors, who, as they coaſted Egypt, and the moſt northern part of Ethiopia, nam'd ſucceſſively thoſe nations, a knowledge of whom he had attain'd to by geography. Such were the Troglodytes, ſo call'd from the caverns in which they dwelt, to ſcreen themſelves from the exceſſive heat of their climate: The Adulites, ſlaves who had eſcap'd out of Egypt, and built a fort there, call'd, Aduliton. The ſouthern Blemyes, men whoſe heads were ſo low and ſquat, that the firſt who diſcover'd them ſaid, they had none at

all;

all; and that their eyes, noſe, and mouth were on the upper part of their breaſts. They ſhew'd the dwellings of other people, who were no otherwiſe diſtinguiſh'd one from the other, than by their different ſorts of diet: As the Riſophagi, who ſubſiſted wholly on roots: The Icthyophagi, who being border'd on the ſea-ſide, by an inacceſſible ſhore, and towards the land by frightful precipices, have no manner of communication with other men, and live only on fiſhing *: The Struthiophagi, a little farther within land, who paſs their lives in hunting the Struthio-camelus, a great bird, with the feet of a camel, with which they throw ſtones behind them at thoſe who purſue them, and that make no other uſe of their wings, which are very ſhort, but to run the lighter.

BEFORE they arriv'd at the Streights, they came near to the Sabean Arabia, otherwiſe call'd, Arabia Felix, by reaſon of the beauty of its meadows, but above all, for the abundanee and variety of its aromatick plants. The approach to this excellent country is known long before you diſcover land. Diodorus expreſſes himſelf very eloquently on this ſnbject: " Nothing, ſays he, can " equal the pleaſure which this compound

* Diodorus mentions theſe Icthyophagi; but he ſeem's to place them in Arabia.

" fragrancy

" fragrancy gives even to those who but coast
" this shore, and partake of it at a distance.
" The land-breezes bring these precious ex-
" halations from the midst of the country
" even to the sea: they steal, as it were,
" into the very innermost of the soul, and
" proceeding actually from the very bosom
" of nature, they give travellers an idea of
" the ambrosia, which poets feign to be the
" delight of the gods."

THEY at last arriv'd at the Streights, of which Cheres heard some of the ship's crew saying, that it was not long since they were believ'd to be clos'd up. Indeed, a certain Damastes, mention'd by Strabo, had been of that opinion. They gave to this passage, at its discovery, a name of evil omen, by calling it, *Sthenæ Deiræ*, the fatal Streights, or the rolling Promontory of Ethiopia, or the isles which meet there: Some authors even call it, *Ostium Luctus* *, the Haven of Mourning. Not that it is so very difficult or dangerous to pass; but in these first times, when long navigations were very hazardous, they thereby signify'd, that those who had the presumption to pass these Streights, in order to go farther, run the risk of never returning.

* This is the signification of its Arabian name, Babel-mendeb.

THEY enter'd, however, into this ſea, which waſhes the ſouthern coaſts of Arabia to the Perſian gulph, and to which the antients gave the name of Red-ſea, rather than to that which is incloſ'd between Egypt and Arabia, ſeldom calling the latter otherwiſe than the Arabian Gulph. Continuing their coaſt toward the eaſt, they row'd within ſight of the coaſts of Carmania and Gedroſia, maritime provinces of Perſia; and they diſcover'd to the ſouth of them that number of little iſlands [the Maldives] which the ſea does but juſt ſeparate one from the other, and ſome of which are not a furlong in circumference: Ptolemy accounts three hundred ſeventy-eight; but ſome travellers affirm there are twelve thouſand, which they ſay are all ſubject to one king.

As they had been above a month on their paſſage, Cheres was perfectly recover'd. The general, call'd Aſtartus, a man of knowledge and experience, and even known to Cheres by his fame, obſerv'd more and more ſomething noble in his phyſiognomy, and a certain air of diſtinction in his whole perſon. He gave great attention to his anſwers, which, without departing from that modeſty, which his preſent condition ſeem'd to require, ſhew'd him poſſeſs'd of a great elevation of mind and thought; but he was truly ſurpriz'd at the

the extent of his knowledge, which had already ſerv'd to redreſs ſome obſervations of the pilots by rules or methods ſurer and more agreeable than theirs; and which ſeem'd equal in all the natural ſciences, as well as in the hiſtory, laws and manners as well of Egypt, as of all other nations whom they undertook to queſtion him about. Cheres manag'd this advantage with art, and only ſaying upon every occaſion what was neceſſary, he made his knowledge appear inexhauſtible: For, in ſhort, tho' he would not be known for the perſon he was, he did not refuſe the eſteem and conſideration he could attain to naturally, and without ſeeming to ſeek it. All the reputation he had gain'd as Sethos, was of no ſervice to him, and he was oblig'd to raiſe a new fame as Cheres. However, tho' alone, depriv'd of every thing, and having loſt to the very leaſt tokens of his birth, he did not deſpair, in the great views he had for the benefit of mankind, to ſee himſelf ſoon chief of that fleet, into which he came as a ſlave. The general, being at an uncertainty with regard to him, without changing, in outward appearance, the condition of a ſoldier and priſoner, which Cheres had himſelf taken, acted in other reſpects with him, as with a perſon from whom he ought to bring no reproaches upon himſelf for the future; and he put in practice, on his account, the very wiſe maxim of reſpecting the unknown. To ſay true, the name of an Egyptian, kept up in this ſtranger by a perſonal merit, was ſufficient for Aſtartus to make the chief officers of his fleet approve his conduct. Even theſe began to regard Cheres as a young man of noble birth, whoſe too diſtinguiſh'd education had made the queen of Memphis jealous of him; ſo they made no difficulty of conferring with him, and they were even ſollicitous to engage him in the intereſt of the Phœnicians.

THE time ſoon came which made them more ſenſible of the purchaſe they had made in him. They already coaſted the weſtern ſhore of the peninſula on this ſide of the Ganges, at the point of which is the promontory, call'd, Cory. Oppoſite to this promontory, at the diſtance of ſixty miles towards the eaſt is the northern port of Taprobane [Ceylon]. This iſland, which was formerly call'd Paleſimundus, is now call'd Salica. If I would give an example of the variations which have happen'd in the names of moſt places in the world, and of the difficulty there is in knowing the preſent world in the antient geographers, I ſhould add, that the firſt name of this iſland was Lamcab, * or Lamca; the ſecond, Ilanarus; and the third, Tratane; of which, it is ſaid, the Greeks have made

* See the notes on the leſſer geogr. of the Oxford edition, cap. 1. pag. 76.

Taprobane.

Taprobane. I purposely omit the history of Jambolus *, who having been put, with his companions only, into a bark, by the Ethiopians, as expiatory victims, pretend to have landed safe on this island; because this history appears in that author, with all the absurdity of a fable. Taprobane was accounted, a long while, the biggest island in the Southern Ocean; whether it was that those which are larger were not then known, or whether it was suppos'd to have been of a greater extent than it really is. And indeed, the charts, made according to the geographical graduations of Ptolemy, extend it under the Equator, tho' it be at about ten degrees northern distance from it.

After a very fortunate voyage, more with the help of their sails than their oars, the Phœnicians were at the height of Cory, when the rising sun discover'd to their view, on the side of the island, a fleet twice as large as theirs. They easily perceiv'd, by the difference of their flags, that the three kings of Taprobane had combin'd to oppose their passage. Astartus, who began to be uneasy that no boat came off to him, to inform him in what condition the affairs

* Diodorus mentions this author, and his voyage, towards the end of his second book.

of

of the colony were, did not doubt but they were entirely deſtroy'd. Not daring to take upon himſelf alone to attack the enemy at ſuch a diſadvantage, and without having had an opportunity of ſpeaking with any of the Phœnicians of the iſland, he aſſembled a council of war. He made Cheres ſtay in the cabbin, under pretence of doing ſome ſervice. The plurality of votes was for returning; For, in ſhort, ſaid they, if our country-men are exterminated, as their ſilence, with regard to us, gives us reaſon to believe, we have not brought along with us ſufficient proviſions, to make a new ſettlement in Taprobane alone, and by force. If we are defeated, we ſhall have no retreat, and victory itſelf will be of no ſervice to us. Aſtartus, who had a private commiſſion, but in good form, which conſtituted him intendant of the eaſtern commerce, annex'd to the employ of the chief of the colony, with whom they were not ſatisfy'd, was uneaſy to find their opinions run this way. Before he gave his vote, he bethought himſelf to aſk Cheres, as if by chance, whether the Egyptians, in ſuch a caſe, would be of the ſame mind? Cheres coming nearer, and ſtanding, thus addreſs'd himſelf to the officers; My lords, tho' I am but a ſtranger in your company, I have, methinks, a greater reluctancy to be ſo near Taprobane, and not to land there, than you have to return into Phœnicia, without being able to give the leaſt account of your country-men. If they are murder'd, don't you owe to the intereſt of your nation, which has ſettlements in many other places, the example of chaſtiſing their murderers? And, if your brethren are in chains, don't you owe to them your utmoſt endeavours for their deliverance? Are not you better combatants by land or ſea than theſe Barbarians whom you fear? Valour and experience in war are very little worth, if they won't be an equivalent for a number of ſhips which does not exceed the double of yours. The general, to encourage Cheres yet more, ſaid; Your arguments would be juſt, if we had a prince Sethos with us, whoſe genius and courage might ſerve inſtead of the ſoldiers we want. But the greater part of our company is compos'd of men fitter for trade than war, and who would be more aſſiduous in preſerving their merchandizes than in acquiring glory. My lord, reply'd Cheres, all Egyptians, at leaſt thoſe who have been bred in the ſame ſchool of virtue, and who have paſs'd the ſame trials, are equal. Attempt the combat only, I will endeavour to keep up among you the honour of my country, and perhaps ſhall encourage your ſoldiers to revenge theirs. Theſe words, ſpoken in a tone which Cheres had not before aſſum'd, made the whole

whole council come to a resolution of attacking the enemy's fleet. All the officers returning to their vessels, carry'd the same resolution thither, with which Cheres had inspir'd them. They told their people, that the gods had sent a man amongst them, in the person of an Egyptian, who had inherited the wisdom and valour of prince Sethos, whose fame they had heard so much of at the White Port; and that with such an assistance victory could never fail them.

CHERES had already put on armour, the lightest he could find in the vessel, and had even cover'd himself with it but in part, that he might be more active: but he had provided himself with a large sabre. He had desir'd the general to let him have the office of carrying his orders throughout the whole fleet, to have, by that means, a continual communication with him, upon all that might offer to be done in the heat of the battle. To begin the exercise of his function, Cheres went, within the space of an hour, to every vessel in the Phœnician fleet. He did not always make use of a boat to pass from one ship to the other, but, putting in practice the agility he had acquir'd, he jump'd from one to the other of those which were nearest together. He generally descended from the highest decks by the planks on the outside, with such dexterity as astonish'd the most hardy sailors. The surprize which he thereby caus'd to men, who were very little accustom'd to the most common exercises of the Egyptians, contributed as much as his discourses to heighten their hopes. In most armies, said he, soldiers look upon their adversaries as enemies to their prince or general, and not as their own. Thence it is that they fight only to avoid reproach or punishment, to deserve their pay, or, at most, strictly to accomplish their duty, and to withdraw from peril as soon as is possible. You, on the contrary, as traders, at two thousand leagues distance from your country, ought to regard these islanders as your personal enemies, whose victory, if you suffer it to be on their side, would be much more fatal to every one of you than to your king or your commander. Defend yourselves in this consideration: you won't give a stroke in vain; each of you will, in some measure, clear himself, danger will disappear in your own eyes, and you will find yourselves conquerors, perhaps, without the loss of one of your lives. The combat began about three or four in the afternoon; the islanders began by shooting a vast number of arrows, weapons which are often lost by land, and almost always by sea. The Phœnicians withstood this not very perilous storm, without doing any thing,

thing, but warding it off as much as they could. When the ſhips drew nearer, they began to make uſe of their long poles with iron ſpikes at the end of them. This was the beginning of the combat, hand to hand; and the Phœnicians, remembring the exhortation Cheres had given them, overthrew a good number of their enemy, without loſing a man themſelves. They at laſt came to boarding.

THE people of Taprobane had, in their naval combats, a cuſtom, which gave their courage an appearance of ferocity and deſpair, but which was ſometimes fatal to themſelves. They never boarded an enemy's veſſel but they endeavour'd to faſten it to their own, by means of grappling-irons made for that purpoſe; ſo that if they would, afterwards, they could not, without a great deal of pains, diſengage themſelves. Thus the ſhip that was defeated was of courſe a prize to the other. Cheres being inform'd of this cuſtom was reſolv'd to take the advantage of it. The general, after having regulated in his preſence the general diſpoſitions for the battle, had declar'd to him, that he had his authority to go every where, as he thought fit, and to give orders as from him, for every thing he ſhould judge neceſſary, 'till he recall'd this general order. But if he had not given him this authority, he would have taken it more than once in every ſhip he was in. For, on ſharp and perilous occaſions, the man who is boldeſt and moſt active is always the moſt follow'd. Cheres, neverthelefs, leaving the officers in all things the honour and extent of their functions, only told them what was neceſſary to be done, to ſecond him in what he might undertake alone, and as a common ſoldier.

THE veſſel he was then in was the firſt that was faſten'd. As ſoon as he ſaw the iſlanders grappling-irons fix'd, and that the attack was begun on each ſide, without entrance, he leap'd over their heads into the middle of their veſſel, and with his ſabre, which he knew how to manage with a wonderful dexterity, he made himſelf an impenetrable buckler, which dazled the eyes of every one, and made a terrible havock among all who were within his reach. This frightful maſſacre drew the enemy from their ſhip's ſide to defend themſelves in the middle; the Phœnicians, ruſhing in at the ſame time, made a terrible ſlaughter, and ſoon became maſters of the veſſel. In the ſhort time they were employ'd in ſecuring thoſe who had deliver'd up their arms, they ſaw Cheres doing juſt the ſame thing in another veſſel, tho' they had not perceiv'd which way he went out of their ſhip, or how

how he got into the other. He purſu'd his victory in this manner in five or ſix, which all became prey to the Phœnicians, while the other veſſels, which he could not get at, defended and attack'd in a different manner, but every where with great advantage. The iſlanders were not, however, as yet, diſcourag'd. In the mean time the day drew near its end, and the night, which in theſe climates ſucceeds almoſt without any twilight *, was going to put an undecided end to the combat. Cheres, who had foreſeen this inconvenience, had caus'd all ſorts of combuſtible matters to be got together, and deſign'd to put an end to a victory by fire, which the ſword had not ſufficiently advanc'd. He repair'd on board the general's veſſel, to inform him of his deſign. He propos'd to him to ſacrifice three of the veſſels they had taken, the priſoners of which might be put on board of another. Theſe three he propos'd to fill with combuſtible matters, which ſhould not take fire 'till a certain fix'd time, and after the Phœnicians, who at firſt ſhould appear on the deck, were got into the boats which muſt be in readineſs to receive them. The obſcurity of the night would, ſaid he, favour this deſign, and ſoon afterwards theſe burn-

* For want of a greater denſity in the Atmoſphere in hot Countries.

ing veſſels, if they ſhould have no other ſucceſs, would ſerve at leaſt to give light enough to continue the combat. The general having approv'd the plan, Cheres departed to put it in execution. He choſe for each of the three veſſels forty of the braveſt and moſt active men of the fleet, and inform'd them, that as ſoon as the ſun was ſet, their buſineſs was to advance near enough to the enemy's fleet, to give the iſlanders room to board them on both ſides. He order'd them to make an appearance of reſiſtance, while they were faſtning their grappling irons, according to cuſtom; but that done, they ſhould immediately run to the poops of their three veſſels, and let themſelves down by ropes, which he had caus'd to be plac'd there for that purpoſe, into the boats which ſhould be ready to receive them, and which he would command himſelf. All this was executed at the time and in the manner propos'd. The three veſſels having taken fire, ſoon communicated it to thoſe which were grappled to them on the right and on the left, and had the appearance of three floating Ætna's. The iſlanders held it no longer at this ſight; but fearing that ſeveral other ſhips of the Phœnician fleet might conceal the ſame ſnares, they diſpers'd, by force of ſails and oars, ſome one way, ſome the other, as they ſaw themſelves

themſelves purſu'd by the Phœnician veſſels.

THE general ſeeing night come, and perceiving the flames of the burning veſſels inſenſibly decreaſe, would not venture further in the dark, and without knowing what fortifications the enemy might have on the ſhore. He order'd the ſignal to be given for his veſſels to retire, and place themſelves in a line 'till morning. Cheres was the firſt to obey this order, and ſoon appear'd before Aſtartus. As they were beholding together a remainder of the iſlanders, who with lamentable cries were jumping into the ſea from the tops of their burning veſſels, others who were yet ſwimming, and again others who were drowning; Cheres, tho' the author of their misfortune by his invention, told Aſtartus, that he could not reflect upon the cruelties of war without ſome grief. That it was not to be excus'd in a king or the head of a republick, but by the extreme juſtice of his cauſe; and that it ought not to be reſolv'd upon, but with a view to ſacrifice ſome private perſons to the general good of ſociety. But ſoon retaking a more gay aſpect, he added, That his grief for the fate of theſe wretches, whom he did not know, was eaſily remov'd by the ſhouts of joy with which his victorious fleet eccho'd on every ſide. That he very

very much approv'd the orders he had given for wine and other refreshments to be distributed to his soldiers. That such indulgences properly plac'd made them forget a long sequel of toils, and encourag'd them to expose themselves the next moment to new dangers. Astartus took all these maxims in good part, and was even charm'd to know the character of his Egyptian to the bottom, that he might employ him more to the purpose. He invited the chief officers of his fleet to a sumptuous repast on board his ship. Cheres was plac'd in an honourable manner at the table, where, as well by his discourse as his noble, discreet, and winning behaviour, he, without exciting any uneasiness or jealousy, confirm'd them in an opinion of his being every way superior to them.

THE general, whose mind was justly taken up with reflecting on the continuance of his enterprize, sent them all away at midnight, with orders to let their ships companies immediately betake themselves to rest, that they might be fit to enter into action again in six hours, and at day-break. Cheres obey'd like the rest, and was soon plung'd into a profound sleep, after the fatigues of the foregoing day. The design of Astartus was to employ the night in examining the prisoners about the state of the colony,

lony, of which he had, 'till then, no news. He was just upon his departure to the vessels where they were confin'd, when his outermost centry let him know, that two men in a small boat had made the usual signal, to acquaint him, they desir'd to speak with the general. He order'd them to be brought to him, and knowing them, notwithstanding their wither'd and pale countenances, to be two officers, who had formerly serv'd under him, he shut himself up with them alone in his council-chamber. The eldest of them said to him, My lord, we come here as deputies from Pheletes, the chief of our colony, who six months ago engag'd in an enterprize which appear'd of advantage to our nation. It has since been attended with fatal consequences. But if you pursue the victory you have just obtain'd yet a little farther; this undertaking, which has hitherto succeeded but badly, may have, from this night, an happy accomplishment. You know, my lord, with what readiness the islanders of Taprobane suffer'd us to settle at Galiba, the fairest, and most convenient for us, of all their maritime cities. From thence we have, in the course of the five first years of our settlement, carry'd on a profitable trade to the Chersonesus Aurea [Siam] to the three Sabadibæ [Sumatra, Java, and Borneo] and even to the kingdom of Serica [Northern China.]

China]. Our chief obſerving, that beſides the great number of Phœnicians which were in Galiba, our trade had drawn thither a great many of the inhabitants of the neighbouring iſlands, all at our command, he projected the deſign of making himſelf maſter of the city. Thinking every thing was lawful againſt Barbarians, he took the opportunity of a dark night to ſurprize the governor and gariſon of Galiba. The firſt was kill'd in his bed, and the latter put to the ſword; and having poſſeſs'd ourſelves of the citadel, the reſt of the city immediately ſubmitted to us. All went well ſo far; and our chief had even taken the time when the king of the Galibians, (whoſe capital is, however, in the country, and is call'd Anurogrammum) was at war with the two other kings of the iſland, and when it was thought it would be acceptable to them. But, on the contrary, as ſoon as they knew it, they at once concluded a peace with him, and promis'd him their aſſiſtance to drive us out of the city, of which we had taken poſſeſſion. Pheletes's deſign was not to inform the court of Phœnicia of his project 'till it was accompliſh'd, to pleaſe the king the more with the relation of a conqueſt already made. But being inform'd that the three kings had immediately begun their march to retake Galiba, he did not preſume to let them know at Tyre the true cauſe of the

rupture

rupture between the iſlanders and us, for fear of being reproach'd with having undertaken an ill-concerted project. He only entreated the king to ſend him a ready and powerful ſuccour againſt the kings of the iſland, who threaten'd our colony with a ſpeedy expulſion. Theſe letters were ſent away a little before the ſiege was form'd: and he took care that there were no other letters but his in the packet, which he ſent by a truſty meſſenger. But ſince that time it has been impoſſible either for him or us to have any communication from without. The kings caus'd a triple chain to be extended, from one point to the other, of the two moles which form the entrance into the port, ſupported from ſpace to ſpace by flat boats. Their ſhips cruize continually before this chain, to ſhut out all ſuccours that might be ſent us from Phœnicia, and my boat had not eſcap'd, but under favour of the diſorder which your victory has caus'd in their fleet. I muſt now inform you, my lord, that the enemy has juſt beyond, and to the ſouth of Galiba, a convenient baſon, fenc'd on the ſea-ſide by a long chain of rocks. Thither the ſhatter'd remains of their fleet are already retir'd. On the other ſide, towards the north, oppoſite to which you now are, is a high plain, and at the end of it are downs, the foot of which is waſh'd by the ſea. From thence it is their land-forces

beſiege

besiege the city. The height and thickness of the walls has defended it against them for almost six months. But we must confess, that the famine to which they have reduc'd us, by investing us so closely both by sea and land, had put us out of a condition to hold out a week longer; when from the tops of our towers we perceiv'd your fleet, as an auspicious star, rising to preserve our lives. Now, my lord, what our chief proposes to you, and begs you would put in execution this very night, to compleat the work you have so happily begun, is this. A little more to the north you will be, at about twenty furlongs from the city, in an excellent road, and will have before you a low shore of the breadth of a furlong. There, under favour of the darkness, and with the help of your boats, we desire you would land all the armed men you have. I offer to be their guide, while my companion will return with your answer to the chief of the colony: you will run no hazard in the descent, since your victory has dispers'd the enemy's vessels which defended that coast. In the mean time, the soldiers of your fleet being landed, and getting, by an easy ascent, up to the downs, will have the army of the besiegers between them and our garison, which will make a vigorous sally upon the enemy, at the same time that you attack them behind.

THE

THE general, not a little ſupriz'd at what he had heard, ſaid to the officer; I believe, dear comrade, you yourſelf are ſenſible of the raſhneſs of this undertaking of your chief. The king, our maſter, when he ſent him into theſe ſeas, gave him a full power to do all that he ſhould think expedient for the good of the colony; and if he did not tie him down to ask and wait for the orders of the court for too diſtant expeditions; even this confidence renders him more blameable by the ill uſe he has made of it. Be it however as it will, I conſent to purſue my victory. The animoſity of the kings of the iſland againſt us muſt now be ſo great, that, without diſpute, nothing but their entire defeat can bring them to a reſolution of allowing us to reſide in Taprobane, even upon the footing we were before. The intent of the Phœnician court was not that you ſhould make a conqueſt of it, of leſs advantage to our trade than the favour and amity of a people ſo friendly as theſe iſlanders were to us. But our ſettlement being once made, to the ſatisfaction of the inhabitants, the king of Tyre will now maintain it, either by good-will or by force. I ſhall therefore immediately undertake the deſcent you propoſe. I accept of you for my guide, and will inſtantly ſend your companion back to carry my anſwer

to

to Pheletes. I only desire your chief, said Astartus, speaking to the second deputy, to attempt nothing before day; and even not to attack the enemy 'till I shall give him the signal, by hoisting red colours, that I am ready to fall upon them on my side. The general accordingly sent away the second deputy immediately, who got into the city as happily as he came out: but turning to the first, he said; For you who remain with us, I can't enough recommend to you an exact silence to our whole fleet, with regard to the conduct of your chief. We have an Egyptian here with us, a man of a distinguish'd merit, who conceals himself under the form of a common soldier of Memphis, made prisoner in a battle which his king lost against the king of Thebes, a little before our departure. It is to this Egyptian you owe your deliverance: It was he who determin'd the officers of our fleet to hazard a combat which appear'd so unequal to them: It was he, in short, who, by his skill and courage, has made the victory turn to the least in number. But since he has been in my vessel, I have observ'd such principles of virtue in him, as would not favour the proceedings of Pheletes. If he should have any knowledge of them, it would extremely allay his fervency, and, of course, that of our soldiers, whom he encourages, by his example and discourses:

In

In a word, it is for your intereſt, that he be not made acquainted with the cauſe of your misfortune, 'till after your deliverance.

AT the ſame time, Aſtartus, tho' his fleet had enjoy'd but three hours reſt, inſtead of ſix, which he had propos'd, gave orders for the deſcent. How numerous ſoever the boats were which they had in their veſſels, the troops they had landed could not be upon the downs 'till ſun-riſing. The enemy, having ſeen them at a diſtance marching in good order, ſent immediately three heralds to them. The chief of them, directing his diſcourſe to Aſtartus, who was at the head of his army, with Cheres by his ſide, ſaid; My lord! the three kings of Taprobane, who are on the other ſide of the intrenchments which you ſee before you, propoſe to you, by me, before you engage, to accept of a conference with them in the midſt of this plain: They will come thither, attended only by a guard of ſixty men, counting even the lords who will accompany them, and will think it very proper for you to take the ſame number on your ſide. They offer their word, and deſire yours, That the conference be held quietly; and that, if the peace cann't be concluded in it, that hoſtilities may not begin again on either ſide, 'till two hours after it be broke up.

 They

They earnestly intreat you will cause Pheletes, the chief of the Phœnician colony, who is shut up in Galiba, which we besiege, to be present at this conference. They will allow him all the safe-guard necessary for him to pass our camp, unless you chuse to send for him in one of your vessels. Our kings are, against their wills, greatly at variance with Phœnicia. The fact alone carries its decision with it, and we have no distrust of the equity either of your king, or of you: but as either side may be prejudic'd in their own cause, our kings are willing to accept of a third as arbiter. The fame of the Egyptians in general is spread throughout the whole world: but some prisoners, which we yesterday took from you, have given us such encomiums of the singular virtues of an Egyptian who is in your company, and who contributed so much to your victory, that our kings are willing to refer every thing to his judgment. Astartus immediately answer'd; That he consented to all the kings desir'd: That he would send one of his vessels to fetch Pheletes, with only ten of the chief officers he had with him in the city, and that he would lessen by so many the number of those who should accompany him: That he would suffer the Egyptian to give his opinion on the dispute in question; and that he himself had a decision to give, with which, he flatter'd himſelf, both parties would be ſatisfy'd. He even added; That being yet the only one in his army who knew the bottom of the caſe, he would not prepoſſeſs any one, but give their judgments a greater liberty upon an affair which would not be brought to light 'till the conference.

THE heralds being departed, extremely ſatisfy'd with their anſwer from Aſtartus, he inſtantly diſpatch'd one of his veſſels to fetch Pheletes, with ten of the chief officers of his colony. He was inraged, to find that a quarrel, which, under the preſent circumſtances of things, ſeem'd to him ſo advantageous to be determin'd by force of arms, ſhould degenerate into a treaty. He plainly perceiv'd it would not turn to his advantage: but he had reduc'd himſelf to a neceſſity of obeying a man, who ſeem'd to be come only to his aſſiſtance, above whom his employ would have plac'd him, in the natural courſe of things, and who, in the common ſituation of affairs, ought to have receiv'd orders from him.

IN the mean time both ſides were preparing the ſpot of ground neceſſary for the conference: They pitch'd upon it at an equal diſtance between the intrenchments of the Taprobane army, and the firſt line of the Phœnician army. The iſlanders furniſh'd a large tent, under which they might be ſhelter'd from the rays of the ſun. Aſtartus, who perfectly knew how to treat with an enemy, was preſent himſelf at the regulation of every thing, and caus'd all the prerogatives of honour to be plac'd on that ſide deſtin'd for the three kings. He order'd their three ſeats to be plac'd upon an elevation, while there were on his ſide only benches ſet in a ſemicircle over-againſt other benches rang'd in the ſame manner for the lords of Taprobane, at the feet of their kings. Pheletes being come, both parties enter'd into the tent. Aſtartus took advantage, in a very graceful manner, of the right, which his victory had given him, to regulate in ſome meaſure the ceremonials of the aſſembly; and, by his conduct, he prevented all thoſe cavils which generally delay, and ſometimes even break off, the moſt important treaties. On his ſide he plac'd Pheletes on his right-hand; and next to him, on the ſame ſide, the ten officers of the colony. He himſelf ſate next to Pheletes on the left-hand; and in the ſame manner plac'd the ten chief officers of his fleet on his left-hand. Cheres, who was the laſt in their row at the bottom, was almoſt between the two nations, by the circular form of the benches.

EVERY thing being thus diſpos'd, the king of the Galibians, being ſeated in the middle of the two other, open'd the conference: He ſaid, That tho' the two kings his allies, himſelf, and all the officers of the iſland who were in the tent, underſtood the Phœnician tongue, ſince the Phœnicians had ſettled in their iſland, yet it was ſome trouble to them to ſpeak it: That therefore he hop'd Aſtartus and his officers would conſent, that the herald, whom he had already ſent as deputy to him, and who had dwelt a long time in Phœnicia, might ſpeak in his place. This propoſal having been accepted of, by a ſign of general conſent, the herald aroſe, and began firſt, by giving a lively image of the hoſpitality which the king of the Galibians had afforded the Phœnicians the firſt day, when their fleet, ſhatter'd with the tempeſt, appear'd before his port. He next ſhew'd the zeal with which he ſoon after had procur'd them the friendſhip of the two other kings of the iſland: But he expatiated far more upon the advantage the Phœnicians had drawn from their factory at Galiba, to carry on their trade to the moſt eaſtern ſhores of the Indian ſea. He repreſented, that it was by the conveniency of this factory the Phœnicians had enrich'd the preſent world with the diſcovery of Serica, farther from Taprobane eaſtward than Phœnicia is towards the west; and that this new world had prodigiously increas'd their own riches, by that fine and shining wooll which certain precious insects produc'd on the leaves of trees, He did not forget the circumstance of so many strangers which the kings of Taprobane had receiv'd in all the ports of their island, upon the credit of the Phœnicians: That (said he) was the first cause of our misfortune and theirs. Without this perfidious assistance, their chief would never have attempted an undertaking, which we very well know was disapprov'd of by his principal officers here present. He massacred in one night the governor and the whole garison of Galiba. He made himself master of the city, an abode quieter and more delicious, before this attempt, for him and the Phœnicians, than for our inhabitants themselves. He has made of this general rendezvous of all the Indies, a place of famine and horror, Our kings having been oblig'd to invest this city on all sides, in order to retake it, have, with regret, reduc'd their own subjects to the greatest extremities; because a single man, a traitor with respect to our citizens, and a tyrant with regard to his own countrymen, has persisted for six months, notwithstanding both, in an unwarrantable pretension. This is the only cause of the war we have made against the Phœnicians, and on on which, Astartus, our kings accept of the virtuous Egyptian, whom you yourself have brought with you, as arbiter; they are willing to accept of him for their judge, tho' he be of a nation which has always declar'd itself a friend of your's, and which is even concern'd for its commerce and increase.

ASTARTUS answer'd; That, previous to every thing else, he thought it would be just, to hear the reasons and defence of Pheletes, if he thought fit to alledge any. Upon which, he arising with an appearance of anger, with which he endeavour'd to hide his confusion, spoke thus; I don't know whether it be with the consent of the king our master, that Astartus has accepted of a conference with the kings of Taprobane; at least, I think that the victory he obtain'd yesterday, and which might this day be follow'd by another, dispens'd him from taking so soon the ways of accommodation. He leaves me here no excuse for an attempt, which had been in his power to have render'd reasonable and glorious. The same decorum is not requir'd in war, as at a conference. It has never been a custom to ask the consent of a nation to take its cities or provinces; and it is generally the gods, and fortune, and not their conquerors, that vanquish'd people reproach for their fate. A military under-

undertaking needs no other juſtification but its ſucceſs. If the general himſelf, who is ſent to my aſſiſtance, makes me fail in this, at a time when his own victory has render'd it ſecure, it is the king of Tyre, and not the kings of Taprobane, I ſhall trouble with my complaint. Pheletes having ſate himſelf down again after theſe few words, Cheres roſe up, and ſaid; The fortune of war, made me fall into the hands of the Phœnicians, and, which they, however, don't know, tho' ſince my captivity I have never been out of their ſight, my choice alone has plac'd me in their company. I have reaſon to be ſatisfy'd with the regard they have been pleas'd to have for me, and which is far beyond the condition under which I myſelf have preſented myſelf to them. I ſhan't boaſt that I have recompens'd their goodneſs by the ſervices I render'd them yeſterday, in the naval combat they gain'd over the kings of Taprobane. Theſe ſervices, from that moment, would become involuntary. The eſteem I have for the Phœnician general, and for the officers who are under him, makes me believe they themſelves diſclaim their victory. Their attack at leaſt, to which I confeſs I greatly contributed, was only grounded, as well on their part as mine, on the ignorance we were in of the real ſtate of the diſpute: But before Aſtartus diſcovers his reſolution

on

on this affair, which is now known, I ſhan't let the opportunity eſcape, of diſcovering myſelf, what every one may expect from me, during the whole courſe of my life. The gods, by making me captive, have increas'd the liberty of my ſoul; and being depriv'd of all fortune's favours, I am more ſtrictly devoted to the love of virtue and juſtice. I acted againſt you, O ye kings of Taprobane, while I thought you had exterminated from your iſland the Phœnicians, of whom we ſaw none appear before the battle. I decide againſt you, O ye Phœnicians, 'till you have puniſh'd the traitor, who has actually committed the ſame crime againſt the iſlanders, which I ſuſpected them to be guilty of againſt you. At theſe words, Pheletes roſe up in a fury, and ſaid; Aſtartus, when will you ſtop the mouth of this unknown perſon, your priſoner and ſlave, who takes upon him, in your preſence, an authority which I ſhould not ſuffer from you yourſelf? Cheres then taking that air of authority, which a diſtinguiſh'd birth, and heroick courage, are, upon all occaſions, capable of giving a man who is poſſeſs'd of them, ſaid; I proclaim thy death, thou who ſpeakeſt; and my warrant is, the intereſt of thy nation, which is under a neceſſity thereby to eſtabliſh its blemiſh'd honour, and to open again to its fleets the ports of every ſea, which the example of thy treachery unpuniſh'd, unpunish'd, would keep for ever shut against them.

At this instant Astartus arose, and stretching out his hand between the two disputants, said; 'Tis neither the one or the other of you two who will decide the matter; but the king of Tyre, who is going to speak, by his orders, which I have about me. Ye kings of Taprobane, you will now see, that Egypt is not the only nation that knows what equity and justice is. As a faithful subject to my master, I should not fear either the wicked or the good, in the execution of his will; but his wisdom is going to give peace to the Phœnicians, and to the Islanders. You would have sav'd yourselves the loss you suffer'd yesterday, if the confidence you put in the number of your vessels, had not hinder'd you from having recourse to a conference which you did not propose 'till this day. You gave us reason, against our will, to let you see the Phœnicians know how to make themselves fear'd by their enemies; and they themselves will now shew you, that they know how to make themselves esteem'd by their allies. Astartus having finish'd this discourse, sate down in his place again, and taking the letters patent from the king of Tyre from under his cuirass, he gave them to his gentleman to read, who was plac'd standing opposite

opposite to the herald who had spoken in the name of the kings of Taprobane. After the first lines, which were only the title, they imported, that the king gave commission to Astartus to carry his fleet, compos'd of fifteen ships, laden with merchandizes, and equipp'd for war, to Taprobane: That the forces of this fleet should be employ'd to support or re-establish the colony of that island, which was threaten'd with an expulsion, for reasons which they had but a confus'd notion of, and which seem'd to have been conceal'd by Pheletes the chief of the colony. The king said further, That he had shewn his acknowledgments in due time to the king of the Galibians, and to the two other kings of Taprobane, for the favourable reception they had given the Phoenicians at their first landing: but that this courtesy being at bottom no more than an observance of the laws of nature and nations, he insisted upon its being preserv'd, either by good-will, or force, upon the conditions formerly regulated, or that might for the future be regulated, as occasion requir'd: That the Phoenician nation made no difficulty of allowing that they obtain'd great advantages in trade, by their factory in Taprobane; but that the islanders had likewise had a very great share in these advantages, by the gold and silver which had on this occasion circulated in their island,

and

and by the vend of their cinamon, which the Phœnicians diſpers'd throughout the whole world: That, with reſpect even to the troubles, the true circumſtances of which were unknown at Tyre, the king, being willing to give all manner of ſatisfaction to his dear and much-honoured allies the kings of Taprobane, appointed Aſtartus chief of the Phœnician colony; grounding this choice on the great ſervices this commander had done him by ſea and land; but particularly on the prudence with which he had always behav'd himſelf among foreign nations, having more than once ſo gain'd the affections even of thoſe people whom he had conquer'd, that they were enter'd into bonds of friendſhip and alliance with Phœnicia: That, with reſpect to Pheletes, of whom he was already inform'd that he was not belov'd by the iſlanders, and had been cruel to the Phœnicians themſelves, he charged Aſtartus to go back to the riſe of theſe ſuſpicions and complaints; and if he ſhould find that Pheletes had been guilty only of imprudence, or involuntary failings, that he ſhould ſend him back to Phœnicia, with the uſual honours, promiſing him all manner of indulgence on the king's part: but if it appear'd that he had been the aggreſſor, and had offer'd the kings of Taprobane any injury that was capital, or tending to promote diſcord between the two people; that,

that, in ſuch caſe, Aſtartus ſhould form a council of war, compos'd of twenty of his principal officers, viz. ten of the colony, and ten of the fleet, in which he ſhould preſide: That Pheletes ſhould be arraign'd before this council; and the ſentence there pronounc'd againſt him ſhould be executed in the ſight of the Phœnicians and the Iſlanders. At theſe words, Pheletes ſaid; I ſhall ſave you the trouble, and know how to puniſh myſelf for having attempted to ſerve my country. Immediately, preventing all diſpoſitions that might have been made to ſtop him, he ran croſs a diſtance of about forty paces between the tent and the brink of the downs, and threw himſelf into the ſea.

THE end of this man, who was more blind than wicked, rais'd ſome ſenſe of compaſſion in the whole aſſembly, which was in ſome confuſion, waiting to ſee what would be the end of his running with ſo much precipitation out of the tent: However, the kings and Aſtartus caus'd the whole aſſembly, each on their own ſide, to take their places again, in order to come to a final reſolution on affairs which began to change their face. They ſoon came to an agreement, That all things ſhould be reſtor'd to the ſame condition they were in before this undertaking of Pheletes, whoſe condemnation

tion was to secure more than ever a mutual confidence between the two nations. They were breaking-up, to go and publish these tidings to the besieged, and to the besiegers, when Cheres stepp'd forward, and intreated a moment's audience. Ye kings of Taprobane, (said he) and you my lords Phoenicians! How urgent soever the publication of the peace, and the deliverance of the city, may be, allow me, now you are so happily assembled, to propose an undertaking equally advantageous to both nations. The gods seem to me to have prepar'd every thing for the execution of this design with which they have inspir'd me, to make the world acquainted with nations unknown, and to give you new allies. My views are towards Africa, in which my country is situated; but it is to discover the southern part of it, with which the Indian seas will give you an easy communication from hence. Tho' I have not perform'd the voyage I propose, I have a peculiar knowledge of it, the source of which I am not allow'd to discover: but this I can assure you in general, I shall find nothing on all the coasts I propose to survey, but what I am already acquainted with. Give me a fleet of twelve vessels; six of the Phoenicians, whom I name first, because I first devoted myself to their service; and six of the Islanders, because their natural good-

ness,

neſs, and their friendſhip for the Phœnicians, make them worthy to be partakers with them of the profits of this new commerce. Theſe veſſels muſt be equipp'd for war; becauſe among the people we ſhall meet with, there are ſome very untractable and unſociable, and ſuch as are only fit to be your ſlaves. As for the ammunitions and proviſions which we ſhall have occaſion for, and advice-boats to bring you tidings of us, while we are compaſſing the coaſts of Africa, theſe are articles which cann't be regulated here, and for which you have all the leiſure neceſſary, while we wait for the moſt proper ſeaſon for our departure. The kings and Aſtartus anſwer'd almoſt at the ſame time, That they did not reject this propoſal, and that they would examine it with him, as well in their ſeparate as united councils; but that, as he himſelf had inſinuated, the moſt urgent at preſent, was, to go and bring joy to both nations, and to carry the beſieged all manner of refreſhments, which might make them forget the long continuance of the evils they had ſuffer'd.

A DESCRIPTION of the rejoicings which were made on both ſides on this occaſion is foreign from my main ſubject. I ſhall only ſay, that while the king of the Galibians and Aſtartus were entring the city in ceremony, Cheres rambled, out of curioſity, into ſeveral ſtreets

ſtreets and ſquares. There were in Galiba ſeveral Egyptian prieſts in the habits of merchants, as it was uſual for them in foreign countries. They conform'd with ſo much diſcretion to the cuſtoms of every place, and behav'd themſelves with ſo much prudence, that they were never obſerv'd; or at leaſt they were only diſtinguiſh'd by the good they found opportunities of doing. Among theſe were fourteen or fifteen prieſts of Memphis, and ſome officers of the ſecond order. Two of theſe prieſts, who met Cheres, knew him immediately. He, at the ſame time, gave them the ſign of religious ſecrecy, which was, by laying his hand on his heart. He related his whole hiſtory to them; and they immediately offer'd him their treaſure, which the length of the ſiege had not yet exhauſted, and which was going to increaſe greatly by the return of thoſe ſums they had lent to the citizens during the publick calamity. Cheres took advantage of an offer which was a right to all initiates: but he told them, that he had left his jewels in the hands of the prieſts of Memphis, and that his deſign was, they ſhould open the box, and take out as many as would pay all the ſums he might borrow of them. To this end, he begg'd of them to conduct him to the houſe where they lodg'd, that he might write to the high-prieſt of Memphis, and leave his letter in their hands, to be carry'd by one of them, or their officers,

cers, who might first return into Egypt. In this letter, after an ample relation of his adventures, he took notice of the debt he had just contracted, and those he might yet contract; begging the high-priest to reimburse himself out of what he had put into his hands, and which he desir'd him yet to keep for the same use, and especially as it contain'd the late queen his mother's ring, the only exterior token of his birth which fortune had left him. He inform'd him of his resolution, and the hopes he was in of undertaking to coast round Africa, without delay, in a fleet of which he was to have the command in chief; and sooner or later to return that way to the Mediterranean-sea, and into Egypt. He promis'd to write to him, during his voyage, by every safe opportunity that might offer: But above all, he engag'd him, under the seal of religious and sacerdotal secrecy, to leave the whole world, and especially the court of Memphis, in their persuasion of his death; being convinc'd that was the most infallible means to overthrow, in time, all those measures which had been taken upon this false supposition; whereas, if his enemies knew he were living, they would, at their leisure, take such as might be effectual to exclude him from the succession to the throne which was his right. But if the high-priest should, before his return, receive the certain and unquestionable news of his death, he referr'd himſelf entirely to him for the publication he might make of the truth of things, if he thought it neceſſary, for the ſatisfaction of the good, and the confuſion of the wicked.

CHERES return'd ſoon enough towards the palace, deſtin'd for the chief of the colony, to enter into it with his retinue; and in the evening, taking Aſtartus aſide, he offer'd him his ranſom, what he knew he had given to the Phœnicians who brought him on board his veſſel. He begg'd of him to receive it, tho' it were but out of a formality, to which he very well knew the idea of liberty was annex'd in publick opinion. My lord, ſaid he, don't be ſurpriz'd at the ſum I give you. I have found in Galiba ſome Egyptians, unknown, in their habit, from the merchants of your nation. It is an eſtabliſh'd rule, eſpecially with thoſe amongſt us, who are ally'd by a religious aſſociation, that their goods are in common in foreign countries. This it is which places me above all neceſſity for my perſon here. I preſume, however, to beg a lodging of you in your palace, becauſe I ſhall be the more at hand to purſue, near your perſon, the preparations for the voyage I have propos'd. Aſtartus anſwer'd him, That even before his ranſom, which he only accepted of to oblige him, he held him free; and that the ſervices he had render'd the Phœnicians, would have cancell'd all the engagements in the world. He added, that at the firſt word he heard him ſpeak, and by the bare tone of his voice, he had believ'd him to be of a quality far above what he aſſum'd, and even above the common race of men: But that, in ſhort, he had regard for his ſecret, and the reaſons he had to conceal himſelf, promiſing him, with an oath, not to communicate to any one the thoughts he had of him, and which he ſtifled when he ſpoke to him himſelf. He aſſur'd him, that he would immediately uſe all poſſible diligence to put the fleet he had deſir'd in a condition to depart as ſoon as he ſhould think expedient; and that he would repreſent this expedition to the king, his maſter, as the moſt advantageous that could be propos'd for the world in general, and for Phœnicia in particular. Aſtartus was as good as his word, and wrote to the king of Tyre not only what he had promis'd Cheres, but added, without his knowledge, that the unknown Egyptian had, by his merit and valour, acquir'd ſo happy an aſcendant over the minds of every one, as promis'd all ſucceſs to his undertaking: But that he ſhould likewiſe be accompany'd by ſuch officers and pilots with whom the intereſt of Phœnicia might be intruſted. The new chief of the colony haſten'd of himſelf the imbarkation; becauſe at his arrival at Galiba he was inform'd, that three

Phœnician veſſels were departed from Taprobane two months before the ſiege for the great iſland of Menuthias [Madagaſcar]; and that they had been promis'd they ſhould ſoon be follow'd by others.

ASTARTUS being more and more confirm'd in the opinion he had of the probity and knowledge of Cheres, caus'd ſix large veſſels to be fitted out, and provided with the moſt excellent Phœnician officers, and the moſt expert pilots of that nation. They did not forget the aſtronomical tables, nor the inſtruments for obſervation, which would be more neceſſary for them in unknown ſeas than in others. The kings of the iſland, who had been prepoſſeſs'd in favour of Cheres, even before they had ſeen him; whoſe part he had ſo generouſly taken in the conference, and which he had ſince improv'd with a great deal of care during their ſtay at Galiba, furniſh'd the ſame number. With the conſent of Aſtartus, the partition of ſuch poſſeſſions and ſettlements, as in their diſcoveries might be to be made between the iſlanders and the Phœnicians, was left to the ſole diſpoſition of Cheres. Theſe firſt veſſels were follow'd by twelve others of leſſer bulk, which were to carry, and bring back again ſucceſſively, proviſions and merchandizes, as occaſion might require. They took care to furniſh themſelves in abundance with all the little utensils, which, being put to the most common uses, are of small value among civiliz'd nations; but which must seem very curious to savages who have no idea of the conveniences of life. Some of the priests of Memphis, who knew Cheres personally; and who, according to their general maxim, travell'd to the different parts of the world, as soon as they were discover'd, desir'd to accompany him in his voyage. He would by no means refuse the pleasure and assistance he had to hope from their conversation, advice and ingenuity. The Phœnicians and the islanders of Taprobane had already their priests, according to the religious customs of the ancients, who never went to sea without them. For this reason the poets have feign'd, that the Argonauts took Orpheus with them, and that the Greeks made Calchas accompany them to the siege of Troy. Cheres was so urgent and assiduous, that every thing was ready within a month; he then went on board of the most gallant vessel, as commander; and this fleet, at its departure from Taprobane, was attended with the blessings of the two nations, who lin'd the shore a long way off.

AT their departure from the port of Galiba, the wind bore them away to the southward, which was their course to the island of Menuthias: but it was the custom of those days to keep the coast; a timorous way of sailing, which continu'd among us till Hipalus *, a famous mariner under the emperor Claudius, taught the Romans to traverse the main sea in their voyages to the Indies. So this northerly wind was contrary to the course Cheres's pilots propos'd to take; which was, to return the same way they came from the Arabian Gulph to Taprobane, and then to pursue the African coasts from the north to the south. Cheres was sorely griev'd to go so much about, because he had very little curiosity to view those coasts which had already been seen by himself or others: therefore, taking advantage of this circumstance of a contrary wind that favour'd a design, which without this pretext he would hardly have ventur'd to have propos'd: he call'd the pilots together, and said to them; Comrades, dare you put trust in my presage? The heavens seem to point out to us the way which we ought to take. We are going in quest of new lands; but we shan't be the first who have procur'd this advantage to mankind; and your nation is already famous for these sorts of discoveries. Let us teach future navigators something newer, and more considerable, and which will render you famous among the Phœnicians themselves. Let us make the world ac-

* Dodwel, de autore & ætate Peripli maris Erythræi, cap. 16.

quainted

quainted with the main sea; and let us open a passage thro' it by our example. Let us take this opportunity of a favourable wind to do designedly, what tempests and currents have oblig'd those vessels to do which have landed on islands at a great distance from the shores of the continent. Experience has taught us, that in crossing the sea we are generally less subject to sands and rocks than in coasting voyages. Those among you who have been at Menuthias by other ways, have determin'd the situation of this island; so you know what course you have to take. The certain advantage of a voyage, shorten'd at least the half, by sailing in a direct line, seems, in my opinion, to outweigh the hazard of it, tho' not yet attempted. What would our navigation now have been if your fathers had not undertaken things which none before them had presum'd to do? They saw the times, in which not only passengers landed every night, but the pilots drew their vessels on shore. Yours are too great to follow them in this lamentable way of working, which you leave to the Greeks; the greater part of whom don't yet venture, I don't say out of the Mediterranean, but hardly out of the neighbourhood of the Archipelago. You allow, that you pass your nights more securely in your vessels, either at anchor, or even continuing your course, than by exposing yourself on desart coasts, or those where you mistrust the inhabitants. Navigation of itself is look'd upon as the boldest attempt mankind has ever been capable of; but we may say, it is become the more secure, in proportion as it has been attempted with the greater boldness. I don't despair but this trial, which I propose to you, will exempt you, in future times, from a thousand shipwrecks and encounters: Besides, the birds * which you carry along with you, according to custom, will, by their flight, direct you where those islands or continents lie, which you are to avoid running upon. As soon as we suppose ourselves in the neighbourhood of them, we will send some of our small vessels or boats to sound the way before us. These are only particular methods: but for the general direction of our course, I build very much upon the knowledge you have of the stars. Mariners of other nations have no other guide but the Great Bear; a constellation, tho' very visible, which discovers the northern region to us, but in an undetermin'd manner. You alone know how to guide yourselves by the Cynosura † or Lesser Bear; the point of whose tail directs you exactly to the polar star. 'Tis true, as soon as we have pass'd the line, the northern pole will disappear from our sight; and I know, that

* Pliny, lib. 6. cap. 24.

† Namque Helice Graios, Tyrios Cynosura per altum parva regit. Festus Avienus in Arateis, & alii.

the nearest star to the southern pole, which we must then have in view, is distant from it above fifteen degrees. This inconveniency might seem capable of reducing us to a pretty great uncertainty. But, not to mention the assistance we shall have by easy reckonings, it is certain, that bearing from hence to the southwest, as you know we must to steer in a direct line for Menuthias, we shall likewise then find ourselves very near to Africa; which we shall afterwards coast, according to the manner of common sailing, during the whole remainder of our course.

THE pilots, being won by a discourse which Cheres had wisely turn'd in their favour, and by which he seem'd to put confidence in their knowledge, accepted of this proposal with joy. And moreover, this trust which he profess'd to repose in them, was, as it generally happens, the measure of theirs in him. In the mean time they doubled their diligence, as well in taking every day the height of the sun, and every night that of different stars, as to discover at as great a distance as possible, the islands they were to meet with in their passage. The continual vigilance, which new dangers oblig'd them to, procur'd them the satisfaction, not only of rendring themselves more expert than they had been before, but of finding themselves in reality more so than they expected to be.

Cheres,

Cheres, in order to exempt those who were to follow him from the painful uncertainty into which he ran himself for their sakes, caus'd a very exact journal to be kept of whatever they observ'd either in the firmament or the seas. As they were then in the middle of our winter, as soon as they had pass'd the line, they made great advantage of the east wind, call'd, *Apeliotes* or *Subsolanus*. This regular wind, which always follows the sun in these seas, from one tropick to the other, and which extremely qualifies the heat of its perpendicular rays, carry'd them in less than a month within sight of the most southern coasts of the island of Menuthias. We find it call'd in some of our authors, *Cerna Ethiopica*, to distinguish it from *Cerna Atlantica*, [the island of Madera] situate over-against the western and northern point of Africa. My anecdote authors relate, that the first, of which we are here treating, had been already discover'd by the Phœnicians, in the following manner:

During the first years that Pheletes govern'd the Phœnician colony of Taprobane, one of his boldest pilots propos'd to him, to extend the knowledge they already had of the eastern coasts of Africa yet farther. As Pheletes was puff'd up with the advantageous ideas which had been given him of the Chersonesus Aurea and Serica, he flatter'd himself

self

ſelf with the hopes of greater profit for his colony and himſelf from thence, than what he could expect from Africa; of which he had heard no other mention made but as of a country hideous not only for its inhabitants but for its deſarts. Thus, whatever inſtances they could make him, he would only grant one veſſel to him who propos'd this undertaking. This pilot, after having taken the common tour to come at the cape of Aromata [Gardafuy] which is the moſt eaſtern promontory of Ethiopia above Egypt, join'd with ſome Ethiopian merchants, who accompany'd him to Rapta, over-againſt the middle of the iſland of Menuthias. There they told him, they were never accuſtom'd to go farther; tho', according to an opinion ſpread among them, by advancing a little farther, they would find the mines of Sophir or Ophir [now Sophala]. Not, added they, that any ſtranger has ever ſeen them. If there be any, they are barr'd from us by Anthropophagian Ethiopians, who, without doubt, don't know their own riches: but being animated by a more brutiſh paſſion, they aſſemble in numerous bodies, to lay hold of all travellers who have the miſfortune to be caſt on their coaſts; and they carry them away to eat them. Thus we have no other evidence of their poſſeſſing mines of gold, but ſome duſt of that metal which has been found mix'd with the ſand on their coaſts.

UPON this advice the Phœnician pilot, conſidering that he was not of force enough, either for an aſſault, or to defend himſelf, was ſatisfy'd, as he paſs'd the night on this coaſt, with ſending a boat to fill a barrel with this ſand in haſte. He then ſtood away for Menuthias, where he had been told the inhabitants had not much more underſtanding, but were more humane than the ſavages of Sophir. He doubled the iſle towards the ſouth, and landed there: he took a juſt account of the height of it, and brought away from thence ſeveral refreſhments, which he purchas'd for ſome trifles of little value. Being return'd to Taprobane by the way he came, he preſented the chief of the colony his barrel of ſand; out of which they drew, by barely waſhing, a pretty large quantity of gold. At the ſight of this, Pheletes conſented to equip three veſſels, which were to land on the ſouthern coaſt of Menuthias, a little beyond the tropic, at the port, which would be eaſily found by the firſt pilot he ſent; and he made them hope, as we have obſerv'd above, that they ſhould ſoon be follow'd by a reinforcement. The reaſon Pheletes alledg'd was, that the firſt thing they had to do was to eſtabliſh themſelves at Menuthias, that they might there concert the moſt expedient meaſures to make war with the ſavages of Sophir. But tho' it was near a year that theſe three veſſels were departed,

departed, they did not arrive at this iſland till eight days after Cheres, with his fleet, was got thither, which was a great honour to the undertaking he had juſt perform'd of croſſing the main ſea.

ASSOON as this fleet, which conſiſted of twenty-four veſſels, appear'd in the road, they obſerv'd that the iſlanders, men and women, terrify'd with a ſight, the like of which, without doubt, they had never ſeen, fled to a great diſtance, and driving before them all their cattle which they could get together, left an open country. The Phœnicians immediately enter'd into a very large haven, which nature * alone had form'd. It is a kind of lake, ſcreen'd from every wind, upon which were a great number of fiſhermens barks, made out of one piece of hollow'd timber, and laden with ſtrong wicker baſkets, which ſerv'd the inhabitants for nets. They landed in a pleaſant and fertile plain, water'd with ſeveral rivers and brooks, which fall into the lake, and full of cabins cover'd with leaves, to ſcreen both men and beaſts from the great heat of the ſun. They found every where proviſions of ruſtick food; and in ſeveral places ſome old men and children, who had wanted ſtrength to leave their dwellings. Cheres gave orders to his whole com-

* Dapper upon the iſland of Madagaſcar.

pany

pany to appeaſe the fear, which their accoutrements of war had caus'd in theſe ſavage peaſants, by all tokens of friendſhip. And, in the mean time, they took poſſeſſion of a place which the cowardice of the poſſeſſors had made ſtrangers, who deſir'd no more than a courteous hoſpitality, the maſters of. After having paſs'd ſome days in marking out the ground they believ'd they might want for themſelves, and for thoſe who would follow them, they began to fortify it, for fear the fugitives might return with ſome unknown ſuccours. For this work they at firſt imploy'd their rowers, but they ſoon had other workmen. The inhabitants came one by one, to ſee whether the ſtrangers were departed. Cheres and his people, by their geſtures and the engaging tone of their voices, prevail'd upon thoſe of the old men and children, who were able to walk a little, to go and meet their relations, and to aſſure them they had nothing to fear of theſe ſtrangers. This expedient ſucceeded beyond all hopes; and the inhabitants return'd in a few days to their cabins. It is true, they were now no longer maſters there; but whether it was that they were ſenſible they had loſt their independancy by their own fault; or whether they perceiv'd the ſuperiority which civiliz'd nations had over them, they ſubmitted to their bondage without reluctance. As they before aim'd at nothing more than a livelihood, and they

had

had never attain'd to it without labour, their condition ſeem'd to be hardly chang'd. On the contrary, the inhabitants of this ſouthern canton having never had any chief in common to them, and conſequently no neceſſary and abſolute judge in their quarrels; they ſeem'd, by the loſs of the propriety of their goods, to have procur'd a more peaceable enjoyment of them. To conclude, one of the comforts of theſe people was, that this new government freed them from the injunctions which their ſoothſayers laid upon all mothers, of expoſing their children, when they found by their obſervations that they were born under inauſpicious omens *.

THE firſt thing Cheres did, was, to make particular laws for this kind of ſlaves. He ordain'd, that they ſhould only be call'd bonds-men or ſervants. He regulated their food, ſuch as they enjoy'd before. He divided their hours equally between work and reſt; but he promis'd them particularly, in the name of the kings, their new ſovereigns, that as long as they behav'd themſelves with that ſubmiſſion they had till then ſhewn, they ſhould never be carry'd out of their iſland againſt their wills. Theſe diſpoſitions being made, they employ'd them in building a fort, walls and dwellings, with the moſt proper materials they found in the neighbour-

* Dapper, pag. 468.

hood.

hood. At laſt, Cheres, by virtue of the power given him at his departure, determin'd, that the fort, the new city, and all the territory which ſurrounded it, ought, on account of the neighbourhood, to appertain as a ſovereignty to the kings of Taprobane, as well as all conqueſts they might for the future make in every iſland.

HE ſent two of his leſſer veſſels, to inform the kings of his diſpoſition, and of the conditions upon which he had made them ſovereigns of the iſland, and maſters of its inhabitants, or at leaſt of that part which was actually conquer'd. One of theſe veſſels carry'd a column of ebony wood, of a prodigious length and thickneſs. All their people, to the very ſailors, had quantities of topazes, granates, amethyſts, and other precious ſtones; which, as they ſaid, and was agreeable to the truth, they had gather'd in the rivers and brooks *. Cheres, in his letter, exhorted the kings to ſend a ſmall fleet, with a certain number of men and women, to begin a ſettlement in the form of a colony at Menuthias. He adviſ'd them to ſend officers and ſoldiers with them, that they might have a gariſon in this iſland, and a fleet in its haven; becauſe he ſhould carry all the veſſels and people he had with him in queſt of farther diſcoveries. He adviſ'd them, however, not to let their

* Dapper, page 446.

people advance farther into the country, till after ſome time, and when, by a mild and juſt dominion over their new ſervants, they were ſure of having zealous ſoldiers in them. He even exhorted them not to extend their conqueſts but in the ſame manner as they had been begun; that is, by convincing the inhabitants of the inward parts of the iſland, that a reaſonable ſervitude would be infinitely more eaſy to them than the ſavage liberty in which they then liv'd. He concluded, that if the kings of Taprobane would but never ſo little haſten the imbarkation he propos'd to them, they might yet find him in the ſame place, becauſe the paſſage between the two iſlands was now no more a tedious voyage.

HE wrote a private letter to Aſtartus; in which he obſerv'd, that he had thought it moſt expedient to make this firſt preſent to his allies, to cement their reconciliation with the Phœnicians, who ſtood in need of their factory of Taprobane for their trade to the Indies. That beſides, theſe allies having fewer maritime forces, and leſs correſpondence in trade than Phœnicia, he had been glad to give them a poſſeſſion, which they might with eaſe keep and improve: But that his deſign was to make the Phœnicians lords of all the eaſtern coaſts of Africa, from Raptum to the moſt ſouthern point of this part of the world. That the correſpondence they already had with the northern Ethiopians would soon make it easy to them to carry on their trade directly to all Africa without going to Taprobane, or even stopping at Menuthias. He advis'd him, that he was going to make a beginning by the mines of Sophir, situate in a barbarous country, whose inhabitants destroy'd and devour'd all those who fell into their hands. That he reckon'd he had men enough to subdue them, and would inform him from thence what troops the Phoenicians would want to maintain their conquest. That after having made as many slaves as he possibly could of these inhuman people, he would employ them in building upon all the coasts such forts as he should judge necessary to secure to Phoenicia those possessions which were advantageous in themselves, or would serve for factories to depart from thence to places where they would have a profitable commerce. He added, that he talk'd of reducing this part of the eastern coast of Africa to slavery, only because it was inhabited by monsters in human shape, uncapable of all society. But that he hop'd to find on the western coast nations with whom they might enter into some treaties of alliance or commerce. That it was not for the interest of Phoenicia to go every where sword in hand: That they would ruin themselves by so tedious an expedition, or at least their dominion would be of no long duration: That it were to be wish'd wish'd for them, they might always find people who would receive them as they had been receiv'd at Taprobane. That he should be so far from destroying, that he would not subdue all the Barbarians, who might at first make some resistance: but that he would make use of his victories, as Astartus himself had more than once given him an example, to reduce the conquer'd to a friendship with the conquerors. That if he had made the inhabitants of Menuthias bonds-men, it was because having found no form of general and constant government among them, he could not apply himself to any of them, in order to treat in safety with the nation: That therefore he could bring them no otherwise but by servitude to that communication of good offices, to which he believ'd all the people of the earth were oblig'd one towards the other. That in consideration, however, of their natural goodness, he had taken all possible measures, that their yoke might rather be advantageous than burthensome. That, in a word, he had acted very differently with them from what he was going to do with the Anthropophagi, those enemies to mankind, of whom he would endeavour to exterminate one part, that he might make the remainder real slaves. But that in general he was persuaded, the natural inhabitants of each country were only truly capable of cultivating and preserving the fruits and production of nature in their own lands, and to traffick with them advantageously for those people themselves who want to purchase them there. That thus it would be to ruin trade in its infancy, not only to exterminate, but even to scare away or to alienate those people who were to be gain'd by prudence and humanity. That, for his part, he had only offer'd his service to Phœnicia and its allies in this view. That his most fervent wishes were, to civilize the savages themselves, who might be found susceptible of any manners, by the intercourse he would procure them with polite nations. In a word, that all he aspir'd to in his undertaking was, to make men advantageous one to the other.

CHERES, while he was waiting the return of his two ships, so hasten'd the works he had begun, that the families of Taprobane found, at their arrival some months afterwards, habitations finish'd, both in the city and in the country. Their commander or governor had orders from the three kings to distribute them according to the advice and dispositions of Cheres, and to conform himself to the regulations he should receive from him in what concern'd this conquest. These orders were accompany'd with a letter of praises and acknowledgements to Cheres: but he was more pleas'd with the approbation which

which Aſtartus gave, in his anſwer, to the motives of his conduct; not only becauſe Phœnicia having as yet not had their ſhare, this approbation ſeem'd more diſintereſted; but becauſe he was chiefly concern'd for the good of the Phœnicians, and believ'd by ſerving them, he more immediately ſerv'd Egypt itſelf.

As Cheres only waited for the iſlanders of Taprobane to put their colony in poſſeſſion of a country he had won for them; as ſoon as that was ſettled, he refitted his whole fleet; and having furniſh'd it abundantly with ammunition and proviſions, he ſet ſail for Sophir.

His deſign was to reach the coaſts of Africa at the river Raptus [Cuama]; where, as has been already obſerv'd, the Ethiopian merchants always ſtopp'd, by reaſon of the dread they had of the Anthropophagi: But a violent ſtorm, ſuch as is very common between Africa and Menuthias, ſoon interrupted the paſſage of his fleet into this canal, which he would not venture into but with a very favourable wind. The calm was not intirely ſettled, when his veſſel, being ſeparated from all the reſt by a tempeſt, was found to be off of a point of land, which he knew to be the promontory of Praſon, and which Ptolemy afterwards plac'd in the fifteenth degree of southern latitude. But as there is no point of land beyond that of Raptum to the south till you come to this promontory; which in my anecdots I find situated under the tropick of Capricorn, I conclude this is the Cape, which Ptolemy knew the name of, without knowing the situation of it, tho' it was truly describ'd to him by Marin of Tyre, whom he quotes on this same subject *. Cheres calling to mind that this was the bounds of Africa, known by the geographers of his time, resolv'd to land there, and took his measures for the descent.

He had perceiv'd, at a distance, a crowd of inhabitants on the shore; and he imagin'd that these people, having discover'd several of his vessels, were only assembled in so great a number to defend themselves, in case they offer'd to approach them. He therefore thought immediately of rejoining his fleet; and afterwards, that the savages might the sooner separate, he got it quite out of their sight. In short, he order'd matters so, that by favour of a night, which was the fifth after the tempest, three of his smaller vessels, which he commanded himself, fill'd with chosen soldiers, and back'd by the remainder of the fleet at a convenient distance, attempted to land. He had observ'd, as a land-mark, some cabins almost on the brink of the cape, at

* Lib. i. cap. 7.

the mouth of a river [the Inhambane]; and he judg'd, by the nature of the ground, the descent would be easy there. His conjecture prov'd true; and they even found no one to oppose them: so marching silently, with sword in hand, they went up to these cabins, guided by the light of some wood, which they saw burning there. About thirty savages, who guarded the entrance into them, awak'd, and immediately made a great cry; which was a signal for their own death. This expedition was pursu'd with so much diligence, that not one of them had time to arm himself with his bow and arrows, which he had by his side, or means to escape, to give notice to his comrades at a distance.

CHERES and his company enter'd immediately into a sort of large stable, supported from space to space by stakes. They found there about fifty men, almost naked, lying upon leaves, and ty'd to these stakes by branches of palms, twisted into the form of chains. These men, who spoke different languages, all agreed in their tokens of joy and supplicating tone of their voices. Cheres made signs to them by favourable gestures to let one of them, who seem'd to be more zealous than the rest, speak for them all: My lord, said he, you who are at the head of these Phœnicians, whom I know by their armour, as being a Phœnician myself: Heaven has, without doubt, ſent you to be the deliverer of us miſerable wretches, who are here deſtin'd to ſerve for food to the cruel inhabitants of this country. We have been drove on ſhore here at different times by contrary winds. They come hither in ſhoals, as ſoon as they perceive a ſtorm, with a deſign to ſeize the prey it may bring them. For otherwiſe, they have not the courage to go to ſea to attack any veſſels they think capable of defending themſelves. They take advantage of the ſtate of imbecility, fatigue and agony, to which travellers, batter'd by the waves, and almoſt drowned, are reduc'd to, to reſerve thoſe wretches for a death by far more terrible than that they have eſcap'd. They keep us here in vaſt paſtures full of flocks, from whence they take their daily food, and with which they nouriſh us, in order to make the ſame uſe of us at their feſtivals as of their flocks: we are liable every month to the frightful choice they come to make of us by the brutal eſtimate of the plight we are in. Oh! young hero, whoever you are, give us our lives, or at leaſt preſerve us from a death ſo unworthy of the human ſpecies. We may, perhaps, be of ſome ſervice to you againſt theſe barbarians, of whoſe genius and cuſtoms, a fatal experience has given us ſome knowledge. Receive us among the meaneſt of theſe brave warriors, who have follow'd you in this glorious expedition, and who ſeem

ſeem as intirely devoted to your perſon, as fill'd with admiration of your valour.

CHERES immediately caus'd the bonds of theſe priſoners to be cut; and ſent orders to the whole fleet to repair immediately into the haven or baſon, which forms the mouth of the river. Seeing himſelf at laſt in this deſir'd land, where he was beginning his labours for the benefit of mankind, he was ſenſible of that joy which travellers, after long voyages, have at their return into their own country. He ſoon learnt from theſe ſtrangers he had juſt deliver'd, that there were at different places on this coaſt, going to the north, on the way to Sophir, more of theſe infamous markets, where the Anthropophagi traffick'd with one another for the men they took. He thought proper, before he went to clear the ſhore of ſo many aſſaſſins, to form a ſettlement at the promontory for his fleet; which might afterwards remain for the uſe of the Phœnicians. It did not appear very difficult to him. He ſaw he had to do with men, who being terrify'd, had abandon'd the whole plain ever ſince he had landed, and who only appear'd on the top of the hills; from which they immediately deſcended on the other ſide as ſoon as they made a ſhew of approaching them. By this example he was confirm'd in the opinion he had always had, that cruelty and barbarity are generally

the

the companions of the vileſt cowardice: He was very glad, at the ſame time, he ſhould have leſs occaſion for blood-ſhed than he thought, in the reducing of theſe ſavages: but their buſineſs was to ſeize as many of them as they could alive; and in the execution of this deſign, the ſtrangers were of great help to him.

As there were ſeveral Ethiopians among them, who had obſerv'd that the language of the ſavages did not differ entirely from theirs, they offer'd Cheres to endeavour at bringing them back again. They told him, that provided they were arm'd, they were not at all fearful of them. They ſaid, they would give them to underſtand, that their flocks, their fruits, and their cabins being in the plain, the ſureſt means for them would be to truſt to the mercy of the conqueror. Yes, ſaid Cheres, and you may aſſure them, that beſides their lives, which I promiſe them, I will employ 'em in ſomething more advantageous to themſelves, than that horrible profeſſion which has made them the abomination of the whole world. Don't forget to add, that I will make a great difference between thoſe who ſhall ſubmit upon your remonſtrances, and thoſe who will put us to the trouble of purſuing them.

THESE deputies being departed, to the number of twenty, their greatest trouble was, to get near these savages; whom they call'd to come to them in the most pacifick tone and gestures. But as soon as they could in any wise get to speak with them; they soon made them sensible, that being us'd to plenty as they were in their meadows along the shore, they would soon perish with misery, if they were to seek their sustenance for themselves and their families, with their bows and arrows, upon barren mountains and desart plains. These, and the like discourses, passing from one to the other, brought back, in a few days, two or three thousand, and more follow'd. Cheres receiv'd them courteously. He distributed them into several companies; at the head of which he plac'd a Phœnician to command them, and an Ethiopian to be their interpreter. He employ'd them to prepare the ground for a small colony which he sent to desire of Astartus, while he employ'd himself in disposing every thing for a greater settlement in the neighbourhood of Sophir. He did not put these slaves to more tedious labour than he had done the islanders of Menuthias. And he even order'd them a more solid nourishment, in consideration of the custom they had contracted.

THE greater part of his company were ſurpriz'd at this humanity, and theſe regards; and they rather expected to have ſeen them chaſtis'd exemplarily for their late inhumanity. But Cheres told them, there was a vaſt difference to be made between crimes committed by private perſons againſt eſtabliſh'd laws in a civiliz'd country, and cuſtoms ariſing from the ignorance and barbarity of a whole nation. That pains inflicted upon them before they were inſtructed, would be a criminal revenge, and not a lawful puniſhment. That he made no ſcruple of exterminating men who were pernicious to mankind; and that upon this principle, he had no reluctance in maſſacring the thirty ſavages who guarded the ſtables, becauſe he then thought it neceſſary. But that now he knew the character of theſe barbarians better, he ſhould think himſelf very blameable to deſtroy a people whom he was going to render of ſervice, by their labours, to the Phœnicians themſelves, and by the continuance of their commerce to all the nations on earth.

HOWEVER, all the ſavages were not in a humour to abandon their idleneſs, and the hopes they yet had of remaining canibals, in exchange for tolerable but regular labours. It was ſoon known, that ſome of them, keeping

ing along the coaſt as far as Sophir, were gone in companies to the other Anthropophagi, to keep them in a body, by telling them they were threatned with ſuch an invaſion as had driven them from the promontory. That therefore they ought to prepare for their defence, and turn their courage againſt their common enemy; which they had hitherto only exerciſed in deſtroying one another ſingly, for private and perſonal quarrels. Cheres being inform'd of theſe proceedings, reſolv'd to go in ſearch of theſe ſavages by land, that he might take them on all ſides. But as it was near a hundred leagues from Praſon to Sophir, he imagin'd horſes would be of ſervice to him; and the more, as the vigour and ſwiftneſs of theſe animals, which this people had never yet ſeen, would infallibly ſtrike terror in their moſt numerous troops.

UPON this he diſpatch'd four veſſels of his fleet, commanded by Phœnicians, but with ſeveral Ethiopians in their company. He gave them a ſum of gold ſufficient to purchaſe ten thouſand horſes in Ethiopia, where they are in great numbers, beautiful, and ſo hard of hoof, that without being ſhod, they aſcend and deſcend the moſt rocky mountains *. He did not think much of this ex-

*. Dapper, pag. 419.

pence,

pence, which he hoped would be abundantly reimburs'd out of the mines of Sophir. These four vessels, which were the largest of his fleet, were to serve as a convoy to the flat-bottom'd vessels which were to bring the horses and their leaders. He foresaw that in this interval of time the Phœnician colony would arrive; and that they being sufficient to guard the promontory, he might take his whole army with him.

PRESENTLY after the return of the vessels which he had sent into Ethiopia, and the arrival of the Phœnician colony which he expected from Taprobane, he began his march towards Sophir. He order'd his fleet to coast along the shore, with all sorts of necessaries that they might want in crossing the country, which was not every where equally fruitful. It was likewise design'd to harbour the sick and wounded, if there should be any, and the slaves he hop'd to make. And as he had only mounted six thousand soldiers, the flat-bottom'd boats transported the remainder in case of need.

THE savages, who were not ignorant of these motions, had the courage to advance within three days journey of Prason. They were assembled in a plain, at the foot of an eminence which Cheres was to pass, not an army, but a great number of men, who all thought

thought that nothing was requiſite for a battle but numbers. For that very reaſon, knowing his arrival on the other ſide of the eminence, which ſeparated them, they had the aſſurance to ſend him a threatning deputation; becauſe they had heard of the Ethiopians, who were ſent to them at the beginning, that among all nations deputies were inviolate. The three ſavages being preſented to Cheres in his tent, were ſtruck with the majeſty of his appearance and countenance; and whether it was that they were ſenſible of the natural ſuperiority, which it has been always ſaid the blacks obſerve in white men; or whether frightned with their habits of ſteel, and helmets adorn'd with plumes and tufts of feathers, which they ſaw not only on Cheres, but on all the officers who were about him, they did not dare to open their mouths. Inſtead of ſpeaking, they repeated continually their proſtrations, ſuch as they were us'd to before their idols. Cheres was oblig'd to let them know by the Ethiopians, who ſerv'd as their interpreters, that they ſhould put an end to their ridiculous compliments, and inform him of their commiſſion. The deputies, trembling and ſtammering, gave him to underſtand, that if he advanc'd farther, their chiefs would immediately burn alive all the ſtrangers they had in their markets. Cheres anſwer'd, They might do as they thought fit; and that they would them-

themſelves mark out the meaſure of their own puniſhment: But that a deſire to change the kind of death of ſome hundreds of men ſhould not hinder him from purging human nature of ſuch monſters as they were. Theſe poor negroes carry'd the impreſſions of their fear to their chiefs, which did not hinder them from cauſing all the ſtrangers they had in a neighbouring market to be maſſacred; becauſe, finding themſelves preſs'd to prepare for battle, they did not think they had time to put them to more lingring torments.

THEY form'd a ſort of ſquare batallion, very cloſe, ſo that there were not above two or three of the firſt rows, who could aim at the enemy when they drew their arrows, and the remainder were oblig'd to ſhoot in the air at random. Theſe arrows were pointed with little ſharp ſtones; which naturaliſts finding ſow'd in the plains of Africa, have ſince taken for thunder-bolts, and call'd them *Ceraunia.* * They had behind them a very ſtrait mountain, the top of which was cover'd with the incorruptible wood of Thya, a ſort of cedar, which render'd this country famous in ancient times. There they had conceal'd their wives and children, and thither they propos'd to retire themſelves in caſe of bad

* Mem. of the Academy of Sciences. An. 1723. By M. de Juſſieu.

ſucceſs.

succeſs. Cheres, having obſerv'd this diſpoſition, order'd the two wings of his army, compos'd each of two thouſand horſe, to ride full ſpeed, as ſoon as they were got on the top of the eminence, to get behind the batallion of the ſavages, by the two ſpaces they had very imprudently left, one on each ſide of them; while he himſelf would face them with the ten thouſand men which remain'd. The barbarians expected theſe horſes, which ſeveral among them had perceiv'd before; but had deſcrib'd them to their comrades as animals, which were very ſlow in the march they had ſeen. They were therefore in a ſtrange conſternation, when having hardly had time to place their arrows in their bows, they ſaw their batallion inclos'd the firſt moment, their ranks broken in the ſecond, and in the third the moſt of them thrown down, and trodden under the horſes feet: they but eſcaped one ſword to meet with another: They found they were conquer'd at the firſt onſet; and their reſiſtance was hardly as long as my deſcription. They ſtretch'd out their arms to beg quarter; and the combat ceaſing at once, they were convey'd to the ſhips by thouſands, where they were put in irons. In the mean time, Cheres finding the ſtable where they had juſt murder'd the ſtrangers, he pick'd out the chief of the barbarians, and order'd them to be hang'd along the ſea-ſhore to intimidate the reſt, and to shew travellers that they might with safety not only pass that channel, but land on that shore.

AFTER this execution, he made the Ethiopians publish an amnesty, by which he promis'd all the savages of the country, who would abandon their former barbarity, and acknowledge themselves slaves to the Phœnicians, not only their lives, but a favourable reception. This brought in the wives and children of those who were in chains. They were separated into families; and Cheres promised them, in his own name, and in the name of the Phœnicians their masters, to join them always after that manner in the labours they should impose upon them. He excepted from this rule none but the young men who were not marry'd, of whom he made rowers, in the stead of those he had brought from Taprobane, who were converted into soldiers, to increase his troops. But he promis'd all these new captives to take off their chains as soon as they had given sufficient proofs of their fidelity. These marks of goodness from a conqueror, who had appear'd so dreadful, was some comfort to them in their defeat and slavery. Those whom he left in their own country took, with less regret, to those labours which are plac'd in the list of punishments for criminals, but to which many other men willingly submit

submit only to get a livelihood; I mean the mines which they were made to open in the territory of Sophir, whither Cheres arriv'd without any opposition, and deliver'd in his passage all the captives of the Anthropophagi.

THESE mines appear'd to be surprisingly rich; and tho' the Phœnicians were great artists in the management of this sort of works, which were not new to them, the Egyptian priests, who were with Cheres, taught them the real secret of separating the gold from the fragments of stone which is taken with it from the mines. This they did before, by grinding it to powder with prodigious labour, and afterwards by reiterated meltings. The Egyptian priests taught them, that quicksilver poured upon the stone, when but slightly pounded, would imbibe the precious metal: That it was easy afterwards to separate this amalgation or mixture from the sand or gravel which yet clog'd it; and that lastly, they had nothing to do but to make the quicksilver evaporate by fire, which would leave the pure gold at the bottom of the vessel *. They farther acquainted them, that this property of the quicksilver extended itself even to silver, but had no effect upon

* Pero Fernandez de Valasco gave this secret to the Spaniards in 1571; who employ'd it in the mines of Potosi. Mer. Ind. p. 1. c. 4. and Rohault has explain'd this effect in his physicks, p. III. c. 6. art. 27.

baſer metals, with which it would not unite; tho' they only wanted it for the former at the mines of Sophir: And we know that, in the following ages, they furniſh'd the moſt renown'd nations not only with the gold, with which they cover'd the temples of their gods and the palaces of their kings, but with precious ſtones without number, with which their women adorn'd themſelves. Not to mention thoſe whoſe names are common, it was from thence they had the pantarba, which had, as it is ſaid, the virtue of repelling the operation of fire; and the ſideropœcilus, a kind of load-ſtone, to which was aſcrib'd the yet more fabulous property of keeping up enmity among thoſe who carry'd it about them *.

ASTARTUS having given an account of theſe advantages, obtain'd of the king of Phœnicia himſelf a more numerous colony for this ſettlement, which was already provided with ſlaves, than the Phœnicians of Taprobane could have made up. This people, who were accuſtom'd at Tyre and Sidon to all the delights of life, found no want of them in this new habitation. They built houſes of ſeveral ſorts of vein'd timber of all colours, of great luſtre, and fitter for carving than marble. Beſides ſalutary as well as delicious

* Heliod. cap. 4. & 8. But ſee M. Huet de Navigatione Salomonis, c. 6. p. 179.

food,

food, which both land and sea afforded in abundance, the plains were fill'd with peacocks, parrots, monkeys and other animals, which, for the beauty of their form or singularity of their qualities, were worth sending, as they were long afterwards, to all those nations who had money to spend in amusements. To conclude, tho' Cheres had no design that the islanders of Taprobane should partake with the Phœnicians in the dominion of Sophir, or in the propriety of its mines, he assign'd them here, as well as during his whole course in every settlement, a quarter for them to dwell in, and gave them a proper interest in the Phœnician commerce. The kings of Taprobane had themselves intimated, that tho' they were overjoy'd that he would teach their subjects trade and navigation, they were not desirous of acquiring very distant possessions, for which they would have enough to do to furnish colonies.

THE settlements Cheres had procur'd for the two nations, who had furnish'd him with their soldiers, were no settlements for him. His mind being fill'd with more extensive projects for the advantage of the whole world, and even with the desire of returning into his own country with all the glory and authority which great actions could intitle him to, he found he was yet very short of his aim. He had actually at heart the finding

ing out the utmost point of Africa; a design really new, that would give a facility to trade; the value of which was very well known, but the hopes of it look'd on as chimerical. Being return'd from Sophir to the promontory, it was in that part he imbark'd for this new expedition. He had increas'd the number of his people by a great many of the strangers whom he had deliver'd. They had themselves desir'd to follow him, after he had granted them full liberty of returning into their own country, loaded with the gold of Sophir. As there were among those who devoted themselves to his service, merchants of every nation, and even Phœnicians already establish'd in the most northern parts of the Atlantick-sea, and who had pass'd the Mediterranean to come and imbark in the Red-sea; he was very glad to have in them proper interpreters for the coasts he was to attempt. He thought it proper to take with him all the horses, after the service they had done him against the Anthropophagi. But before he departed from Sophir, he chang'd his flat-bottom'd boats, which had brought them from Ethiopia, into vessels which drew more water, and were fitter to hold out against a tempest.

END of VOL. I.

CPSIA information can be obtained
at www.ICGtesting.com
Printed in the USA
LVHW021442210421
685121LV00012B/736

9 781166 202378